EXPERIMENTS MANUAL

ELECTRICITY

Principles and Applications

Fifth Edition

Richard J. Fowler

D0025924

Glencoe
McGraw-Hill

New York, New York   Columbus, Ohio   Woodland Hills, California   Peoria, Illinois

Cover photos: Charles Thatcher/Tony Stone Images; background: David McGlynn/FPG.

Safety section photos: Page x (*top*): Lou Jones/The Image Bank; (*bottom*): © Cindy Lewis.

Glencoe/McGraw-Hill

A Division of The **McGraw·Hill** Companies

Experiments Manual for
Electricity: Principles and Applications, Fifth Edition

Send all inquiries to:
Glencoe/McGraw-Hill
8787 Orion Place
Columbus, Ohio 43240

ISBN 0-02-804848-2

3 4 5 6 7 8 9   045   06 05 04 03 02 01 00

Contents

Editors' Foreword

The Glencoe *Basic Skills in Electricity and Electronics* series has been designed to provide entry-level competencies in a wide range of occupations in the electrical and electronic fields. The series consists of coordinated instructional materials designed especially for the career-oriented student. Each major subject area covered in the series is supported by a textbook, an experiments manual, and an instructor's productivity center. All the materials focus on the theory, practices, applications, and experiences necessary for those preparing to enter technical careers.

There are two fundamental considerations in the preparation of materials for such a series: the needs of the learner and needs of the employer. The materials in this series meet these needs in an expert fashion. The authors and editors have drawn upon their broad teaching and technical experiences to accurately interpret and meet the needs of the student. The needs of business and industry have been identified through personal interviews, industry publications, government occupational trend reports, and reports by industry associations.

The processes used to produce and refine the series have been ongoing. Technological change is rapid and the content has been revised to focus on current trends. Refinements in pedagogy have been defined and implemented based on classroom testing and feedback from students and instructors using the series. Every effort has been made to offer the best possible learning materials.

The widespread acceptance of the *Basic Skills in Electricity and Electronics* series and the positive responses from users confirm the basic soundness in content and design of these materials as well as their effectiveness as learning tools. Instructors will find the texts and manuals in each of the subject areas logically structured, well-paced, and developed around a framework of modern objectives. Students will find the materials to be readable, lucidly illustrated, and interesting. They will also find a generous amount of self-study and review materials and examples to help them determine their own progress.

Both the initial and on-going success of this series are due in large part to the wisdom and vision of Gordon Rockmaker who was a magical combination of editor, writer, teacher, electrical engineer, and friend. Gordon has retired but he is still our friend. The publisher and editors welcome comments and suggestions from instructors and students using the materials in this series.

Charles A. Schuler,
Project Editor
and
Brian P. Mackin,
Editorial Director

Basic Skills in Electricity and Electronics

Charles A. Schuler, Project Editor

New Editions in This Series
Electricity: Principles and Applications, Fifth Edition, Richard J. Fowler
Electronics: Principles and Applications, Fifth Edition, Charles A. Schuler
Digital Electronics: Principles and Applications, Fifth Edition, Roger L. Tokheim
Other Series Titles Available:
Communication Electronics, Second Edition, Louis E. Frenzel
Microprocessors: Principles and Applications, Second Edition, Charles M. Gilmore
Industrial Electronics, Frank D. Petruzella
Mathematics for Electronics, Harry Forster, Jr.

Preface

This experiments manual contains a wide variety of tests and experiments designed to aid students in understanding electrical principles and applications. The structure and content of this experiments manual parallel the theory presented in the companion textbook, *Electricity: Principles and Applications, Fifth Edition*. Students using this manual will find that working with basic circuits will enhance their understanding of the theory.

The fifth edition has two new features: troubleshooting experiments and computer simulations. Some of the troubleshooting experiments can be performed by using real components and instruments or by using electronic-circuit simulation software. Other troubleshooting experiments are designed specifically for computer simulation. Many experiments from the previous edition have been modified so that they can also be completed using either real components or circuit simulation software. Further, new experiments have been added to almost all chapters for this edition, and a number of them are designed for simulation software. A number of these simulation experiments refer to figures with the extension ".ewb," which are Electronics Workbench files contained in the *Instructor's Productivity Center*. Overall, one-third of the experiments are new to this edition.

In this fifth edition, the experiments presented in the first seven chapters are primarily concerned with direct current, and those in Chaps. 8 through 13 deal with alternating current. Chapter 14 covers ac and dc motor characteristics, and Chapter 15 covers instruments for measuring dc and ac quantities. Together, these 15 chapters constitute a complete, integrated coverage of basic electricity. Although not all the experiments in each chapter need to be used in the classroom, it is recommended that the chapters be covered in sequential order.

The manual also includes a selected group of advanced problems. All of the experiments and advanced problems will enhance and foster skills used by electrical technicians. The advanced problems may be chosen to serve the needs of a particular class or group of students, as well as the physical facilities available (such as shops and labs). The parts required for the experiments are standard materials available from many different hardware and electrical parts distributors. Whenever possible, the same components are used in more than one experiment. All of the experiments and advanced problems have been thoroughly classroom-tested.

Students are encouraged to see beyond the exercise of recording data, drawing lines, and creating curves. The collected data serves to reinforce the classroom theory, and laboratory experience also demonstrates the proper and practical use of test equipment. Students are encouraged to look and think beyond each experiment for trends and consistency of theory presented.

Each chapter begins with a comprehensive test that covers the chapter's content. The test may be taken in one or two class sessions depending upon class needs. It is suggested that even-numbered questions be given on one day, and odd-numbered questions on the next. This approach results in similar content coverage on both days. This same type of split is recommended when both a pretest and a posttest for the chapter are desired. If the textbook and this manual are studied simultaneously, the test may be given after each chapter is completed in both the text and the experiments manual.

The experiments manual concludes with three appendixes, the first covering tools and soldering techniques, the second breadboarding, and the third maintaining a lab notebook, as recommended by the ISO and ANSI.

Every effort has been made to develop experiments that support modern theory and current practice. Instructors and students recommended many of the changes and improvements to this edition. Comments from both instructors and students are again most welcome.

Richard J. Fowler

Safety

Electric and electronic circuits can be dangerous. Safe practices are necessary to prevent electrical shock, fires, explosions, mechanical damage, and injuries resulting from the improper use of tools.

Perhaps the greatest hazard is electrical shock. A current through the human body in excess of 10 milliamperes can paralyze the victim and make it impossible to let go of a "live" conductor or component. Ten milliamperes is a rather small amount of electrical flow: It is only *ten one-thousandths* of an ampere. An ordinary flashlight uses more than 100 times that amount of current!

Flashlight cells and batteries are safe to handle because the resistance of human skin is normally high enough to keep the current flow very small. For example, touching an ordinary 1.5-V cell produces a current flow in the microampere range (a microampere is one-millionth of an ampere). This amount of current is too small to be noticed.

High voltage, on the other hand, can force enough current through the skin to produce a shock. If the current approaches 100 milliamperes or more, the shock can be fatal. Thus, the danger of shock increases with voltage. Those who work with high voltage must be properly trained and equipped.

When human skin is moist or cut, its resistance to the flow of electricity can drop drastically. When this happens, even moderate voltages may cause a serious shock. Experienced technicians know this, and they also know that so-called low-voltage equipment may have a high-voltage section or two. In other words, they do not practice two methods of working with circuits: one for high voltage and one for low voltage. They follow safe procedures at all times. They do not assume protective devices are working. They do not assume a circuit is off even though the switch is in the OFF position. They know the switch could be defective.

As your knowledge and experience grow, you will learn many specific safe procedures for dealing with electricity and electronics. In the meantime:

1. Always follow procedures.
2. Use service manuals as often as possible. They often contain specific safety information. Read,
and comply with, all appropriate material safety data sheets.
3. Investigate before you act.
4. When in doubt, *do not act*. Ask your instructor or supervisor.

General Safety Rules for Electricity and Electronics

Safe practices will protect you and your fellow workers. Study the following rules. Discuss them with others, and ask your instructor about any you do not understand.

1. Do not work when you are tired or taking medicine that makes you drowsy.
2. Do not work in poor light.
3. Do not work in damp areas or with wet shoes or clothing.
4. Use approved tools, equipment, and protective devices.
5. Avoid wearing rings, bracelets, and similar metal items when working around exposed electric circuits.
6. Never assume that a circuit is off. Double-check it with an instrument that you are sure is operational.
7. Some situations require a "buddy system" to guarantee that power will not be turned on while a technician is still working on a circuit.
8. Never tamper with or try to override safety devices such as an interlock (a type of switch that automatically removes power when a door is opened or a panel removed).
9. Keep tools and test equipment clean and in good working condition. Replace insulated probes and leads at the first sign of deterioration.
10. Some devices, such as capacitors, can store a *lethal* charge. They may store this charge for long periods of time. You must be certain these devices are discharged before working around them.
11. Do not remove grounds and do not use adaptors that defeat the equipment ground.
12. Use only an approved fire extinguisher for electrical and electronic equipment. Water can con-

duct electricity and may severely damage equipment. Carbon dioxide (CO_2) or halogenated-type extinguishers are usually preferred. Foam-type extinguishers may also be desired in *some* cases. Commercial fire extinguishers are rated for the type of fires for which they are effective. Use only those rated for the proper working conditions.

13. Follow directions when using solvents and other chemicals. They may be toxic, flammable, or may damage certain materials such as plastics. Always read and follow the appropriate material safety data sheets.

14. A few materials used in electronic equipment are toxic. Examples include tantalum capacitors and beryllium oxide transistor cases. These devices should not be crushed or abraded, and you should wash your hands thoroughly after handling them. Other materials (such as heat shrink tubing) may produce irritating fumes if overheat-ed. Always read and follow the appropriate material safety data sheets.

15. Certain circuit components affect the safe performance of equipment and systems. Use only exact or approved replacement parts.

16. Use protective clothing and safety glasses when handling high-vacuum devices such as picture tubes and cathode-ray tubes.

17. Don't work on equipment before you know proper procedures and are aware of any potential safety hazards.

18. Many accidents have been caused by people rushing and cutting corners. Take the time required to protect yourself and others. Running, horseplay, and practical jokes are strictly forbidden in shops and laboratories.

Circuits and equipment must be treated with respect. Learn how they work and the proper way of working on them. Always practice safety: your health and life depend on it.

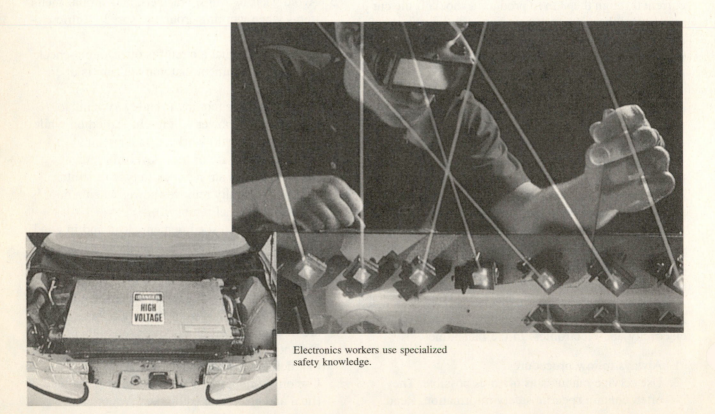

Electronics workers use specialized safety knowledge.

Chapter 1

Basic Concepts

TEST: BASIC CONCEPTS

For questions 1 to 9, determine whether each statement is true or false.

1. Many energy-conversion processes are 100 percent efficient.   1. _____

2. Neutrons and protons are contained in the nucleus of the hydrogen atom.   2. _____

3. The nucleus of any atom has a positive charge.   3. _____

4. Positively charged particles repel each other.   4. _____

5. Atoms which have five or more valence electrons become negative ions when ionized.   5. _____

6. Protons have a larger diameter than electrons do.   6. _____

7. There are as many elements as there are types of atoms.   7. _____

8. An electric lamp converts electric energy to heat energy and light energy.   8. _____

9. The symbol (or abbreviation) for energy is J.   9. _____

For questions 10 to 17, choose the letter that best completes each statement.

10. Energy is defined as   10. _____
    a. A force in newtons
    b. A weight in kilograms
    c. The ability to do work
    d. A negative charge

11. The base unit of energy is the   11. _____
    a. Watt   c. Newton
    b. Joule   d. Nucleus

12. All matter is composed of   12. _____
    a. Atoms   c. Ions
    b. Compounds   d. Newtons

13. A generator that is turned by a mechanical device   13. _____
    a. Creates electric energy
    b. Converts heat energy to electric energy
    c. Converts electric energy to heat energy
    d. Converts mechanical energy to electric energy and heat energy

14. An object that possesses negative static charge has   14. _____
    a. An excess of electrons
    b. A deficiency of atoms
    c. An excess of neutrons
    d. A deficiency of protons

15. Which of the following electrons of a silver atom will be at the highest energy level (possess the most energy)?
   a. An electron in the first shell
   b. An electron in the second shell
   c. An electron in the valence shell
   d. An electron that has just escaped the valence shell

15. _____

16. A positive ion is an atom which has
   a. Gained a valence electron
   b. Lost a valence electron
   c. Gained a proton
   d. Lost a proton

16. _____

17. A lightning bolt is visible because
   a. Protons are jumping from atom to atom
   b. An air column is ionizing and deionizing
   c. Electric energy is being converted to heat energy
   d. Heat energy is being converted to electric energy

17. _____

For questions 18 to 20, solve each problem.

18. How much work is done when an object is moved 2.1 m by a force of 1.8 N?

18. Given: _____
_____

Find: _____

Known: _____

Solution: _____

Answer: _____

19. What is the efficiency of a portable radio receiver which uses 900 J of energy from its battery to produce 190 J of sound energy?

19. Given: _____
_____

Find: _____

Known: _____
_____

Solution: _____
_____

Answer: _____

20. A device is 37 percent efficient and requires an input of 10,867 J of energy. What is its output energy?

20. Given: _____
_____

Find: _____

Known: _____
_____

Solution: _____
_____

Answer: _____

For questions 21 and 22, supply the missing word or phrase in each statement.

21. Inefficiency in a light bulb is caused by electric energy being converted to _____ energy.

21. _____

22. A precipitator uses _____ electricity to remove dust from an air stream.

22. _____

1-1 LAB EXPERIMENT: STATIC CHARGES

PURPOSE

This experiment is designed to familiarize you with some of the characteristics of static charges.

MATERIALS

Qty.

1 rod (glass or plastic) approximately 12 in. long and ⅛ to ½ in. in diameter

1 wire (magnet or hookup), 18 to 22 gage, about 14 in. long

1 ½-in. square of notebook paper or newspaper

1 thread, lightweight sewing, approximately 10 in. long

Qty.

1 piece of tape (masking, electrical, or transparent) approximately 1½ in. long

1 piece of cloth (silk, wool, or polyester) or leather about 10 × 10 in.

1 piece of Styrofoam cup approximately ¼ in. wide and 1 in. long

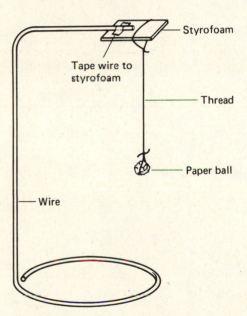

Fig. 1-1 Setup for checking static charge.

1. Bend the magnet or hookup wire into a stand as illustrated in Fig. 1-1. Set the stand on your table or desk. Crumple the ½-in. square of paper into a ball and tie the thread around it. Tie the other end of the thread around one end of the strip of Styrofoam. Tape the other end of the Styrofoam to the end of the wire stand (Fig. 1-1). Be certain that the tape does not touch the thread. Adjust (bend) the top of the stand until the ball clears the table top by at least 1 in.

2. Stroke the glass rod against the cloth or leather two or three times. Then slowly bring the end of the rod toward the free-hanging paper ball. Observe that the paper is attracted to the rod and makes contact with the rod; then the paper is quickly repelled (pushed away) from the rod. (Note: After being repelled, the paper ball may again be attracted to the rod if the charge on the rod is not very strong. If the charge on the rod is too weak, it may reattract and hold the paper for long periods of time.)

a. What causes the paper to be initially attracted to the rod?

_____

_____

b. What causes the paper to be repelled by the rod?

_____

_____

3. Tie another paper ball and thread to the Styrofoam (Fig. 1-2). Adjust the length of the new thread so that the two papers are hanging side by side. Separate the two threads just far enough so that the two paper balls are not touching.

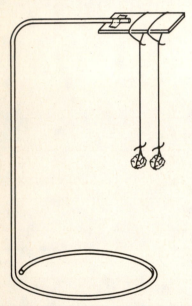

Fig. 1-2 Setup for checking the reaction between two charged objects.

4. Again charge the glass rod by stroking it two or three times against the cloth or leather. Now bring the rod toward the two hanging paper balls and touch both of them at the same time. Then pull the rod down and away from the papers. (If the threads tangle up, straighten them and try again.) Note that the two papers repel each other.
   a. Do the two balls have the same type of charge? _____ Why?

   _____

   _____

   b. How can a manufacturing industry use the principles you have just observed?

   _____

   _____

   _____

   _____

Chapter 2

Electrical Quantities and Units

TEST: ELECTRICAL QUANTITIES AND UNITS

For questions 1 to 10, supply the missing word or phrase in each statement.

1. An electron possesses a _____ electric charge.

   1. _____

2. Ions can be current carriers in either _____ or _____.

   2. _____

3. The type of current which periodically reverses direction is _____ current.

   3. _____

4. Energy in motion or being converted is _____ energy.

   4. _____

5. A coulomb is the amount of charge possessed by _____ electrons.

   5. _____

6. The type of materials used in insulators is classified as a _____.

   6. _____

7. Another name for specific resistance is _____.

   7. _____

8. The nonmetric unit for electric power is _____.

   8. _____

9. _____ describes a change in resistance caused by a change in temperature.

   9. _____

10. Atoms that have gained or lost electrons are called _____.

    10. _____

For question 11 to 37, choose the letter that best completes each statement.

11. The symbol for electric charge is
    a. *C*
    b. *W*
    c. *Q*
    d. *P*

    11. _____

12. "Coulomb" is the base unit for
    a. Current
    b. Power
    c. Resistance
    d. Charge

    12. _____

13. The abbreviation for coulomb is
    a. W
    b. C
    c. Q
    d. P

    13. _____

14. An electric current may be defined as the movement of
    a. Protons through a copper conductor
    b. Ions through a copper conductor
    c. Charges in a specified direction
    d. Charges in random directions

    14. _____

15. Current is represented by the letter   15. _____
    a. *E*
    b. *I*
    c. *C*
    d. *A*
16. The watt is the base unit of   16. _____
    a. Current
    b. Amperage
    c. Voltage
    d. Power
17. "A coulomb per second" is the definition of   17. _____
    a. An ampere
    b. A watt
    c. A joule
    d. A volt
18. The abbreviation for the base unit of current is   18. _____
    a. W
    b. V
    c. C
    d. A
19. Voltage can be defined as   19. _____
    a. Opposition to current
    b. Potential energy difference
    c. Movement of charges
    d. Rate of doing work
20. "*P*" is the symbol for   20. _____
    a. Voltage
    b. Power
    c. Energy
    d. Current
21. The voltage of a battery is available   21. _____
    a. At the negative terminal
    b. At the positive terminal
    c. Between the two terminals
    d. At either the negative or the positive terminal
22. "Volt" is the base unit for   22. _____
    a. Wattage
    b. Amperage
    c. Voltage
    d. Power
23. The base unit of voltage is defined as one   23. _____
    a. Ampere per second
    b. Coulomb per second
    c. Volt per second
    d. Joule per coulomb
24. The abbreviation for volt is   24. _____
    a. W   c. V
    b. P   d. A
25. Which of the following devices does not produce voltage?   25. _____
    a. Solar cell
    b. Crystal
    c. Conductor
    d. Chemical cell
26. Resistance is defined as   26. _____
    a. Ability to conduct voltage
    b. Ability to do work
    c. Rate of doing work
    d. Opposition to current

6

27. Electric energy is converted to heat energy by
    a. Neutrons
    b. Resistors
    c. Insulators
    d. Conductors

27. _____

28. Which of the following materials is the best conductor?
    a. Iron
    b. Copper
    c. Wood
    d. Aluminum

28. _____

29. The base unit of resistance is the
    a. Joule
    b. Ampere
    c. Ohm
    d. Coulomb

29. _____

30. The symbol for resistance is
    a. R
    b. Q
    c. P
    d. Ω

30. _____

31. The abbreviation for the base unit of resistance is
    a. V
    b. Ω
    c. Q
    d. R

31. _____

32. "Rate of converting energy" is the definition for
    a. Current
    b. Kinetic energy
    c. Work
    d. Power

32. _____

33. "Ampere" is the base unit for
    a. Current
    b. Work
    c. Power
    d. Voltage

33. _____

34. "Joule per second" is a definition of the base unit for
    a. Current
    b. Work
    c. Power
    d. Voltage

34. _____

35. The abbreviation for the base unit of power is
    a. C
    b. Ω
    c. W
    d. V

35. _____

36. "V" is the symbol for
    a. Voltage
    b. Power
    c. Current
    d. Energy

36. _____

37. Which of the following units is not a metric unit?
    a. Horsepower
    b. Coulomb
    c. Second
    d. Watt

37. _____

For questions 38 to 43, solve each problem.

38. Determine the energy stored in a 12-V dry cell that has a charge of 2000 C.

38. Given: _____
_____
Find: _____
Known: _____
Solution: _____
_____
Answer: _____

39. How much current is flowing when a charge of 4 C, all moving in the same direction, passes a specified point in 2 s?

39. Given: _____
_____
Find: _____
Known: _____
Solution: _____
_____
Answer: _____

40. If K = 0.004 $\Omega \cdot$cm at 20°C, what is the resistance (at 20°C) of 250 cm of a solid conductor with a cross-sectional area of 0.02 cm²?

40. Given: _____
_____
Find: _____
Known: _____
Solution: _____
_____
Answer: _____

41. A 500-W heater operates continuously for 3 h. How many watthours of energy does it convert?

41. Given: _____
_____
Find: _____
Known: _____
Solution: _____
_____
Answer: _____

42. What is the efficiency of an electric device requiring 51,600 joules every minute to produce 602 W of useful power output?

42. Given: _____
_____
Find: _____
Known: _____
Solution: _____
_____
Answer: _____

43. How much input power (in watts) is required by a motor that is 56 percent efficient and produces ¾ hp?

43. Given: _____
_____
Find: _____
Known: _____
Solution: _____
_____
Answer: _____

For questions 44 to 49, complete the conversions.

44. 210 mA = _____ A

45. 2,000,000 = _____ (expressed in powers of 10)

46. 5.3×10^{-6} = _____ (expressed in base 10)

47. 68,000 Ω = _____ kΩ

48. 3 mA = _____ μA

49. 2.2×10^3 Ω = _____ kΩ

44. _____

45. _____

46. _____

47. _____

48. _____

49. _____

2-1 LAB EXPERIMENT: CONDUCTORS, INSULATORS, AND RESISTANCE

PURPOSE

In the following experiment, you will determine which materials are conductors and which are not. The last section of the experiment will help you visualize how physical dimensions determine resistance.

MATERIALS

Qty.

1   6-V battery (or other 6-V dc power supply)
1   no. 47 miniature lamp (6.3 V, 0.15 A)
1   lamp holder for no. 47 lamp (T-3¼ bayonet base)
3   test leads with alligator clips on both ends
1   teaspoon of sodium bicarbonate (baking soda)
2   15-cm (6-in.) lengths of bare (untinned) copper wire, 10 to 16 gate

Qty.

1   Styrofoam cup
•   strips of various test materials such as paper, wood, copper, aluminum foil, glass, plastic, cloth, rubber, leather; the strips should be approximately 8 cm (3 in.) long; cross-sectional area is not important as long as connections can be made with alligator clips

PROCEDURE

(*Note:* To prolong the life of the battery, operate the light for as short a time as possible.)

1. Connect the battery, lamp socket, and wires, as shown in Fig. 2-1. Touch together the two alligator clips that will be used to make contact with the test materials. The lamp should light up to full brilliance. This indicates that the connecting wires are good conductors. Separate the alligator clips and the lamp should go off.

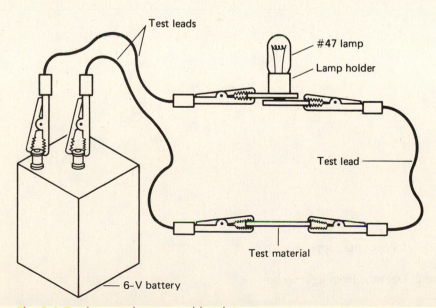

Fig. 2-1 Testing conductors and insulators.

2. Connect a piece of aluminum foil between the alligator clips and observe the brilliance of the lamp. Disconnect the alligator clips from the aluminum. Is aluminum a good conductor? _____

3. Using the procedure outlined in step 2, test the other materials provided by your instructor. Record your results in Table 2-1. The first line of Table 2-1 is completed as an example.

TABLE 2-1 INSULATORS AND CONDUCTORS

Material	Conductor (lamp lights)	Poor Conductor or Insulator (lamp does not light)
Aluminum	✔	
Paper		
Copper		
Wood		
Glass		
Plastic		
Cloth		
Rubber		
Leather		

4. Bend a piece of bare copper wire into the shape of copper wire 2 in Fig. 2-2. The end of the wire should be approximately 1 cm (⅜ in.) from the bottom of the cup. Connect the alligator clip from the lamp socket to this copper wire (Fig. 2-2). Connect the other piece of bare copper wire (copper wire 1 in Fig. 2-2) to the alligator clip that connects to the battery lead. Copper wire 1 and the alligator clip attached to it are held in place by hand when tests are being conducted. At other times, they can be placed on the table beside the cup.

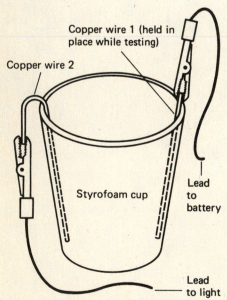

Fig. 2-2 Testing ionized solutions.

5. Fill the cup about two-thirds full of water.
   a. Insert copper wire 1 along the edge of the cup opposite copper wire 2. Does the lamp light? _____
   b. Move copper wire 1 toward copper wire 2. Does the lamp light up before the two wires touch? _____
   c. Is water a good conductor? _____

6. Remove the alligator clip from copper wire 1. Add 1 teaspoon of baking soda to the water in the cup and stir with copper wire 1 (the baking soda will form ions when added to the water). Remove copper wire 1 from the solution and reconnect it to the alligator clip. Now slowly insert copper wire 1 into the solution along the edge opposite copper wire 2.

   a. Does the light come on? _____

   b. Is a baking soda solution a conductor? _____

   c. While observing the lamp, slowly move copper wire 1 up and down in the solution. Does the light get brighter as the copper wire is moved into the solution? _____

   d. With copper wire 1 fully inserted into the solution, slowly move copper wire 1 toward copper wire 2. Does the light get brighter as the wires are brought closer together? _____

   e. Do you see any similarity between the depth that copper wire 1 was inserted into the solution and the cross-sectional area of a conductor? Why? (*Hint:* The current carriers—ions—move between the surfaces of the two copper wires.)

   _____

   _____

   f. Do you see any similarity between the distance copper wire 1 was from copper wire 2 and the length of a conductor? Why?

   _____

   _____

   g. Does increasing the cross-sectional area of a conductor increase or decrease its resistance? _____

   h. Does increasing the length of a conductor increase or decrease its resistance? _____

7. Remove both wires from the solution. Dispose of the baking soda solution and the two copper wires in the manner specified by your instructor.

2-2 ADVANCED PROBLEMS

2-1. How much input power is required by a stereo amplifier that produces 100 joules per second and that is 65 percent efficient? _____

2-2. What is the efficiency of a 1.0-hp motor that uses 6.1×10^6 J in 1 h? _____

2-3. A 120-W stereo amplifier is 60 percent efficient. How many joules of energy does it use in 45 min? _____

2-4. A 20-V battery has 2000 C of charge. It is connected to a 3.7-W electric device. How long will it take to use 50 percent of the battery's energy? _____

2-3 LAB EXERCISE: TEMPERATURE COEFFICIENTS OF RESISTORS

1. Obtain one or more electronics parts catalogs from your instructor or your library. Look in the index for the pages that list resistors. If the index has subheadings under resistors, look under precision, carbon-composition, metal-film, and wire-wound headings. Turn to the indicated pages and read the specifications for these types of resistors. You will not understand most of the specifications, but look for the temperature coefficient (tc) rating.

2. Record the highest and lowest temperature coefficients you can find. Also record the type of resistor (carbon, metal-film, etc.) that has the lowest and the highest temperature coefficient.

_____

_____

_____

a. Do most of the resistor listing include temperature coefficients? _____

b. Why do you think some resistor specifications do not include temperature coefficients?

_____

_____

_____

Chapter 3

Basic Circuits, Laws, and Measurements

TEST: BASIC CIRCUITS, LAWS, AND MEASUREMENTS

For questions 1 to 14, determine whether each statement is true or false.

1. The metal frame of an automobile can serve as a conductor in its electric circuits.   1. _____

2. In an electric circuit, the load converts electric energy to another form of energy.   2. _____

3. The symbol for an insulated conductor is a dashed line between two solid lines.   3. _____

4. The physical arrangement of electric components is indicated by a schematic diagram.   4. _____

5. Schematic diagrams never include the electrical specifications of the components.   5. _____

6. Current is directly proportional to resistance in an electric circuit.   6. _____

7. Doubling the resistance in a circuit halves the current if the voltage is held constant.   7. _____

8. Electron current leaves the positive terminal of the cell and travels through the load to the negative terminal of the cell.   8. _____

9. A digital panel meter is also known as a multimeter.   9. _____

10. A VOM is also known as a multimeter.   10. _____

11. The ohms-adjust setting on a VOM should be checked every time the resistance range is changed.   11. _____

Refer to Fig. 3-1 for questions 12 to 14.

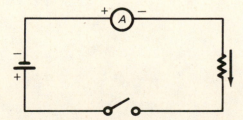

Fig. 3-1 Diagram for questions 12 to 14.

12. In Fig. 3-1, the arrow is pointing in the correct direction to indicate the direction of current (electron flow).   12. _____

13. The polarity shown on the meter is incorrect.   13. _____

14. The circuit contains a protection device.   14. _____

For questions 15 through 20, choose the letter that best completes each statement.

15. Which of the following is not an essential part of every circuit?
    a. Load   **c.** Fuse
    b. Conductor   **d.** Energy source

16. Which of the following is classified as a load for an electric circuit?
    a. Resistor   **c.** Fuse
    b. Conductor   **d.** Insulator

17. A circuit must be physically interrupted to measure
    a. Voltage   **c.** Current
    b. Resistance

18. Power must be removed from a circuit when measuring
    a. Voltage   **c.** Current
    b. Resistance

19. A multimeter cannot measure
    a. Power   **c.** Voltage
    b. Current   **d.** Resistance

20. Which of the following has no schematic symbol?
    a. Fuse   **c.** Conductor
    b. Resistor   **d.** Insulator

15._____

16._____

17._____

18._____

19._____

20._____

For questions 21 to 34, solve each problem. Be sure to include units (mA, V, etc.) in your answers.

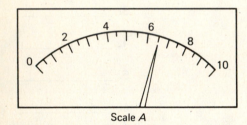
Scale *A*

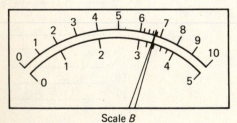
Scale *B*

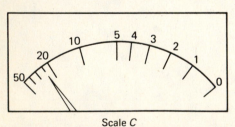
Scale *C*

Fig. 3-2 Meter scales for questions 21 to 25.

21. Scale *A* in Fig. 3-2 represents part of a meter. How much voltage does the meter indicate if it is on the 100-V range?

22. Refer to scale *A* in Fig. 3-2. How much current does the meter indicate if it is on the 10-mA range?

23. Refer to scale *B* in Fig. 3-2. How much voltage is indicated if the meter is on the 1-V range?

21._____

22._____

23._____

16

24. Refer to scale *B* in Fig. 3-2. How much current is indicated if the meter is on the 5-mA range?

25. Refer to scale *C* in Fig. 3-2. How much resistance is indicated if the meter is on the ×100 Ω range?

26. How much current flows through a 40-Ω resistor that is connected to a 24-V battery?

27. How much voltage is required to force 40 mA of current through a 100-Ω load?

28. What is the resistance of a 12.6-V lamp that draws 1.4 A of current?

29. What is the power of the lamp in question 28?

30. How much energy is used by the lamp in question 28 if it operates for 6 h?

31. Assuming that electric energy costs 9¢/kWh, how much does it cost to operate a 900-W toaster for 3 h?

32. How much current is required by a 28-V, 40-W lamp?

33. How much power is required by a circuit in which 5 A flows through a 15-Ω resistor?

34. How much voltage is across a 5-kΩ resistor which has 2.5 mA of current flowing through it?

24. _____
25. _____
26. _____
27. _____
28. _____
29. _____
30. _____
31. _____
32. _____
33. _____
34. _____

3-1 LAB EXERCISE: WORKING WITH SCHEMATIC DIAGRAMS

1. Draw a schematic diagram of the pictorial presentations shown. Show the polarity of the battery and the meter on the diagram. Also indicate the direction of current by an arrow.
   a. Fig. 3-3
   b. Fig. 3-4
2. Refer to Fig. 3-5. Record on each diagram
   a. What is being measured
   b. The correct polarity of the meter if polarity is important for the indicated measurement
   c. The direction of current flow
3. Name each component in Fig. 3-5(*b*).
4. Would the meter reading in Fig. 3-5(*c*) change if the switch were opened? _____ Why?
   _____
   _____
5. Would the meter reading in Fig. 3-5(*a*) change if the switch were opened? _____ Why?
   _____
   _____
6. What might happen if the switch in Fig. 3-5(*d*) were accidentally closed?
   _____
   _____

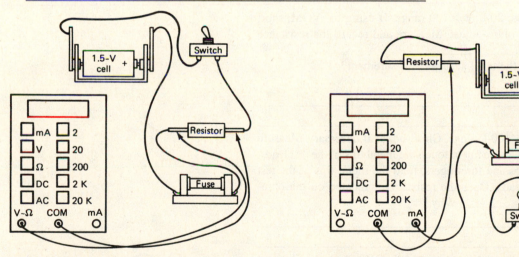

Fig. 3-3 Pictorial presentation for step 1a.

Fig. 3-4 Pictorial presentation for step 1b.

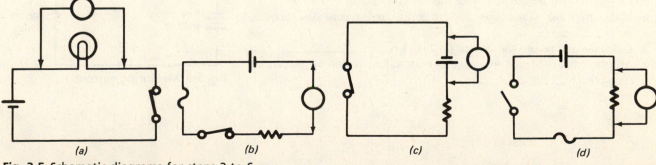

Fig. 3-5 Schematic diagrams for steps 2 to 6.

3-2 LAB EXPERIMENT: MEASURING VOLTAGE, CURRENT, AND RESISTANCE

PURPOSE

This experiment will provide practice in using the multimeter.

MATERIALS

Qty.

1 multimeter (DMM or VOM)
1 6-V dry battery (or other
   6-V dc power supply)

Qty.

1 1.5-V dry cell
1 1000-Ω, ½-W resistor
1 1-MΩ, ½-W resistor

PROCEDURE

1. Set the multimeter to the dc voltage function and the 10-V or larger range.
   a. Observing polarity, measure and record the voltage of the cell and the
      battery. Cell _____ Battery _____
   b. Next, select a range just larger than 1.5 V. Measure and record the volt-
      age of the cell. _____
   c. Did measuring the cell voltage on a lower range yield a higher resolu-
      tion? _____ Why?

   _____

   _____

2. Set the multimeter to the resistance function. Select the 2-k range of the
   DMM or the ×10 range of the VOM. If using the VOM, short the leads
   together and ohms-adjust.
   a. Measure and record the resistance of the resistor that is marked 1000
      Ω. _____
   b. Change the meter to the 20-k or ×100 range. If using the VOM, short
      the leads together and ohms-adjust. Measure and record the resistance
      of the 1000-Ω resistor. _____
   c. Which range provides the most accurate measurement?
      _____ Why?

   _____

   _____

   d. Change to the 2-M or ×100-k range. Ohms-adjust if necessary. Measure
      the 1-MΩ resistor, being sure not to touch the metal tips of the test leads.
      Now, with your thumbs and forefingers, hold the metal tips of the test
      leads to the resistor leads. Does the resistance indicated on the ohm-
      meter change? _____ Why?

   _____

   _____

3. Set the multimeter to the current function and the 10-mA range. Connect
   all but one connection of the circuit shown in Fig. 3-6. Have your instructor
   check your circuit before you make the last connection.
   a. Make the last connection and measure and record the current.

      _____
   b. Calculate and record the current for Fig. 3-6. _____
   c. Are the calculated and measured current values within 10 percent of
      each other? _____

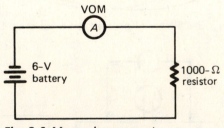

Fig. 3-6 Measuring current.

3-3 LAB EXPERIMENT: OHM'S LAW

PURPOSE

This experiment provides verification of Ohm's law. It also provides additional experience in constructing circuits and using meters.

MATERIALS

Qty.		Qty.	
1	multimeter (DMM or VOM)	1	1.5-V dry cell
1	6-V dry battery or power supply	1	1000-Ω, ½-W resistor
		1	10-kΩ, ½-W resistor

PROCEDURE

1. Refer to the circuit shown in Fig. 3-7(a).
   a. Using Ohm's law and the indicated voltage and resistance, calculate the current:

   $$I = \frac{V}{R} = \frac{6\text{ V}}{1000\ \Omega} = \underline{\hspace{2cm}} \text{ A} = \underline{\hspace{2cm}} \text{ mA}$$

   b. Construct the circuit. Then measure and record the current. Remember that the circuit must be physically interrupted, as shown in Fig. 3-7(b), to measure current. _____
   c. Are the measured and the calculated current about the same (within 15 percent)? If they are not, you have made an error or have faulty equipment. Check with your teacher. _____
2. Change the 1000-Ω resistor in Fig. 3-7(a) to a 10,000-Ω resistor. This increases the resistance by a factor of 10 and provides the circuit shown in Fig. 3-7(c).
   a. According to Ohm's law, what should happen to the current?

   _____

   _____

   b. Measure and record the current with the 10,000-Ω resistor in the circuit. _____
   c. Is this the current you expected? _____
3. Change the battery to a 1.5-V cell and the resistor to 1000 Ω. This will give you the circuit shown in Fig. 3-7(d). Notice the voltage has decreased to one-fourth the value used in Fig. 3-7(a).
   a. What relationship should there be between the currents in the circuits of Fig. 3-7(a) and (d)?

   _____

   _____

   b. Measure and record the current in the new circuit [Fig. 3-7(d)].

   _____

   c. Is this the current you would expect after decreasing the voltage from 6 V to 1.5 V? _____

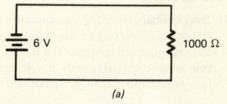

(a)

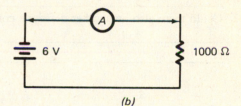

(b)

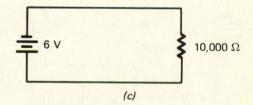

(c)

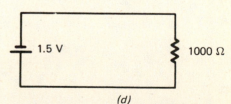

(d)

Fig. 3-7 Circuits for experiment 3-3.

3-4 LAB EXPERIMENT: TROUBLESHOOTING

PURPOSE

Electric circuits do fail. Electrical workers need to develop troubleshooting skills. This experiment will help you do that.

MATERIALS

Qty.

1 multimeter (DMM or VOM)
1 6-V dry cell or power supply
1 no. 47 lamp
1 switch, SPST, 1A, 125 V ac
1 fuse, 0.5 A, with holder
• For simulation software, obtain the file labeled Fig. 3-8.ewb from your instructor.

PROCEDURE

1. The physical circuit for the schematic diagram in Fig. 3-8 has a defective component. Unless your instructor asks you to use electronic-circuit simulation software, construct the circuit with the components provided by your instructor. Using only a voltmeter, determine which component is faulty and explain how you made this determination.

_____

_____

2. Could there also be another defective component in the circuit? Explain.

_____

_____

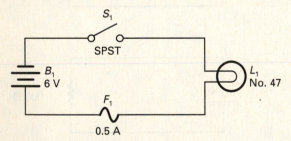

Fig. 3-8 Diagram for defective circuit.

3-5 ADVANCED PROBLEMS

3-1. How much current is flowing through a 40-Ω resistor that dissipates 360 W? _____

3-2. A 98-Ω electric device uses 0.25 kWh of energy in 5 h. How much voltage is connected to the device? _____

3-3. How much power is needed to force 30 C of charge through a 5-Ω resistor in 20 s? _____

3-4. The current through a lamp is 2 A. If it requires 30 J to force 3 C through the lamp, how much power is needed? _____

Chapter 4

Circuit Components

TEST: CIRCUIT COMPONENTS

For questions 1 to 9, supply the missing word or phrase needed in each statement.

1. Cells that can be recharged are called _____ cells.
2. A battery has at least _____ cells.
3. The accumulation of gas ions around an electrode in a cell is called _____.
4. The _____ cell has the longest shelf life of any of the primary cells.
5. A _____ cell uses sulfuric acid in its electrolyte.
6. The _____ of a cell causes its terminal voltage to change with changes in cell current.
7. The specific gravity of a cell can be measured with a _____.
8. The specific gravity of a cell _____ as the cell is discharged.
9. Fast-blow fuses are sometimes called _____ fuses.

1. _____
2. _____
3. _____
4. _____
5. _____
6. _____
7. _____
8. _____
9. _____

For questions 10 to 37, determine whether each statement is true or false.

10. Lead-acid batteries should be stored in a charged state.
11. The cycle life of an alkaline cell is greater than that of a nickel-cadmium cell.
12. For high-current applications, alkaline cells are better than carbon-zinc cells.
13. The carbon-zinc D cell is cheaper than the alkaline D cell.
14. For the same size cell, alkaline cells store more energy than carbon-zinc cells.
15. The alkaline cell has a less constant output voltage than the nickel-cadmium cell does.
16. Alkaline cells maintain a more constant voltage as they are discharged than mercury cells do.
17. Silver oxide cells are commonly used in high-current applications.
18. Miniature incandescent lamps have carbon filaments.
19. An incandescent lamp operated below its rated voltage has a reduced life expectancy.
20. When heated, a bimetallic strip bends.
21. The hot resistance of a lamp is greater than the cold resistance of a lamp.
22. When a neon lamp is operated on dc voltage, both electrodes glow.
23. Neon lamp circuits contain a resistor to limit the current through the lamp.
24. A rheostat is often used as a potentiometer.

10. _____
11. _____
12. _____
13. _____
14. _____
15. _____
16. _____
17. _____
18. _____
19. _____
20. _____
21. _____
22. _____
23. _____
24. _____

25. When used to describe a switch, NC is the abbreviation for "no connection."

26. Power resistors are usually carbon-composition resistors.

27. Conductive plastic is often used for potentiometers.

28. The resistance of a resistor is not related to the physical size of the resistor.

29. The power rating of a resistor is not related to the physical size of the resistor.

30. A switch can control more current in a 208-V circuit than it can in a 120-V circuit.

31. Coaxial cables are often used to connect electric motors to a power source.

32. A 16-gage wire has half as much resistance per foot as a 19-gage wire.

33. The amount of current a copper conductor can carry depends only on the cross-sectional area of the conductor.

34. Electric motors are usually protected with slow-blow fuses or long-time-lag circuit breakers.

35. Some resistors have essentially 0 Ω of resistance.

36. All circuit-protection devices produce an open circuit when they are tripped or blown.

37. An SMD has short leads for soldering into holes in a printed circuit board.

25. _____

26. _____

27. _____

28. _____

29. _____

30. _____

31. _____

32. _____

33. _____

34. _____

35. _____

36. _____

37. _____

For questions 38 to 42, choose the letter that best completes each statement.

38. The energy storage capacity of a cell or battery is specified in
   a. Watthours
   b. Joule-hours
   c. Volt-hours
   d. Ampere-hours

39. Which of the following cells is a secondary cell?
   a. Lithium
   b. Carbon-zinc
   c. Nickel-cadmium
   d. Mercury

40. Which of the following switch types can perform the most complex switching?
   a. Rotary
   b. Toggle
   c. Rocker
   d. Push-button

41. Which of the following switch types can be either shorting or nonshorting?
   a. Rotary
   b. Rocker
   c. Toggle
   d. Push-button

42. The cross-sectional area of a round conductor is specified in
   a. Mils
   b. Circular mils
   c. Circular meters
   d. Square meters

38. _____

39. _____

40. _____

41. _____

42. _____

Using the color code below, determine the resistance and tolerance indicated by the sequence of colors listed in questions 43 to 46.

Black	0	Blue	6
Brown	1 or 1 percent	Violet	7
Red	2 or 2 percent	Gray	8
Orange	3	White	9
Yellow	4	Gold	0.1 or 5 percent
Green	5	Silver	0.01 or 10 percent

24

43. Green, brown, silver, gold
44. Gray, red, green, silver
45. Brown, black, black, black, brown
46. Red, black, green, red, red

43. _____
44. _____
45. _____
46. _____

For questions 47 to 51, solve each problem. Be sure to include units (W, Ω, etc.) in your answers when appropriate.

47. What is the terminal voltage of a voltage source with a nominal voltage of 20 V and an internal resistance of 0.45 Ω when the source is providing 2.1 A to its load?

47. _____

48. A 560-Ω, 5 percent resistor is at the high end of its tolerance. How much power does it dissipate when it carries 240 mA?

48. _____

49. In an electric device, a 100-Ω, 10 percent resistor will draw 100 mA of current. What power rating should the resistor have?

49. _____

50. How much current is drawn by a lamp rated at 12.6 V and 31.5 W?

50. _____

51. What is the hot resistance of the lamp in question 50?

51. _____

4-1 LAB EXPERIMENT: LAMP SWITCHING CIRCUIT

PURPOSE

The following experiment will provide experience in using switches and fuses. It also provides experience in building circuits from diagrams.

MATERIALS

Qty.

1 multimeter (DMM or VOM)
1 6-V dry battery or power supply
2 SPDT toggle switches (1-A, 125-V ac rating)

Qty.

1 0.5-A fuse, 32 V (or greater)
1 fuse holder
1 no. 47 lamp
1 lamp holder for no. 47 lamp

PROCEDURE

1. Using an ohmmeter, check for continuity between the center terminal and the outside terminals of one of the toggle switches. Change the switch to its other position and again check for continuity. Now check for continuity between the two outside terminals with the switch in one position and then the other. Which terminal of the switch is the pole? _____

2. Construct the circuit shown in Fig. 4-1.
   a. Throw S_1 back and forth while observing the lamp. Does the lamp turn off and on? _____
   b. Throw S_2 back and forth. Does the lamp turn off and on? _____
   c. Can S_1 control the lamp with S_2 in either position? _____

3. While the lamp is on, remove F_1 from its holder. Removal of the fuse gives the same effect as a blown fuse. Now measure the voltage across the terminals of the fuse holder. Reinsert F_1 and again measure the voltage across its terminals. Can a voltmeter be used to indicate the condition of a fuse in a circuit? _____ How?

   _____

   _____

4. Turn the lamp off with S_2. Now measure the voltages between the center terminal and the outside terminals of S_2. Next measure the voltages between the center terminal and the outside terminals of S_1. Can a voltmeter indicate whether a switch is open? _____

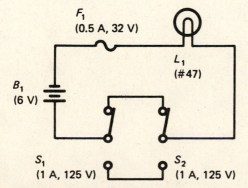

Fig. 4-1 Lamp switching circuit.

4-2 LAB EXPERIMENT: DETERMINING THE RESISTANCE OF A LAMP

PURPOSE

Completion of this experiment will acquaint you with the characteristics of incandescent lamps. The experiment will also give you additional experience in measuring current.

MATERIALS

Qty.

1 6-V dry battery or power supply
1 lamp holder

Qty.

1 no. 47 lamp (6.3 V, 0.15 A)
1 VOM or DMM

PROCEDURE

1. Measure and record the resistance of the lamp. This resistance is referred to as the "cold resistance" of the lamp. It is not the same as the resistance when the lamp is operated at rated voltage. The resistance at rated voltage is called the "hot resistance." _____

2. Determine the hot resistance by constructing the circuit of Fig. 4-2(*a*) and measuring the current and voltage.
   a. What is the measured voltage across the lamp [Fig. 4-2(*b*)]? _____
   b. What is the measured current through the lamp [Fig. 4-2(*c*)]? _____
   c. Now calculate and record the hot resistance with Ohm's law. _____
   d. How does this resistance compare with the resistance measured in step 1 above? _____

3. a. Using the manufacturer's ratings (6.3 V, 0.15 A), calculate the hot resistance. _____
   b. Is this resistance closer to the resistance determined in step 1 or to that determined in step 2 above? _____

4. a. What is the power rating of the no. 47 lamp? _____
   b. How much power was the lamp using in step 2? _____

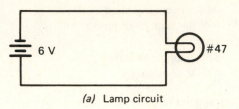

(a) Lamp circuit

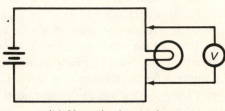

(b) Measuring lamp voltage

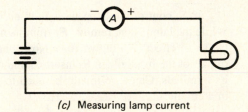

(c) Measuring lamp current

Fig. 4-2 Determining "hot resistance."

4-3 LAB EXPERIMENT: INTERNAL RESISTANCE

PURPOSE

This experiment demonstrates how the internal resistance and the terminal voltage of a cell vary as the load current varies. It also provides additional practice calculating and measuring electrical quantities.

MATERIALS

Qty.

1 multimeter (DMM or VOM)
1 1.5-V dry cell
1 100-Ω, ½-W resistor
1 47-Ω, ½-W resistor
1 22-Ω, ½-W resistor
1 10-Ω, ½-W resistor
1 4.7-Ω, ½-W resistor
1 SPST switch

PROCEDURE

1. Measure and record in Table 4-1 the terminal (N.L.) voltage of the dry cell when it has no resistor connected to it.
2. Construct the circuit shown in Fig. 4-3. Leave S_1 open and use the 100-Ω resistor.

TABLE 4-1   Measured and Calculated Values for Fig. 4-3

Load, Ω	$V_{measured}$, V	$I_{calculated}$, mA	V_{intR}, mV	R_{int}, Ω
N.L.				
100				
47				
22				
10				
4.7				

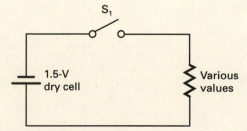

Fig. 4-3 Circuit for experiment 4-3.

3. Prepare the multimeter to measure the voltage across R_1. Close S_1 and measure the voltage across R_1. Open S_1 and record the measured voltage in Table 4-1.
4. Repeat step 3 using the other resistors listed in Table 4-1.

5. Using the measured voltages and the given value of resistance, calculate and record in Table 4-1 the current for each resistor.

6. Calculate and record in Table 4-1 the voltage dropped across the internal resistance ($V_{intR} = V_{N.L.} - V_{load}$).

7. Calculate and record in Table 4-1 the internal resistance for each load condition.

8. Is the decrease in internal resistance proportional to the increase in load current? _____

9. What would have happened if a 2.2-Ω, ½-W resistor had been used as a load?

   _____

10. Calculate and record the power dissipated by the 4.7-Ω load and the 47-Ω load. _____   _____

11. Does the 4.7-Ω resistor draw 10 times as much current as the 47-Ω resistor in this circuit? _____ Why?

   _____

4-4 LAB EXERCISE: RESISTOR TOLERANCE AND STANDARD VALUES

1. Obtain an electronics parts catalog from your teacher or library. Look in the fixed-resistor section for the values of resistors available in ±5 and ±10 percent. List the values of resistors between 400 and 600 Ω that are available in 5 and 10 percent tolerances.

    5% _____   _____   _____   _____

    10% _____   _____   _____   _____

2. Notice that there are fewer values available in 10 percent resistors than in 5 percent resistors. For example, in a 5 percent resistor you can obtain values of 470, 510, and 560 Ω. Only the 470- and 560-Ω values are obtainable in 10 percent tolerance. This is because the minimum value of a ±10 percent, 560-Ω resistor is less than 510 Ω. And the maximum value of a ±10 percent, 470-Ω resistor is greater than 510 Ω.

3. Standard 680- and 750-Ω resistors are available in 5 percent tolerance.
    a. Without referring to the catalog, determine whether or not a 715-Ω, ±5 percent resistor is available. Is it? _____ Why?

    _____

    _____

    b. Would it be available in a 10 percent resistor? _____
    c. Would it be available in a 1 percent resistor? _____

4-5 LAB EXERCISE: USING WIRE CHARTS AND TABLES

This exercise requires the use of wire tables. These are available in electrical handbooks and manufacturers' catalogs. Obtain a copy of the appropriate tables from your teacher or the library.

1. An electric saw is to be operated on a 100-ft extension cord. The saw requires 10 A of current.
   a. What size conductors will be required? _____
   b. Why does a 125-ft cord require a larger conductor than a 100-ft cord to carry 10 A of current?

   _____

   _____

2. What is the resistance of 140 ft of 16-gage solid copper wire at 20°C?
   _____

3. In residential wiring, the electrical code permits a 14-gage copper conductor to carry 15 A under certain conditions. What is the rating of this conductor in circular mils per ampere? _____

Chapter 5

Multiple-Load Circuits

TEST: MULTIPLE-LOAD CIRCUITS

For questions 1 to 8, supply the missing word or phrase in each statement.

1. All the voltages in a _____ circuit are equal.

2. All the currents in a _____ circuit are the same.

3. The reciprocal formula is used to calculate total resistance in a _____ circuit.

4. Adding another series resistor to a series circuit will _____ the total conductance.

5. In a parallel circuit, the total resistance must be _____ than the lowest individual resistance.

6. Ammeters have a very _____ internal resistance.

7. The total power of a parallel circuit _____ when one load opens.

8. The _____ resistance drops the most voltage in a series circuit.

1. _____

2. _____

3. _____

4. _____

5. _____

6. _____

7. _____

8. _____

For questions 9 to 20, determine whether each statement is true or false.

9. In a parallel circuit, one end of a resistor must be disconnected from the circuit to measure its resistance.

10. The total current in a series circuit can be measured by inserting an ammeter in series with any load in the circuit.

11. A deficiency of electrons always exists at the positive end of a resistor.

12. The total resistance of a series circuit is always less than the lowest resistance.

13. The voltage measured across an open load is approximately equal to the source voltage.

14. In a parallel circuit, the lowest resistance uses the least power.

15. When one load is removed from a parallel circuit, the total resistance decreases.

16. Maximum power transfer in a circuit leads to maximum efficiency.

17. For maximum power transfer, the load resistance should be not more than half as high as the source resistance.

18. A low resistance has more conductance than a high resistance.

19. When any one of the resistors in a parallel circuit is removed, the conductance of the circuit increases.

20. Three 33-Ω resistors connected in parallel provide 99 Ω of total resistance.

9. _____

10. _____

11. _____

12. _____

13. _____

14. _____

15. _____

16. _____

17. _____

18. _____

19. _____

20. _____

For questions 21 to 29, choose the letter that best completes each statement.

21. A series-parallel circuit is classified as a   **21.** _____
    a. Single-load circuit
    b. Single-path circuit
    c. Multiple-load circuit
    d. Multiple-path circuit

22. The formula $P_T = P_{R_1} + P_{R_2} + P_{R_3}$ is used with   **22.** _____
    a. Series circuits
    b. Parallel circuits
    c. Series-parallel circuits
    d. All the above circuits

23. The formula $I_T = I_{R_1} + I_{R_2} + I_{R_3}$ is used with   **23.** _____
    a. Series circuits
    b. Parallel circuits
    c. Series-parallel circuits
    d. All the above circuits

24. The formula $R_T = R_1 + R_2 + R_3$ is used with   **24.** _____
    a. Series circuits
    b. Parallel circuits
    c. Series-parallel circuits
    d. All the above circuits

25. The highest resistor dominates the circuit if the circuit is   **25.** _____
    a. Series
    b. Parallel
    c. Series-parallel
    d. Any of the above

26. The total resistance of 68-, 82-, and 100-Ω resistors connected in parallel will be   **26.** _____
    a. Less than 68 Ω
    b. Between 68 and 82 Ω
    c. Between 82 and 100 Ω
    d. Greater than 100 Ω

27. When estimating the total resistance of the circuit in Fig. 5-1, which resistor would you omit from your calculations?   **27.** _____
    a. R_1 **c.** R_3
    b. R_2 **d.** R_4

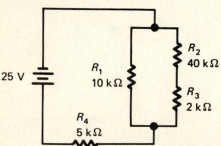

Fig. 5-1 Circuit for questions 27, 28, 29, and 34.

28. In Fig. 5-1, increasing R_1 to 15 kΩ will   **28.** _____
    a. Increase I_T **c.** Increase P_T
    b. Increase R_T **d.** Increase V_T

29. In Fig. 5-1, decreasing R_2 to 10 kΩ will   **29.** _____
    a. Decrease V_{R_4} **c.** Decrease V_{R_1}
    b. Decrease V_{R_3} **d.** Decrease V_T

Solve the following problems and record your answers. Be sure to specify units as well as numbers.

30. Find the values for V_{R_1}, R_2, R_3, P_T, and R_T for Fig. 5-2.

30. _____
_____
_____
_____
_____

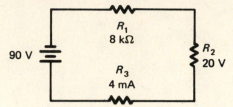

Fig. 5-2 Circuit for question 30.

31. Find the values for I_{R_1}, I_{R_2}, R_2, P_T, and P_{R_1} for Fig. 5-3.

31. _____
_____
_____
_____
_____

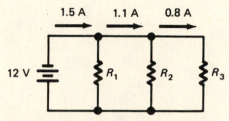

Fig. 5-3 Circuit for question 31.

32. Three resistors—22, 44, and 66 Ω—are parallel-connected to a 6-V battery. Determine the values for R_T, I_T, P_T, and G_T.

32. _____
_____
_____
_____

33. For the circuit of Fig. 5-4, find the values for V_{R_1}, V_{R_3}, I_{R_1}, R_1, and R_T.

33. _____
_____
_____
_____
_____

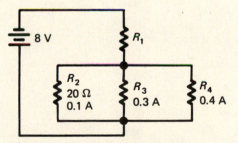

Fig. 5-4 Circuit for question 33.

34. Determine R_T, I_T, and P_T for Fig. 5-1.

34. _____
_____
_____

5-1 LAB EXPERIMENT: SERIES CIRCUITS—
GENERAL PROPERTIES

PURPOSE

This experiment is designed to illustrate the major characteristics of a series circuit. It will also provide experience in constructing and testing series circuits.

MATERIALS

Qty.		Qty.	
1	6-V dry battery (or 6-V dc power supply)	1	4.7-Ω, ½-W resistor
2	no. 47 lamps	1	33-Ω, ½-W resistor
2	lamp holders for no. 47 lamps	1	VOM or DMM
		•	test leads and wire

PROCEDURE

Note: If using a battery, operate the lamps for the shortest time possible to conserve the battery.

1. Connect the circuit shown in Fig. 5-5(*a*).
    a. Do the lamps glow with equal brilliancy? _____ Why?

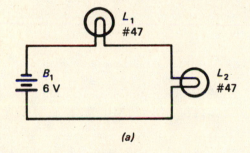

(a)

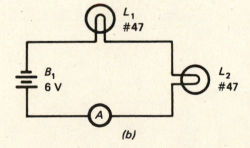

(b)

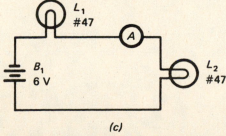

(c)

Fig. 5-5 Series lamps.

b. Does either lamp glow with normal brilliancy? _____ Why?

_____

c. Should $V_{L_1} + V_{L_2}$ equal the battery voltage? _____

d. Measure and record the voltage across each lamp and across the battery.

V_{L_1} _____ V_{L_2} _____ V_{B_1} _____

e. Does $V_{L_1} + V_{L_2}$ equal the battery voltage? _____

f. Interrupt the circuit between the positive terminal of the power source and L_2. Insert the DMM (current function, 500-mA range) as shown in Fig. 5-5(*b*). Measure and record the current at this location in the circuit.

_____

g. Should the current be the same if measured between L_1 and L_2, as indicated in Fig. 5-5(*c*)? Check your answer by reconnecting the DMM according to the diagram of Fig. 5-5(*c*). _____

h. Is the current measured in Fig. 5-5(*b*) and (*c*) the same?

_____

2. Remove the DMM from the circuit and reconnect the circuit as in Fig. 5-5(*a*).

a. Will L_2 become more brilliant or less brilliant if L_1 is shorted out? _____ Why?

_____

_____

b. Short out L_1 by connecting a jumper lead from one terminal of the socket to the other terminal of the socket. Does the brilliancy of L_2 change as you expected? _____

c. Remove the jumper from the socket of L_1. If L_2 is shorted out, what will the effect be on the brilliancy of L_1? Check your conclusion.

_____

_____

3. Remove any shorting jumpers so that the circuit is back to what is shown in Fig. 5-5(*a*).

a. Now remove L_1 from its socket. Removing L_1 has the same effect as L_1 burning out. What happened to the light output of L_2? _____ Why?

_____

_____

b. How much voltage would you expect across L_2 when L_1 is removed? _____ Why?

_____

_____

c. Verify your answer by measuring and recording the voltage across L_2.

_____

d. How much voltage would you expect across the terminals of the socket from which L_1 was removed? _____ Why?

_____

_____

e. Verify your answer by measuring and recording the voltage across the terminals of the socket. _____

f. Do your results support the statement that "the voltage across an open load equals the source voltage in a series circuit"? _____

4. Construct the circuit shown in Fig. 5-6, using a 4.7-Ω resistor for R_1. Note the brilliancy of the lamp.

a. How does it compare with the brilliancy it had when the circuit of Fig. 5-5(*a*) was used?

_____

_____

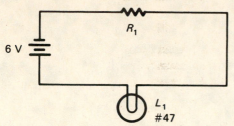

Fig. 5-6 Controlling lamp current.

b. Which do you think is dropping more voltage, R_1 or L_1?
_____ Why?

_____

_____

c. To test your conclusions, measure the voltages across R_1 and L_1. Which has more resistance, R_1 or L_1? _____

d. If the 4.7-Ω resistor at R_1 is replaced with a 33-Ω resistor, will L_1 get brighter or dimmer? _____

e. Test your answer by changing R_1 to 33 Ω. Is the voltage across R_1 or L_1 greater now? _____

f. Is the resistance of R_1 greater or less than the resistance of L_1?
_____

g. Could a 100-Ω rheostat at R_1 control the output of L_1 from no light to full brilliancy? _____

5-2 LAB EXPERIMENT: PARALLEL CIRCUITS—GENERAL PROPERTIES

PURPOSE

This experiment illustrates the major characteristics of parallel circuits. Additional practice in constructing circuits and making electrical measurements is also provided.

MATERIALS

Qty.

1 6-V dry battery (or 6-V dc power supply)
2 no. 47 lamps
2 lamp holders for no. 47 lamps

Qty.

1 220-Ω, ½-W resistor
1 VOM or DMM
• test leads and wire

PROCEDURE

1. Construct the circuit in Fig. 5-7(a).

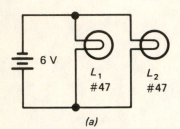

(a)

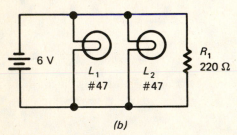

(b)

Fig. 5-7 Parallel loads.

    a. Measure the voltage across the terminals of the battery and across the terminals of each lamp socket. Are all measured voltages the same? _____

    b. Remove L_1 from its socket and measure the voltage across the terminals of the L_1 socket. Did the voltage at the terminals of the L_1 socket change when L_1 was removed? _____ Why?

_____

_____

    c. Did the brilliancy of L_2 change when L_1 opened (was removed)? _____

    d. Put L_1 back in its socket and remove L_2. Did removal of L_2 affect the brilliancy of L_1? _____

    e. Reinstall L_2 in its socket. Add a 220-Ω resistor in parallel, as shown in Fig. 5-7(b). Did the addition of the resistor change the brilliancy of L_1 and L_2? _____

    f. Do your data indicate that each branch of a parallel circuit is independent of the other branches? _____

2. Set the DMM to the current function and the 500-mA range. Replace the conductor between the negative terminal of the battery and the terminal of L_1 with the DMM. This will measure the total (source) current in Fig. 5-7(*b*).

    a. Remove L_1. Did the total current increase or decrease?

    _____

    b. Remove L_2. Did the total current increase or decrease?

    _____

    c. Which draws more current from the battery, the 220-Ω resistor or L_2?

    _____

    d. Does the sum of the branch currents equal the total current?

    _____

5-3 LAB EXPERIMENT: SERIES-PARALLEL CIRCUITS—GENERAL PROPERTIES

PURPOSE

The following experiment provides experiences in constructing more complex circuits. It will allow you to determine some of the major properties of series-parallel circuits. This experiment provides clear visual evidence of the inter-dependency of these circuits.

MATERIALS

Qty.

1   6-V dry battery (or 6-V dc power supply)
4   no. 47 lamps

Qty.

4   lamp holders for no. 47 lamps
•   jumper leads and wire

PROCEDURE

1. Study the circuit in Fig. 5-8 and predict the answers to the following questions:

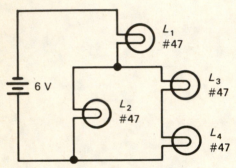

L_1
#47

L_3
#47

6 V

L_2
#47

L_4
#47

Fig. 5-8 Series-parallel lamps.

    a. Which lamp(s) will be most brilliant? _____
    b. Which lamp(s) will be least brilliant? _____
    c. Now construct the circuit of Fig. 5-8 and check your answers to questions a and b. Why is lamp L_1 more brilliant than lamp L_2?

    _____
    _____

    d. Why is L_2 more brilliant than either L_3 or L_4?

    _____
    _____

    e. Why is the brilliancy of L_3 and L_4 equal?

    _____
    _____

2. Again study Fig. 5-8 and predict what will happen to the brilliancy of the other lamps when L_1 is shorted out. Then short out L_1 with a jumper lead and see what happens.
    a. Did L_2 get brighter or dimmer? _____
    b. Did L_3 and L_4 get brighter or dimmer? _____
    c. Explain why the brilliancy of L_2 changed as it did when L_1 was shorted.

    _____
    _____

    d. Remove the jumper lead (short) from L_1. Now predict the effect on the brilliancy of the other lamps when L_2 is shorted. Are you sure of your predictions? If so, short out L_2 and record your results. Did L_1 get brighter or dimmer? _____

e. Did L_3 and L_4 get brighter or dimmer? _____

f. Explain why L_1 and L_3 changed as they did when L_2 was shorted. Remove the short from L_2.

_____

_____

g. If L_3 is shorted, will L_2 get brighter or dimmer? _____

h. If L_4 is shorted, will L_2 get brighter or dimmer? Check your answers by shorting out L_3 and then L_4. _____

i. Why does L_1 get brighter when either L_3 or L_4 is shorted?

_____

_____

j. Why does L_3 get brighter when L_4 is shorted?

_____

_____

5-4 LAB EXERCISE: POLARITIES AND MEASUREMENTS

PURPOSE

This exercise will provide additional experience in determining the polarity of voltage drops in multiload circuits. It will also illustrate current and voltage measurements in these circuits.

PROCEDURE

1. Refer to Fig. 5-9(a). The polarity of the voltage across R_1 is already marked on the diagram.

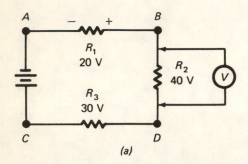

(a)

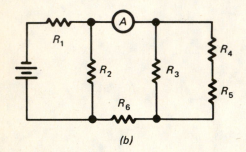

(b)

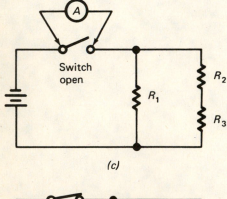

(c)

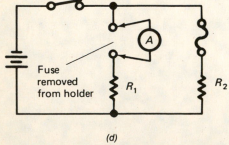

(d)

Fig. 5-9 Polarities and measurements.

a. Mark the polarity of the voltages across R_2 and R_3. Also indicate the polarity of the voltmeter. In Fig. 5-9(a), the voltage at point B is 20 V positive with respect to point A.

b. What is the voltage at point C with respect to point B? _____

c. What is the voltage at point C with respect to point D? _____

2. a. In Fig. 5-9(b), what current is being measured by the ammeter? _____

b. Which lead ($-$ or $+$) of the ammeter should be connected to the junction of R_1 and R_2 in Fig. 5-9(b)? _____

c. Will the current in R_6 flow from left to right or from right to left? _____

3. Usually when current is measured, the circuit must be physically interrupted to insert the ammeter in series. Sometimes the desired current can be measured by connecting the ammeter across an open switch or fuse.

a. What current is being measured in Fig. 5-9(c)? _____

b. Should the negative or the positive lead of the ammeter be connected to the battery side of the switch? _____

c. What current is being measured in Fig. 5-9(d)? _____

d. Which lead of the ammeter should be connected to the R_1 side of the fuse holder? _____

4. In the space next to Fig. 5-9, redraw the circuit of Fig. 5-9(b) and show where an ammeter would be inserted to measure I_{R_3}.

5-5 LAB EXPERIMENT: SERIES CIRCUITS— CURRENT, VOLTAGE, AND RESISTANCE

PURPOSE

This experiment will provide experience in measuring and calculating electrical quantities in series circuits. It will show that measured and calculated values are not exactly equal because of component tolerances.

MATERIALS

Qty.

1   20-V dc power supply
2   10-kΩ, ½-W resistors
1   20-kΩ, ½-W resistor

Qty.

1   1-kΩ, 1-W resistor
1   VOM or DMM
•   test leads and wires

PROCEDURE

1. **a.** Calculate and record the total resistance of the circuit in Fig. 5-10(a). _____

    b. Connect the two 10-kΩ resistors in series (*do not* connect them to the power supply) and measure and record their total resistance. _____

    c. Now connect the circuit of Fig. 5-10(a) and measure and record the total current. _____

    d. Calculate and record the total current. _____

    e. In a series circuit, do equal resistors drop the same amount of voltage? _____

    f. Measure and record the voltages across R_1 and R_2 in Fig. 5-10(a).
    V_{R_1} _____ V_{R_2} _____

    g. Are these two voltages equal (within 10 percent)? _____

    h. Now calculate and record the voltage across R_1 and across R_2.
    V_{R_1} _____ V_{R_2} _____

    i. How much power is required from the battery in Fig. 5-10(a)? _____

    j. Will R_1 and R_2 each dissipate the same amount of power? _____

TABLE 5-1   Electrical Quantities for Fig. 5-10(b)

Quantity	Measured Value		Calculated Value
	Software	Hardware	
R_T			
I_T			
V_{R_1}			
V_{R_2}			

2. **a.** If your instructor asks you to perform this experiment using electronic-circuit simulation software, record the measured values in the Software column of Table 5-1. When you use software, the measured and calculated columns should agree within normal round-off error. Compare them as you do the experiment.

    If you are using physical (real) components, record measured values in the Hardware column of Table 5-1. Keep comparing your measured and calculated values. If they disagree by more than 10 percent, you have probably made an error in either your calculations or your measurements. Repeat either or both, as necessary.

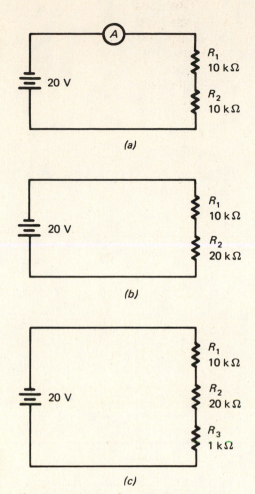

(a)

(b)

(c)

Fig. 5-10 Circuits for experiment 5-5.

Using the circuit of Fig. 5-10(b), make the measurements and calculations needed to fill in Table 5-1. In completing Table 5-1, calculate one quantity and then measure the same quantity. If the two agree, then do the next calculation and measurement. By following this procedure, you will discover and correct mistakes that might otherwise affect the rest of the experiment.

b. Is V_{R_2} twice as large as V_{R_1}? _____

c. Would the voltage across a 30-kΩ resistor be three times as large as the voltage across a 10-kΩ resistor? _____

d. If a 5-kΩ resistor drops 10 V, how much voltage will be dropped across a 20-kΩ resistor? Notice that the voltage drops in a series circuit are in direct proportion to the individual resistances. Mathematically, this statement can be written

$$\frac{R_1}{R_2} = \frac{V_{R_1}}{V_{R_2}}$$

When rearranged to solve for V_{R_2}, this relationship becomes

$$V_{R_2} = \frac{V_{R_1} R_2}{R_1}$$

Check your answer by using this equation (the 5-kΩ resistor is R_1).

e. The power in a series circuit also distributes in direct proportion to the individual resistances. Check this statement by calculating the power of R_1 and R_2 in Fig. 5-10(b).

P_{R_1} _____ P_{R_2} _____

f. Is P_{R_2} twice as large as P_{R_1}? _____

3. Construct the circuit of Fig. 5-10(c).

    a. Would you expect the total current of this circuit to be about the same as the total current of Fig. 5-10(b)? _____ Why?

    _____

    b. Measure the total current. Is it 3 to 4 percent lower than in Fig. 5-10(b)?

    _____

    c. Would you expect V_{R_2} of Fig. 5-10(b) and (c) to be about the same? Measure V_{R_2} in Fig. 5-10(c) to check your answer. _____

    d. Using the formula in step 2d and the measured value of V_{R_2}, predict V_{R_3}. Now measure V_{R_3} to check your answer.
Predicted V_{R_3} _____

    e. Would shorting out R_3 affect the total power by less than or more than 5 percent? _____

    f. Would the total power increase or decrease? _____

5-6 LAB EXPERIMENT: PARALLEL CIRCUITS—CURRENT, VOLTAGE, AND RESISTANCE

PURPOSE

One of the objects of this experiment is to verify Kirchhoff's current law. The other objective is to provide experience in measuring and calculating electrical quantities in parallel circuits.

MATERIALS

Qty.   **Qty.**

1 20-V dc power supply   1 1-kΩ, 1-W resistor
2 10-kΩ, ½-W resistors   1 VOM or DMM
1 20-kΩ, ½-W resistor   • test leads and wires

PROCEDURE

If your instructor asks you to perform this experiment using electronic-circuit simulation software, record the measured values in the Software column of Tables 5-2 and 5-3. When you use software, the measured and calculated columns should agree within normal round-off error. Compare them as you do the experiment.

TABLE 5-2   Electrical Quantities for Fig. 5-11(a)

Quantity	Measured Value		Calculated Value
	Software	Hardware	
R_T			
I_{R_1}			
I_{R_2}			
I_T			
V_{R_1}			
V_{R_2}			

If you are using physical (real) components, record measured values in the Hardware column of Tables 5-2 and 5-3.

1. Refer to Fig. 5-11(a). Would you expect
   a. R_1 to be greater than R_T? _____
   b. I_{R_1} to be greater than I_T? _____
   c. I_{R_1} to be greater than I_{R_2}? _____
   d. Connect two 10-kΩ resistors in parallel and measure the equivalent (total) resistance. Enter the measured value of R_T in Table 5-2. Was your answer to question a correct? Check your response to questions b and c by connecting the circuit and finishing Table 5-2. In completing Table 5-2, make a calculation and then make the corresponding measurement before proceeding to the next calculation.
   e. Do your measured values of current agree with Kirchhoff's current law?

   _____
   f. Compute the values of P_{R_1}, P_{R_2}, and P_T by using the measured data in Table 5-2.
      P_{R_1} _____ P_{R_2} _____ P_T _____
   g. Do your measured data show that $P_T = P_{R_1} + P_{R_2}$? _____

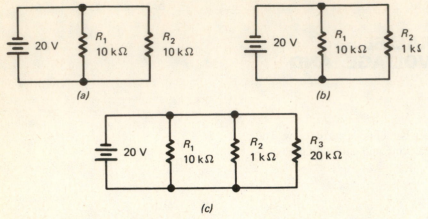

Fig. 5-11 Circuits for experiment 5-6.

2. **a.** Construct the circuit shown in Fig. 5-11(b) and complete Table 5-3. Remember to measure the resistance before power is applied to the circuit.

TABLE **5-3** Electrical Quantities for Fig. 5-11(b)

Quantity	Measured Value		Calculated Value
	Software	Hardware	
R_T			
I_{R_1}			
I_{R_2}			
I_T			

    b. Does changing the value of R_2 from 10 to 1 kΩ affect the current in R_1? _____

    c. Does the sum of the branch currents $(I_{R_1}+I_{R_2})$ equal the total current I_T? _____

    d. Which resistor, R_1 or R_2, uses more power? _____

3. Construct the circuit shown in Fig. 5-11(c).

    a. Measure and record R_T, I_T, and I_{R_3}.

    R_T _____ I_T _____ I_{R_3} _____

    b. Would the measured values of I_{R_1} and I_{R_2} be the same as they were for the circuit of Fig. 5-11(b)? _____

    c. Is I_{R_3} equal to the difference between the total current of Fig. 5-11(c) and the total current of Fig. 5-11(b)? _____

    d. How much current flows in the conductors that connect R_1 to R_2 in Fig. 5-11(c)? Check your answers by measuring the current in the conductors. _____

4. Answer the following questions without referring to your measured or calculated data. Then, check your answers by referring to the data of steps 1 to 3.

    a. Which circuit (a, b, or c) in Fig. 5-11 will

        (1) have the least resistance? _____

        (2) draw the most current? _____

        (3) consume the most power? _____

    b. Will the total resistance of Fig. 5-11(b) be less than or more than 1 kΩ?

    c. Will the total resistance of Fig. 5-11(c) be less than or more than 1 kΩ?

    d. Which resistor in Fig. 5-11(c) will

        (1) draw the least current? _____

        (2) dissipate the most power? _____

        (3) dominate the circuit? _____

5-7 LAB EXPERIMENT: SERIES-PARALLEL CIRCUITS—CURRENT, VOLTAGE, AND RESISTANCE

PURPOSE

This experiment will provide experience in making measurements in multiple-load circuits. It will also give additional practice in computing electrical quantities in series-parallel circuits.

MATERIALS

Qty.

1 20-V dc power supply
2 10-kΩ, ½-W resistors
1 20-kΩ, ½-W resistor

Qty.

1 1-kΩ, 1-W resistor
1 VOM or DMM
• test leads and wires

PROCEDURE

If your instructor asks you to perform this experiment using electronic-circuit simulation software, record the measured values in the Software column of Table 5-4. When you use software, the measured and calculated columns should agree within normal round-off error. Compare them as you do the experiment.

If you are using physical (real) components, record the measured values in the Hardware column.

Look at Fig. 5-12 and visualize how it could be reduced to an equivalent circuit containing two parallel resistors. Now, using this "visualized circuit," estimate the total resistance.

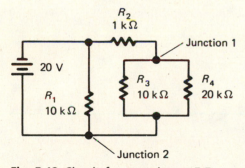

Fig. 5-12 Circuit for experiment 5-7.

1. Will it be greater than or less than 10 kΩ? _____
2. Will the current through R_1 be equal to, less than, or more than the current through R_2? _____
3. Construct the circuit of Fig. 5-12 and complete Table 5-4. Then check your answers to steps 1 and 2.
4. Using measured values of R_T and I_T, compute and record P_T. _____
5. Use your calculated values of R_T and I_T and again compute and record P_T. _____
6. Are your answers to steps 4 and 5 exactly the same? _____
7. If they are not, why do you think they are different?

_____

_____

Table 5-4 Electrical Quantities for Fig. 5-12

Quantity	Measured Value		Calculated Value
	Software	Hardware	
R_T			
V_{R_1}			
V_{R_2}			
V_{R_4}			
I_{R_1}			
I_{R_2}			
I_{R_3}			
I_{R_4}			
I_T			

8. What is the potential difference (voltage) between junction 1 and junction 2 in Fig. 5-12? _____

9. With respect to junction 2, is junction 1 negative or positive? Check your answers to this step and step 8 by connecting the voltmeter between the two junctions. _____

10. Does the current entering junction 1 equal the current leaving junction 1? _____

11. Would removing R_1 from the circuit change the value of I_{R_3}? Check this by temporarily removing R_1 and measuring I_{R_3}. _____

12. Would removing R_4 change the value of I_{R_1}? Again, check your answer by removing R_4 while measuring I_{R_1}. _____

13. Does removing R_4 change I_{R_2}? _____

14. If a 100-Ω resistor were added in parallel with R_4, what would happen to the voltage across R_2? _____

5-8 ADVANCED PROBLEMS

5-1. How many 120-V, 450-W heaters can be operated from a 20-A, 120-V power line? _____

5-2. A 100-ft 14-gage copper conductor extension cord is used to connect a 12-A load to a 120-V outlet. How much voltage will be across the load if the 14-gage copper wire has a resistance of 2.8 Ω per 1000 ft at the operating temperature? _____

5-3. What is the internal resistance of a battery if its terminal voltage drops from 9 to 8 V when a 500-mA load is connected to it? _____

5-4. A 1500-W frying pan and a 900-W toaster are plugged into a 120-V outlet. How much current is drawn from the outlet? _____ What is the total resistance of the circuit? _____

5-5. Refer to Fig. 5-13 and solve for I_{R_2}, R_2, R_3, V_{R_3}, R_4, and P_T.

I_{R_2} _____ R_2 _____
R_3 _____ V_{R_3} _____
R_4 _____ P_T _____

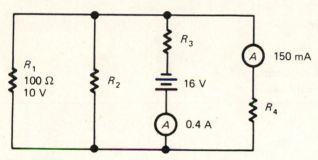

Fig. 5-13 Circuit.

5-9 LAB EXERCISE: SELF-DESIGNED CIRCUITS

PURPOSE

This exercise will give you experience in designing (and testing) circuits to meet specified criteria.

MATERIALS

Qty.		Qty.	
1	DMM and/or VOM	1	470-Ω, ½-W resistor
1	0- to 20-V dc power supply	2	1000-Ω, ½-W resistors
1	10-Ω ½-W resistor	1	2.2-kΩ, ½-W resistor
1	22-Ω, ½-W resistor	1	4.7-kΩ, ½-W resistor
1	51-Ω, ½-W resistor	2	10-kΩ, ½-W resistors
2	100-Ω, ½-W resistors	1	20-kΩ, ½-W resistor
1	220-Ω, ½-W resistor	•	test leads and wires

PROCEDURE

1. Using some combination of the resistors in the above materials list, design, construct, and test the circuits specified below. Remember not to exceed 50 percent of the power dissipation ratings of the resistors.
   a. A two-resistor circuit in which $V_{R_1} = 10V_{R_2}$ and $V_{R_1} = 14$ V.
   b. A two-resistor circuit in which $R_T = 68.75$ Ω and $I_{R_1} = 2.2I_{R_2}$.
   c. A three-resistor circuit in which $I_{R_1} = I_{R_2}$ and $I_{R_1} = 2I_{R_3}$.
2. Write a formal report for this exercise which includes, as a minimum, schematic diagrams, measured and calculated values of electrical quantities, and possible reasons for disagreements between calculated and measured values.

5-10 LAB EXPERIMENT: TROUBLESHOOTING—ONE FAULTY COMPONENT

PURPOSE

Electrical workers and technicians are often required to troubleshoot multi-load circuits and complex systems. This experiment will help you further develop your troubleshooting skills.

MATERIALS

Qty.

4   ½-W resistors (values known only to the instructor)
1   fuse, 0.5 A, with holder
1   20-V dc power supply
1   multimeter (VOM or DMM)
•   test leads and wires
•   For simulation software, obtain the file labeled Fig. 5-14.ewb from your instructor.

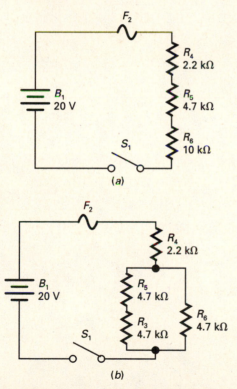

Fig. 5-14 Circuits for experiment 5-10.

PROCEDURE

1. The circuit for the diagram shown in Fig. 5-14(*a*) has one defective component. Unless your instructor asks you to use electronic-circuit simulation software, construct the circuit with the components provided by your instructor. Once the circuit is constructed, no components can be removed or disconnected to make measurements. (Pretend that they are soldered in place.) Use only the voltage and current functions of the multimeter.
   a. Which component is faulty? _____

b. What is wrong with the component?

_____

_____

c. Submit a report explaining how you arrived at the answers to steps a and b. Include calculated values of I_T and R_T and the voltage drop for each resistor using the values shown on the diagrams. Also include the measured value of I_T and each voltage drop.

2. Repeat step 1 for the circuit shown in Fig. 5-14(*b*).

a. Which component is faulty? _____

b. What is wrong with the component?

_____

_____

c. Submit a detailed report as outlined in step 1c.

5-11 LAB EXPERIMENT: TROUBLESHOOTING—TWO FAULTY COMPONENTS

PURPOSE

This experiment will give you experience in locating two faulty components in the same circuit. It will illustrate that an understanding of fundamental circuit laws and relationships is essential when troubleshooting a circuit.

MATERIALS

Qty.

5   ½-W resistors (values known only to the instructor)
1   fuse, 0.5 A, with holder
1   20-V dc power supply
1   multimeter (VOM or DMM)
•   test leads and wires
•   For simulation software, obtain the file labeled Fig. 5-15.ewb from your instructor.

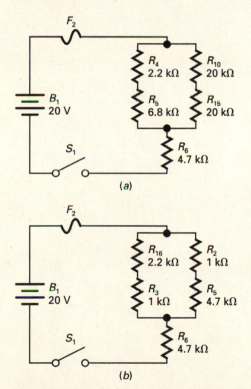

Fig. 5-15 Circuits for experiment 5-11.

PROCEDURE

1. The circuit for the diagram shown in Fig. 5-15(a) has two defective components. Unless your instructor asks you to use electronic-circuit simulation software, construct the circuit with the components provided by your instructor. Once the circuit is constructed, no components can be removed or disconnected to make measurements. (Pretend that they are soldered in place.) Use only the voltage and current functions of the multimeter.

a. Which components are faulty? _____

b. What is wrong with the components?

_____

_____

c. Submit a report explaining how you arrived at the answers to steps a and b. Include calculated values of I_T and R_T and the voltage drop for each resistor using the values shown on the diagrams. Include also the measured value of I_T and each voltage drop.

2. Repeat step 1 for the circuit shown in Fig. 5-15(*b*).

a. Which component is faulty? _____

b. What is wrong with the component?

_____

_____

c. Submit a detailed report as outlined in step 1c.

Chapter 6

Complex-Circuit Analysis

TEST: COMPLEX-CIRCUIT ANALYSIS

For questions 1 to 5, supply the missing word or phrase in each statement.

1. Superposition theorem is applicable only to _____ circuits.
2. Current is independent of load resistance for a _____ source.
3. _____ theorem reduces a circuit to an ideal current source and a parallel resistance.
4. Application of _____ theorem and _____ theorem may not allow one to solve for all values of current and voltage.
5. _____ independent equations are required to simultaneously solve three variables.

1. _____
2. _____
3. _____
4. _____
   _____
5. _____

For questions 6 to 21, determine whether each statement is true or false.

6. When converting a Norton equivalent circuit to a Thevenin equivalent circuit, R_{TH} will be equivalent to R_N.

6. _____

7. When a Norton equivalent circuit is converted to a Thevenin equivalent circuit, the V_{oc} of the two circuits will be the same.

7. _____

8. The short-circuit current of a Thevenin equivalent circuit equals the constant current of a Norton equivalent circuit when both equivalent circuits are derived from the same complex circuit.

8. _____

9. A three-loop complex circuit produces at least four unknown variables in the set of loop equations.

9. _____

10. A complex circuit which requires two loops will have three unknown variables in at least one of the loop equations.

10. _____

11. All loop equations for a given complex circuit will have the same number of unknown variables.

11. _____

12. A Thevenin equivalent circuit represents an ideal (constant) voltage source.

12. _____

13. When analyzing a three-source complex circuit by the superposition method, only one source is shorted out at any given time.

13. _____

14. When the simultaneous solution of loop equations yields a negative value for a current, the assumed direction of the current is incorrect.

14. _____

15. Application of the superposition theorem usually leads to the solution of all voltages and currents without the use of simultaneous equations.

15. _____

16. Application of Norton's theorem always leads to the solution of all voltages and currents without the use of simultaneous equations.

16. _____

17. When thevenizing a circuit, R_{TH} and V_{TH} can always be calculated with series-parallel circuit procedures.

17. _____

18. All but one of the sources in a multiple-source complex circuit are shorted out when calculating I_N for the Norton equivalent circuit.

18. _____

19. Some complex circuits can be analyzed using only series-parallel rules and procedures.

20. If a single-source complex circuit is to be analyzed as a two-terminal network, the ends of the source are usually selected to be the terminals.

21. If V_{RL} for many values of R_L must be determined, a circuit should be thevenized.

19. _____

20. _____

21. _____

Solve the following problems and record your answers. Be sure to specify units when appropriate.

22. What equation results from adding $-2x + 4y = 15$ to $4x + 2y + 4z = -8$?

23. Solve for the values of A, B, and C when $2A - 5B = -4$, $-3B + 4C = 18$, and $3A + 4B - 2C = 5$.

22. _____

23. _____
_____
_____
_____

24. Calculate the value of R_{TH} and V_{TH} when the circuit in Fig. 6-1 is thevenized by using R_2 as the load resistor.

24. _____
_____

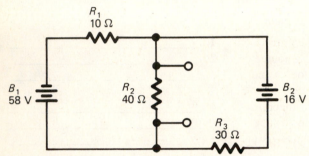

Fig. 6-1 Circuit for questions 24 and 25.

25. Use the superposition theorem to determine I_{R_3}, V_{R_3}, and I_{R_1} in the circuit shown in Fig. 6-1.

25. _____
_____
_____

26. Use the loop-equation technique to compute I_{R_2} and I_{R_3} for the circuit of Fig. 6-2.

26. _____
_____

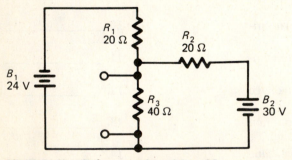

Fig. 6-2 Circuit for questions 26 to 28.

27. Calculate the value of I_N and R_N for the circuit shown in Fig. 6-2. (Do not assume that R_3 is the load resistor.)

27. _____
_____

28. How much current will flow in a 50-Ω resistor connected between the terminals in Fig. 6-2?

28. _____

60

6-1 LAB EXPERIMENT: ANALYZING A BRIDGE CIRCUIT

PURPOSE

This experiment will provide experience in calculating and measuring currents and voltages in a complex circuit. Within the tolerances of the equipment and components, the measured values will verify whether or not the calculations are correct.

MATERIALS

Qty.

1   20-V dc power supply
1   470-Ω, ½-W, 5% resistor
1   1-kΩ, ½-W, 5% resistor
1   2.2-kΩ, ½-W, 5% resistor

Qty.

1   4.7-kΩ, ½-W, 5% resistor
1   10-kΩ, ½-W, 5% resistor
1   VOM or DMM
•   test leads and wires

PROCEDURE

1. In Fig. 6-3, will point A be negative or positive with respect to point B? (Hint: Remove R_5 and determine whether point A or point B is more negative with respect to point C.) _____

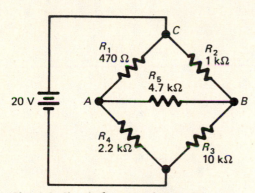

Fig. 6-3 Circuit for experiment 6-1.

2. Using Thevenin's theorem, calculate and record V_{R_5} and I_{R_5} for the circuit in Fig. 6-3. _____   _____
3. Construct the circuit shown in Fig. 6-3.
   a. Measure and record the voltage across R_5. _____
   b. Is the polarity of V_{R_5} as you predicted in step 1? Is the value of V_{R_5} within ±10 percent of the value calculated in step 2? _____   _____
   c. Measure and record I_{R_5} and compare the measured value with the value calculated in step 2. If these two values differ by more than 10 percent, check your measurement technique and your calculations for error. _____
   d. Knowing the value of I_{R_5} and V_{R_5}, can you determine other currents and voltages with just Kirchhoff's and Ohm's laws? _____
   e. If you also knew V_{R_2}, in addition to V_{R_5} and I_{R_5}, could you then compute the other currents and voltages using only Kirchhoff's and Ohm's laws? _____
4. Using Thevenin's theorem, compute and record the value of V_{R_2}, and I_{R_2} for Fig. 6-3. _____   _____

5. Verify your calculations in step 4 by measuring and recording V_{R_2} and I_{R_2}.

   _____ _____

6. Compute and record I_{R_3} by applying Kirchhoff's current law to the junction at point B. Use the values of I_{R_5} and I_{R_2} from steps 2 and 4, respectively. _____

7. Measure and record I_{R_3}. Does the measured value match the value calculated in step 6? _____ _____

8. Compute and record V_{R_4} by applying Kirchhoff's voltage law to the loop which includes R_2, R_5, and R_4. _____

9. Measure and record V_{R_4}. It should be within 10 percent of the value calculated in step 8. _____

10. If you decreased the value of R_5 to 2.7 kΩ, would I_{R_5} increase or decrease? _____

11. Calculate and record the value of I_{R_5} when R_5 is changed to 6.8 kΩ. (Hint: Use the value of V_{TH} and R_{TH} determined in step 2.) _____

12. Will changing the value of R_5 change the value of I_{R_4}? _____

6-2 LAB EXPERIMENT: THE CONSTANT-CURRENT SOURCE

PURPOSE

This experiment will introduce you to a practical constant-current source which uses a transistor, a zener diode, and two resistors. It will illustrate the two major characteristics of a constant-current source: very high internal resistance and a load current that does not vary as the load resistance varies.

MATERIALS

Qty.

1 0- to 20-V dc power supply
1 2N4126 transistor
1 14-V, 1-W, 5% zener diode
1 100-Ω, ½-W, 5% resistor
1 1-kΩ, ½-W, 5% resistor
1 2.2-kΩ, ½-W, 5% resistor

Qty.

1 4.7-kΩ, ½-W, 5% resistor
1 10-kΩ, ½-W, 5% resistor
1 20-kΩ, ½-W, 5% resistor
1 VOM or DMM
• test leads and wires

PROCEDURE

1. Construct the circuit shown in Fig. 6-4. Both Z_1 (the zener diode) and Q_1 (the transistor) are polarized devices, and so you must identify the leads before inserting them into the circuit. Refer to Fig. 6-5 to find out how to identify the leads.

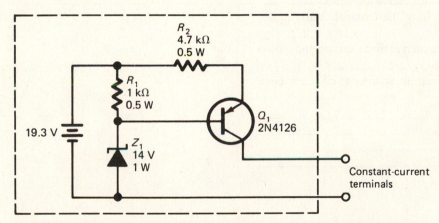

Fig. 6-4 Constant-current source for experiment 6-2. The dotted lines indicate that the complete circuit, including power supply, is the current source.

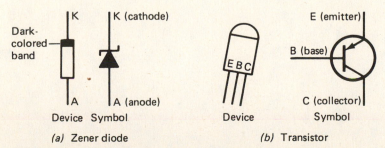

Fig. 6-5 Lead identification for the zener diode and transistor used in the constant-current source for experiment 6-2.

2. Temporarily disconnect the power supply from the circuit you just constructed. Then, using the DMM or the VOM on the ×1k range, measure and record the resistance between the constant-current terminals. Is the measured resistance approximately the value you would expect for a constant-current source? *Note:* The internal resistance of the source does change when power is applied, but for purposes of the experiment the change is not significant. _____ _____

3. Reconnect the power supply to the circuit and adjust it for 19.3 V. Now connect a 2.2-kΩ resistor to the terminals; then measure and record the current through the resistor. Also measure and record the voltage across the resistor. _____ _____

4. Replace the 2.2-kΩ resistor with a 100-Ω resistor and again measure and record the current through and voltage across the resistor. Did the measured value of current change from step 3 to step 4? Did the measured value of voltage change from step 3 to step 4?

_____ _____ _____ _____

5. If you now replace the 100-Ω resistor with a 10-kΩ resistor, how much current should the resistor draw? How much voltage would you expect across the 10-kΩ resistor? Check your answers by changing resistors and making the necessary measurements. _____ _____

6. Remove the 10-kΩ resistor and connect the milliammeter directly across the terminals of the source. Is the short-circuit current the same (within 5 percent) value as recorded in the previous three steps? _____

7. You have probably noticed that constant-voltage sources, like cells and batteries, lose their constant-voltage characteristics when too much current is drawn from them. That is, the voltage at the terminals drops as the load resistance becomes too small.

   Constant-current sources also have limits. When the load resistance, and thus the load voltage, becomes too large, the source loses its constant-current characteristics. That is, the current from the terminals starts to decrease.

   Connect a 20-kΩ resistor to the current source; then measure and record the current through the 20-kΩ resistance. _____

8. List four characteristics of a constant-current source which have been demonstrated by this activity.

   a. _____

   b. _____

   c. _____

   d. _____

6-3 LAB EXPERIMENT: EQUIVALENT CIRCUITS—NORTON'S AND THEVENIN'S

PURPOSE

This experiment will provide additional experience in converting complex circuits into equivalent circuits. It will also verify the relationships between Norton's equivalent circuit and Thevenin's equivalent circuit.

MATERIALS

Qty.

- 1 VOM or DMM
- 1 6-V battery or dc power supply
- 1 0- to 20-V dc power supply
- 1 14-V, 1-W, 5% zener diode
- 4 1-kΩ, $\frac{1}{2}$- or 1-W, 2 or 5% resistors

Qty.

- 1 2N4126
- 1 2.2-kΩ, $\frac{1}{2}$-W, 5% resistor
- 2 4.7-kΩ, $\frac{1}{2}$-W, 5% resistors
- 1 10-kΩ, $\frac{1}{2}$-W, 5% resistor
- 1 20-kΩ, $\frac{1}{2}$-W, 5% resistor
- • test leads and wires

PROCEDURE

If your instructor asks you to perform this experiment using electronics simulation software, record the measured values in the SW (Software) columns of Table 6-1. If you are using physical (real) components, record measured values in the HW (Hardware) columns.

1. Construct the complex circuit drawn in Fig. 6-6(a). Measure V_{R_L} and I_{R_L}. Record these values in Table 6-1 in the first row and the first and second columns. Now change R_L in Fig. 6-6(a) to 2.2 kΩ and again measure and record V_{R_L} and I_{R_L}. Finally, change R_L to 4.7 kΩ and measure and record V_{R_L} and I_{R_L}.

TABLE 6-1 Measured Currents and Voltages for the Circuits of Fig. 6-6

Type of Circuit	Value of R_L											
	1000 Ω				2200 Ω				4700 Ω			
	V_{R_L}		I_{R_L}		V_{R_L}		I_{R_L}		V_{R_L}		I_{R_L}	
	SW	HW	SW	HW	SW	HW	SW	HW	SW	HW	SW	HW
Complex [Fig. 6-6(a)]												
Norton's [Fig. 6-6 (b) and (c)]												
Thevenin's [Fig. 6-6 (d) and (e)]												

2. Using R_L as the load resistor, nortonize the circuit of Fig. 6-6(a). Record your calculated values of R_N and I_N.

_____   _____

3. Measure and record I_N for Fig. 6-6(a) by removing R_L and replacing it with the DMM set on the 1-mA range. (The internal resistance of the DMM on the 1-mA range is very small compared with that of the other resistors in the circuit. Thus, it approximates a short circuit.) Does this measured I_N agree, within 10 percent, with the calculated I_N of step 2?

_____   _____

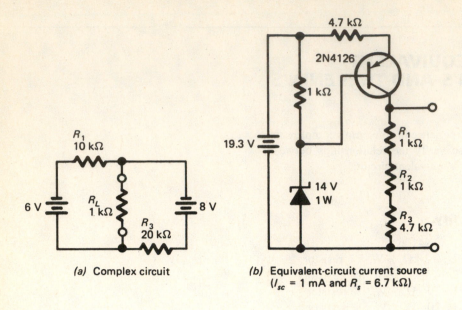

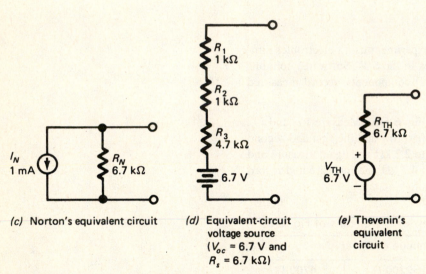

(a) Complex circuit

(b) Equivalent-circuit current source
(I_{sc} = 1 mA and R_s = 6.7 kΩ)

(c) Norton's equivalent circuit

(d) Equivalent-circuit voltage source
(V_{oc} = 6.7 V and R_s = 6.7 kΩ)

(e) Thevenin's equivalent circuit

Fig. 6-6 Circuits for experiment 6-3.

4. The Norton equivalent circuit you developed in step 2 should look like the one detailed in Fig. 6-6(c). If it doesn't, try again! Figure 6-6(b) shows a practical circuit diagram for the Norton equivalent circuit of Fig. 6-6(c). It is composed of the 1-mA constant-current source used in experiment 6-2 and an added 6.7 kΩ (R_1, R_2, and R_3) of internal parallel resistance. The circuits of Fig. 6-6(b) and (c) are electrically equivalent to that of Fig. 6-6(a) when R_L is removed from Fig. 6-6(a).

5. Should a 1-kΩ load across the terminals of Fig. 6-6(b) receive the same current and voltage as the 1-kΩ load (R_L) in Fig. 6-6(a)? _____

6. Connect different values of R_L to Fig. 6-6(b) and make the measurements necessary to complete the second row of Table 6-1.

7. Does the data in rows 1 and 2 of Table 6-1 support Norton's theorem? _____

8. Convert the Norton equivalent circuit you developed in step 2 into a Thevenin equivalent circuit. Record your calculated values of R_{TH} and V_{TH}. _____ _____

9. Reconstruct the circuit of Fig. 6-6(a). Remove R_L from the circuit. Then measure and record the voltage between the points from which you removed R_L. Is this voltage equal (within 10 percent) to V_{TH} calculated in step 8? _____   _____

10. Your Thevenin equivalent circuit from step 8 should look like the one in Fig. 6-6(e). A practical implementation of Fig. 6-6(e) is shown in Fig. 6-6(d). Construct the circuit of Fig. 6-6(d) and measure and record the voltage between its terminals. Should this voltage be equal to the voltage measured in step 9? _____   _____

11. Connect the necessary loads to the circuit of Fig. 6-6(d) and make the necessary measurements to complete the last row of Table 6-1. Do rows 2 and 3 of Table 6-1 indicate that Fig. 6-6(b) and (d) are equivalent circuits? _____

12. When R_L of Fig. 6-6(a) is removed, are all the circuits in Fig. 6-6 electrically equivalent in terms of providing current and voltage to a specific load? _____

6-4 LAB EXPERIMENT: THE SUPERPOSITION THEOREM

PURPOSE

In this experiment you will verify the techniques used in applying the super-position theorem. You will also gain additional experience in working with complex dual-source circuits.

MATERIALS

Qty.

1 6-V battery or dc power supply
1 0- to 20-V dc power supply
2 1-kΩ, ½-W, 5% resistors

Qty.

1 2.2-kΩ, ½-W, 5% resistor
1 VOM or DMM
• test leads and wires

PROCEDURE

1. Calculate and record the value and direction (up or down) of I_{R_1} in Fig. 6-7. _____   _____
2. Construct the circuit shown in Fig. 6-7 and then measure and record I_{R_1}. Did the measured value and direction agree with step 1?

   _____   _____

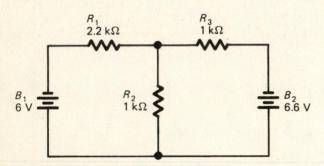

Fig. 6-7 Circuit for experiment 6-4.

3. Replace B_1 with a conductor and then measure I_{R_1}. Record both the direction and value of I_{R_1}. _____   _____
4. Remove the short (conductor) inserted in step 3 and place B_1 back in the circuit. Now replace B_2 with a short circuit and once again measure and record the magnitude and direction of I_{R_1}.

   _____   _____

5. Is the direction of I_{R_1} in steps 3 and 4 the same? Is the magnitude of I_{R_1} in the two steps the same? _____   _____
6. Does the algebraic sum of I_{R_1} in step 3 and I_{R_1} in step 4 equal the value of I_{R_1} measured in step 2? _____
7. Do your results support the superposition theorem? _____
8. Will the direction of I_{R_2} be different when B_1 is shorted from when B_2 is shorted? _____
9. If the polarity of B_2 in Fig. 6-7 is reversed, will the value of I_{R_1} increase or decrease?
10. Check your answer to step 9 by reversing B_2 and measuring and record-ing I_{R_1}. _____

6-5 LAB EXPERIMENT: ANALYSIS OF A VOLTAGE SOURCE

PURPOSE

Completion of this experiment will provide experience in experimentally developing a Thevenin equivalent circuit for an "unknown" voltage source.

MATERIALS

Qty.   **Qty.**

1 "unknown" voltage source   1 470-Ω, ½-W resistor
1 VOM or DMM   1 1000-Ω, ½-W resistor
1 220-Ω, ½-W resistor

DISCUSSION

The Thevenin equivalent circuit of a voltage source can be determined after making two voltage measurements. The first measurement determines the open-circuit terminal voltage (V_{oc}), and the second measurement determines the terminal voltage under loaded conditions (V_{R_L}). Figure 6-8 shows that the loaded voltage source can be treated as a series circuit. Thus, the voltage-divider equation can be applied to the circuit:

$$V_{R_L} = \frac{V_{oc}R_L}{R_L + R_S}$$

Solving this equation for R_S yields

$$R_S = \frac{V_{oc}R_L}{V_{R_L}} - R_L$$

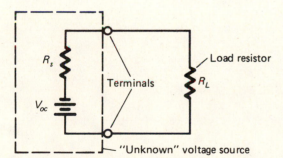

Fig. 6-8 Equivalent circuit of a loaded voltage source.

Since we know the value of R_L and can measure the values of V_{oc} and V_{R_L}, we can calculate the value of R_S using this equation. The values of R_S and V_{oc} are all that we require for the Thevenin equivalent circuit of the voltage source ($R_{TH} = R_S$ and $V_{oc} = V_{TH}$).

PROCEDURE

1. Measure and record the open-circuit voltage of the unknown voltage source.

   _____

2. Connect a 220-Ω, ½-W resistor to the voltage source. Measure and record the voltage across the resistor. Disconnect the resistor. _____

3. Using the data obtained in steps 1 and 2, calculate and record the internal resistance of the voltage source. _____

4. Draw a diagram of the Thevenin equivalent circuit of the voltage source.

5. Using the Thevenin equivalent circuit of step 4, predict—and record—the voltage across a 470-Ω resistor when the resistor is connected to the voltage source. _____

6. Connect a 470-Ω resistor to the voltage source and measure—and record—the voltage across it. Does the measured voltage agree (± 10 percent) with the predicted voltage of step 5? _____   _____

7. Convert the Thevenin equivalent circuit of step 4 to a Norton equivalent circuit. Record the value of the Norton current (I_N). _____

8. Predict and record the current through a 1-kΩ resistor when it is connected to the unknown voltage source. _____

9. Using the 10-mA range of the DMM, measure and record the current through a 1-kΩ resistor when it is connected to the voltage source. Does the measured current agree (± 10 percent) with the current predicted in step 8? _____   _____

6-6 LAB EXPERIMENT: TROUBLESHOOTING A BRIDGE

PURPOSE

This experiment provides troubleshooting experience on a complex circuit. It can be completed with electronic-circuit simulation software and a faulty software circuit (provided by your instructor).

MATERIALS

1   electronic-circuit simulation software with faulty circuit provided

PROCEDURE

1. The Wheatstone bridge shown in Fig. 6-9 has one defective resistor. Your problem is to determine which resistor it is without disconnecting any components. (Assume that all parts are soldered in place.)
2. Which resistor is defective? _____
3. Submit a report detailing how you determined which resistor was faulty.

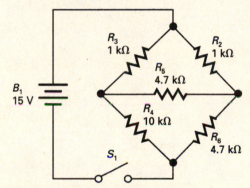

Fig. 6-9 Circuit for experiment 6-6.

Chapter 7

Magnetism and Electromagnetism

TEST: MAGNETISM AND ELECTROMAGNETISM

For questions 1 to 24, determine whether each statement is true or false.

1. Invisible magnetic lines of force surround all materials.

2. All the flux from the north pole of a bar magnet extends out parallel to the bar magnet.

3. The flux from a horseshoe magnet is least dense halfway between its poles.

4. Flux leaves the south pole and enters the north pole of the magnet.

5. Magnetic poles are attracted to each other when their fluxes join together.

6. A magnet's field is usually destroyed when the magnet is broken into two pieces.

7. Continuous loops of flux pass through a bar magnet as well as through the surrounding air.

8. A circular magnet can have both a north and a south pole.

9. Any current-carrying conductor has a magnetic field around it.

10. The current in a coil is flowing clockwise when viewed from the bottom of the coil. The top of the coil is a south pole.

11. Nonmagnetic materials block magnetic flux.

12. A magnetic field is associated with a neutron.

13. Magnetic domains are present in all materials.

14. The domains in a magnetized material are aligned in an orderly fashion.

15. Tin is a temporary magnetic material.

16. The insertion of any magnetic material in the center of a coil carrying direct current increases the pole flux.

17. Permanent magnetic materials can be either magnetized or demagnetized with a dc coil.

18. A piece of steel has more reluctance than a piece of brass of equal size.

19. Current changes in one coil can induce a voltage in a second coil.

20. An electromagnet's strength is increased when its core is replaced with a higher-permeability material.

21. The magnetic polarity of the armature in a dc motor changes as the motor rotates.

22. Relays can be made to operate on either alternating or direct current.

23. The movable part of a solenoid is made from nonmagnetic material.

24. Electromechanical devices used to operate mechanical devices like brakes and clutches are called solenoids.

1. _____
2. _____
3. _____
4. _____
5. _____
6. _____
7. _____
8. _____
9. _____
10. _____
11. _____
12. _____
13. _____
14. _____
15. _____
16. _____
17. _____
18. _____
19. _____
20. _____
21. _____
22. _____
23. _____
24. _____

For questions 25 to 36, supply the missing word or phrase needed in each statement.

25. A _____ is a natural permanent magnet.

26. The lines of force in a magnetic field are called _____.

27. The north pole of a magnet attracts the _____ of another magnet.

28. Parallel conductors with currents flowing in the same direction _____ each other.

29. When other factors are unchanged, increasing the space between the turns of a coil causes the pole flux to _____.

30. A conductor has no induced voltage if it moves _____ to magnetic flux.

31. The permeability of a material _____ as the material saturates.

32. _____ magnetic material is used for the core of electromagnets.

33. Ampere-turn is the base unit of _____.

34. Weber is the base unit for _____.

35. Tesla is the base unit for _____.

36. The part of a dc motor that makes contact with the brushes is the _____.

25. _____

26. _____

27. _____

28. _____

29. _____

30. _____

31. _____

32. _____

33. _____

34. _____

35. _____

36. _____

For questions 37 to 47, choose the letter that best completes each statement.

37. Halving the distance between magnetic poles makes the force between the poles
    a. Twice as great
    b. Four times as great
    c. Half as great
    d. One-fourth as great

37. _____

38. Current flowing in a straight conductor produces a magnetic field with
    a. A north pole at the negative end of the conductor
    b. A north pole at the positive end of the conductor
    c. No north pole or south pole
    d. A flux at 45° to the conductor

38. _____

39. You are viewing the end of a conductor in which the current is flowing away from you. The direction of the magnetic flux of the conductor is
    a. Counterclockwise
    b. Clockwise
    c. Away from you
    d. Toward you

39. _____

40. Which of the following elements is magnetic:
    a. Lead   c. Copper
    b. Tin   d. Iron

40. _____

41. Magnetic shields are made from
    a. Nonmagnetic materials
    b. High-reluctance materials
    c. Low-reluctance materials
    d. Nonmetallic materials

41. _____

42. Field intensity can be increased by
    a. Increasing the current in a coil
    b. Decreasing the reluctance of the magnetic circuit
    c. Decreasing the number of turns in a coil
    d. Increasing the permeability of the magnetic circuit

42. _____

43. When a magnetic material is saturated,
    a. Its reluctance is very low
    b. Its permeability is very high
    c. It is passing as much flux as it can
    d. Its flux density approaches zero

43. _____

74

44. The opposition to magnetic flux is called   44. _____
    a. Flux density
    b. Residual magnetism
    c. Reluctance
    d. Permeability

45. The movable part of a solenoid is called the   45. _____
    a. Armature
    b. Coil
    c. Commutator
    d. Plunger

46. The movable part of a relay is called the   46. _____
    a. Armature
    b. Commutator
    c. Field
    d. Plunger

47. The rotating part of a dc motor is called the   47. _____
    a. Armature
    b. Coil
    c. Field
    d. Brush

Answer the following questions.

48. Determine the flux density at the pole of a bar magnet which is 0.1 m   48. _____
long, 0.03 m wide, and 0.01 m high and produces 0.12 base units of flux.

49. What is the mmf of a 500-turn coil when the coil draws 1.6 A?   49. _____

50. Determine the magnetic field strength of a circuit which has 0.6 A in a   50. _____
200-t coil on a core with an average length of 0.4 m.

7-1 LAB EXPERIMENT: MAGNETIC FIELDS
AROUND CONDUCTORS

PURPOSE

This experiment will demonstrate the existence of a magnetic force around current-carrying conductors. It will show that reversing the current in a conductor reverses the direction of the magnetic field.

MATERIALS

Qty.

1   6-V dry battery
4   masking tape strips, 4 cm
    (1½ in.) long
2   wires, 36 gage, 18 cm
    (7 in.) long

Qty.

•   connecting leads with alligator
    clips

PROCEDURE

1. Tape the two pieces of 36-gage wire to the table top, as shown in Fig. 7-1. The wires must be physically parallel to each other. They should form an arch about 4 cm high [see Fig. 7-1(a)]. The wires must not touch each other under the tape. Touching can be avoided by using two pieces of tape at each end, as indicated in the end view of Fig. 7-1(b). Leave 3 or 4 cm of wire extending beyond the tape for making electric connections. Adjust the arches of wire so that they are about 1 mm apart.

CAUTION The circuits for this experiment rapidly discharge the battery. Therefore, do not leave the circuits connected. The magnetic forces between the two wires are most observable when the connection to one battery terminal is made and broken. To complete these circuits, just touch the lead against the battery terminal.

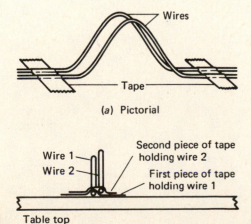

(a) Pictorial

(b) End view

Fig. 7-1 Physical arrangement of conductors for experiment 7-1.

2. Prepare the circuit shown in Fig. 7-2(a), but do not connect the lead to the negative terminal of the battery. One end of the wire arches can be connected by twisting the 36-gage wires together. Notice in Fig. 7-2(a) that the arch wires are electrically in series but physically parallel to each other.

    a. Will the current in the arch wires be in the same or opposite directions?

    _____

    b. Will the two wires attract or repel each other when the circuit is completed? _____

    c. Check your answer to step 2b by touching the connecting lead to the negative terminal of the battery. Do the wires repel or attract each other?

    _____

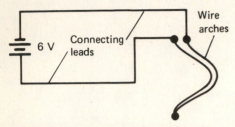

(a) Current in opposite directions

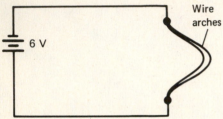

(b) Current in same direction

Fig. 7-2 Circuits for experiment 7-1.

3. Prepare the circuit of Fig. 7-2(b), but leave one lead off the battery terminal. The arch wires can be connected in parallel by twisting together the wires at each end.

    a. Are the currents in the arch wires in the same direction?

    _____

    b. Will the wires repel each other when the circuit is completed?

    _____

    c. Check your response to step 3b by momentarily connecting the circuit. Do the wires attract or repel each other? _____

    d. What causes the arch wires to repel or attract each other?

    _____

    _____

4. A two-conductor cable supplies current to a load such as a large lamp. Will the conductors repel or attract each other? _____ Why?

_____

_____

7-2 LAB EXPERIMENT: MAGNETIC MATERIALS, POLES, AND FIELDS

PURPOSE

This experiment illustrates the existence of magnetic poles and fields. You will identify magnetic and nonmagnetic materials and determine flux concentration in high-permeability materials.

MATERIALS

Qty.

2 magnets, bar, approximately 0.5 × 1 × 3 cm (3/16 × 3/8 × 1 1/4 in.)
1 salt shaker filled with iron filings
1 ferrite rod, approximately 1 cm (3/8 in.) in diameter and 1.5 cm (5/8 in.) long

Qty.

1 sheet of paper, 8 1/2 × 11 in.
3 masking tape strips, 6 cm (2 1/2 in.) long
1 screwdriver
• small samples of iron (nails), copper, brass, aluminum, paper, wood, etc.

PROCEDURE

1. Using one of the bar magnets, determine which materials are magnetic and which are nonmagnetic. Also test the ferrite rod.
   a. List the magnetic materials.

   _____

   _____

   _____

   b. Will the ferrite rod attract iron (nails)? _____
   c. Is ferrite a permanent or temporary magnetic material? _____
2. Stroke the blade of the screwdriver with one end of a bar magnet.
   a. Will the screwdriver now attract magnetic materials? _____
   b. What type of magnetic material is the screwdriver made of? _____
3. Lay one of the magnets on the table and cover it with a sheet of paper. Sprinkle a thin coating of iron filings on the paper and gently tap the paper.
   a. Are the iron filings concentrated at the ends of the poles? _____
   b. In the margin of this page, sketch the pattern made by the iron filings. Remove the lid from the salt shaker and pour the iron filings back into the shaker.
4. Tape one of the bar magnets to the top of a table or desk. Bring one end of the other magnet up to one end of the taped-down magnet. Note the force of either repulsion or attraction. Reverse the ends of the free magnet and note the opposite force.
   a. When the magnets repelled each other, were the poles of the same or opposite polarities? _____
   b. Arrange and tape the two magnets, as shown in Fig. 7-3. The magnets should be about 1 cm (3/8 in.) apart, with unlike poles facing each other. Now cover the magnets with paper and sprinkle on iron filings. Tap the paper gently. Does the arrangement of the filings indicate that lines of force from the two poles join together? _____ Sketch the pattern of the filings around the two poles. Pour the filings back into the shaker.
   c. Reverse either of the two magnets so that like poles are facing each

other. Again tape the magnet so that the poles are about 1 cm apart. Put the paper back over the magnets and sprinkle on a thin coat of filings. Tap lightly. Do the filings indicate that the flux from like poles joins together? _____ In the margin of this page, sketch the pattern of the filings. Return the filings to the shaker.

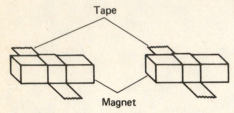

Fig. 7-3 Position of taped-down magnets for experiment 7-2.

5. Arrange the magnets and the ferrite rod, as shown in Fig. 7-4. Allow about 2 mm between the ferrite and the magnets. Have unlike poles of the magnet facing the ferrite rod. Cover the magnets and rod with paper. Sprinkle with iron filings and tap lightly.

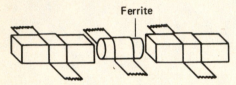

Fig. 7-4 Location of magnets and ferrite rod for experiment 7-2.

a. In the margin of this page, sketch the arrangement of the filings around the ferrite and the poles. Put the filings back in the shaker. Does the filing pattern indicate that the ferrite rod carried most of the flux from one pole to the other? _____

b. Does ferrite have a smaller or larger permeability than air? _____

c. Which has more reluctance, the ferrite rod or the air it replaces? _____

7-3 LAB EXPERIMENT: ELECTROMAGNETISM

PURPOSE

The objectives of this experiment are to verify some principles of electro-magnetism and to magnetize and demagnetize materials. Completing the experiment will provide experience in working with magnet wire.

MATERIALS

Qty.

1   wooden dowel, ¼ in. in diameter × 4 in. long
1   150-ft magnet wire, 23 gage
1   screwdriver, approximately ³⁄₁₆ × 4-in. blade
2   no. 47 lamps with holders
1   6- to 8-V, 2-A ac power supply (a 6-V transformer will do)

Qty.

1   6- to 8-V, 2-A dc power supply
1   sheet of paper, 8½ × 11 in.
12   nails, 3d (3 penny), common
3   nails, 16d
1   resistor, 2 Ω, 10 W
1   soldering gun
•   masking tape, connecting wires

PROCEDURE

CAUTION The soldering gun tip will heat up as you continue this experiment. Do not touch the tip when magnetizing or demagnetizing materials.

1. Put the blade of the screwdriver between the ends of the tip of the soldering gun so that the tip surrounds the blade. Turn the soldering gun on and then off immediately. Remove the screwdriver and see if it will attract the small nails. If it does not, repeat the process.
   a. Has the screwdriver been magnetized? _____
   b. Is it a permanent magnet? _____
   c. Again insert the screwdriver while the gun is off. Turn the gun on and remove the screwdriver while the gun is on. Then turn off the gun. Should the screwdriver now be magnetized or demagnetized? _____
   d. Try to pick up the 3d nails with the screwdriver. Does the screwdriver attract any nails? _____

2. Demagnetize one of the large (16d) nails. Wind a coil on the nail. The coil should be about two-thirds the length of the nail. It should consist of four layers of 23-gage magnet wire. Leave about 25-cm (10-in.) leads on the start and finish ends of the coil. Use masking tape to hold each layer of wire in place. The construction details of the coil are shown in Fig. 7-5. When you have finished winding the electromagnet, remove about 1 cm (⅜ in.) of insulation from the ends of the coil. Now connect the circuit shown in Fig. 7-6. In this figure the two straight lines by the coil represent the iron core (nail) on which the coil is wound. The no. 47 lamp limits the current in the circuit to about 100 mA. _____
   a. Will the electromagnet you have just made attract small nails? _____ Why?
   _____
   _____

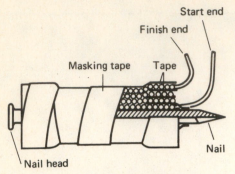

Fig. 7-5 Making an electromagnet.

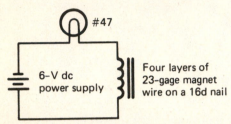

Fig. 7-6 Circuit for experiment 7-3, step 2.

b. Pick up as many small nails as you can with the electromagnet. While holding the electromagnet (and nails) above the table top, disconnect the electric circuit. What happened? _____ Why?

_____

_____

c. Try picking up the small nails again while the electric circuit is disconnected. Is there any magnetism left in the electromagnet? _____

d. What is the name for the magnetism left in a temporary magnet after the magnetizing force has been removed? _____

CAUTION Operate this circuit only for short periods of time. The current in the coil will be about 2 A, which will cause the coil to heat up.

3. Increasing the current in a coil will increase the magnetomotive force (and thus the strength) of an electromagnet.
   a. Connect your electromagnet as shown in Fig. 7-7(a). See how many small nails your electromagnet will pick up now. Has the strength of your electromagnet increased? _____
   b. Disconnect the circuit and check the residual magnetism. Is it any greater than it was before? _____ Why?

   _____

   _____

   c. Now change from a dc to an ac power supply, as shown in Fig. 7-7(b). Connect the circuit and see how many nails the magnet will pick up when powered by alternating current. Disconnect the circuit and check the residual magnetism. Is there a noticeable difference in the strength of the magnet when powered by alternating or direct current?

   _____

   d. Is there any difference in the residual magnetism? _____

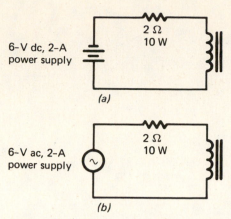

Fig. 7-7 Circuit for experiment 7-3, step 3.

4. Either construct or borrow a second electromagnet. Connect the two magnets in series and power them, as shown in Fig. 7-8. Using the left-hand rule, predict whether the heads of the two magnets will attract or repel.

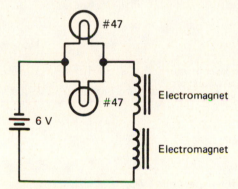

Fig. 7-8 Circuit for experiment 7-3, step 4.

    a. Bring the heads of the magnets together. Do they attract or repel?

    _____

    b. Now reverse the direction of current in one of the magnets by interchanging the start and finish ends of one magnet. Again bring the heads of the magnets together. Do they now attract or repel each other?

    _____

    c. If you reverse the direction of current in the other magnet, would the heads repel or attract each other? _____ Check your answer by reversing current in the second coil.

5. Now you are going to make a coil in which you can use different core materials. The coil will be wound on a paper form. Both the form and the coil will be wound on a ¼-in. dowel. Refer to Fig. 7-9 and fold a sheet of paper into four layers as shown. Next roll and tape the paper around the dowel, as shown in Fig. 7-10. Do not tape the paper to the dowel because the dowel will be removed later. Wind four layers of 23-gage magnet wire on top of the paper. Tape, as shown in Fig. 7-11, both ends of each layer with masking tape. When the coil is finished, remove the insulation from the ends of the magnet wire.

    a. Connect the circuit of Fig. 7-12(*a*) and try to pick up the small nails with the wood-core magnet. Does the magnet attract the nails?

    _____

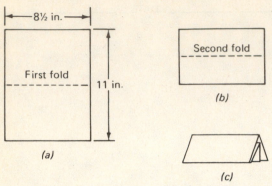

Fig. 7-9 Folding paper for coil form used in experiment 7-3, step 5.

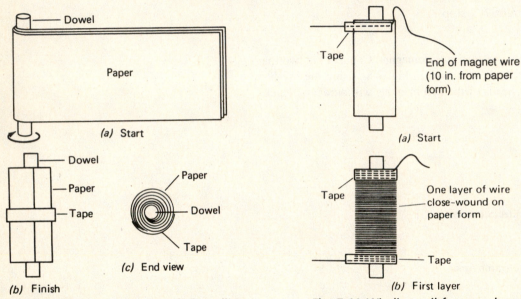

Fig. 7-10 The coil form is made by rolling the folded paper around the dowel.

Fig. 7-11 Winding coil for experiment 7-3, step 5.

b. Remove the ¼-in. dowel by gently pulling and twisting on it. Now try to attract the small nails with the air-core magnet. Does it attract any better than the wood-core? _____ Why?

_____

_____

c. Insert a large (16d) nail into the core of the coil. Now try attracting the small nails with the electromagnet. Does it attract any better than either a wood-core or an air-core magnet? _____ Why?

_____

_____

d. Remove the large nail from the core. Change the electromagnet circuit from that shown in Fig. 7-12(a) to that shown in Fig. 7-12(b). The current in the coil in Fig. 7-12(b) is about 10 times as great in Fig. 7-12(a). Now try to attract the small (3d) nails. Disconnect the circuit so that the coil does not overheat. Will the magnet now attract the small nails? _____ Why?

_____

_____

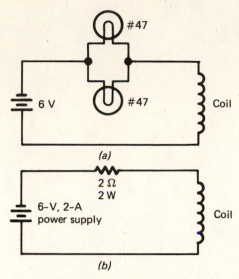

Fig. 7-12 Circuits for experiment 7-3, step 5.

e. Insert a large nail about one-third of the way into the coil. Now reconnect the circuit. What happens?

_____

_____

f. Why did this happen?

_____

_____

g. Hold the coil, with the nail in it and its head facing down, above the desk. Now disconnect the circuit. What happened?

_____

_____

h. Why? (What happened to the mmf?)

_____

_____

i. Could this coil be used to magnetize and demagnetize a screwdriver? _____ Try it!

NAME _____ DATE _____

Chapter 8

Alternating Current and Voltage

TEST: ALTERNATING CURRENT AND VOLTAGE

For questions 1 to 21, determine whether each statement is true or false.

1. Alternating current reverses the direction it is flowing at the end of each alternation.

2. Fluctuating direct current periodically touches the zero reference line of a waveform graph.

3. One hertz is equal to two alternations per second.

4. Electric power is distributed at 120 Hz in the United States.

5. Effective voltage and rms voltage are interchangeable terms.

6. The mechanical and electrical degrees of a two-pole generator are equal.

7. The output voltage of a generator can be changed by changing the flux density of its field.

8. The frequency of a generator can be changed by changing the number of poles in the field.

9. Both the frequency and the voltage of a generator change when the armature speed changes.

10. The rms voltage from a 120-V outlet is greater than the average voltage.

11. An ac generator uses a commutator and brushes.

12. Alternating current is used to excite the electromagnetic field coils of an ac generator.

13. A three-phase system requires only three conductors for its power line.

14. Each phase in a three-phase system is separated 120° from the other two phases.

15. The three phases of a three-phase system never have the same instantaneous polarity.

16. The line current and phase current are equal in a four-wire wye system.

17. The common connection in a wye system is called the star point.

18. The reference ends of the phase windings are connected together in a delta-connected system.

19. The neutral wire of a three-phase, four-wire system carries current under all load conditions.

20. Three-phase systems are more efficient than single-phase systems.

21. Rectified three-phase alternating current is closer to pure direct current than rectified single-phase alternating current.

1. _____
2. _____
3. _____
4. _____
5. _____
6. _____
7. _____
8. _____
9. _____
10. _____
11. _____
12. _____
13. _____
14. _____
15. _____
16. _____
17. _____
18. _____
19. _____
20. _____
21. _____

For questions 22 to 31, supply the missing word or phrase in each statement.

22. The symbol or abbreviation for period is _____.
23. The symbol or abbreviation for frequency is _____.
24. The base unit of frequency is _____.

22. _____
23. _____
24. _____

25. The abbreviation or symbol for the base unit of frequency is
   _____.

26. _____ is the rate at which cycles are produced.

27. When a voltage waveform is plotted, voltage is usually plotted on the _____ axis.

28. Either time or _____ can be plotted on the _____ axis of a waveform graph.

29. The time required to complete one cycle is the _____.

30. There are _____ degrees per cycle.

31. The line voltage is _____ times higher than the phase voltage in a _____ system.

25. _____

26. _____

27. _____

28. _____

29. _____

30. _____

31. _____

For questions 32 to 35, choose the letter that best completes each statement.

32. Commercial power is distributed as a
   a. Circle wave
   b. Triangle wave
   c. Sine wave
   d. Square wave

33. Which of the following does not influence the amount of voltage induced in a conductor?
   a. Flux density
   b. Direction the conductor moves
   c. Speed the conductor moves
   d. Angle at which the conductor cuts the flux

34. A given value of direct current has the same heating effect as an equal value of
   a. Peak ac current
   b. Peak-to-peak ac current
   c. Root-mean-square ac current
   d. Average ac current

35. A three-phase system which provides both 120-V single-phase and 208-V three-phase is the
   a. Four-wire delta system
   b. Four-wire wye system
   c. Five-wire delta system
   d. Five-wire wye system

32. _____

33. _____

34. _____

35. _____

For questions 36 to 42, solve each problem.

36. What is the period of a 500-Hz sine wave?

37. What is the frequency of a waveform that has a period of 0.4 ms?

38. What is the peak-to-peak value of 100 V?

39. What is the rms value of 180 V_{av}?

40. The rms current in a circuit is a 12 A. What is the peak current?

41. What is the frequency of a six-pole generator that rotates at 1000 r/min?

42. What is the line voltage of a wye-connected, three-phase generator that has a phase voltage of 260 V?

36. _____

37. _____

38. _____

39. _____

40. _____

41. _____

42. _____

8-1 LAB EXERCISE: AC WAVEFORMS AND TERMINOLOGY

PURPOSE

This experiment will provide you with more experience in using waveforms to describe ac currents and voltages.

PROCEDURE

1. Figure 8-1(*a*) lists the voltages of an ac waveform for each 15° of the cycle. Using these voltages and corresponding degrees, plot the points of a waveform on the graph in Fig. 8-1(*b*).

Electrical degrees	Volts	Electrical degrees	Volts
0	0.0	195	-18.1
15	18.1	210	-35.0
30	35.0	225	-49.5
45	49.5	240	-60.6
60	60.6	255	-67.6
75	67.6	270	-70.0
90	70.0	285	-67.6
105	67.6	300	-60.6
120	60.6	315	-49.5
135	49.5	330	-35.0
150	35.0	345	-18.1
165	18.1	360	0.0
180	0.0		

(a) Data

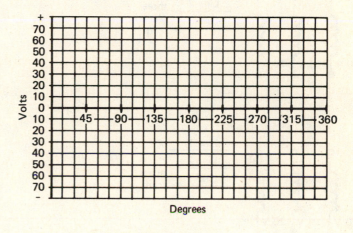

(b) Graph

Fig. 8-1 Plotting a sine wave.

    a. Now connect the points together to finish the waveform.
    b. What type of waveform does it make? _____
    c. Assume each degree of the cycle represents 0.0001 s. What is the period (*T*) of the waveform? _____
    d. What is the frequency of the waveform? _____
    e. What is the rms value of the waveform? _____
    f. What is the average value of the waveform? _____

2. Refer to Fig. 8-2.
    a. What type of waveform is shown? _____
    b. What is the peak-to-peak value of the waveform? _____
    c. What is the peak positive value of the waveform? _____
    d. What is the period of this waveform? _____
    e. What is its frequency? _____
    f. How many cycles of this waveform will be completed in 1 s? _____

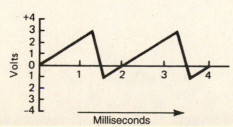

Fig. 8-2 Waveform for experiment 8-1, step 2.

8-2 LAB EXERCISE: THREE-PHASE CONNECTIONS

PURPOSE

The purpose of this exercise is to reinforce your understanding of delta and wye connections.

PROCEDURE

1. The three coils in Fig. 8-3 are the phase windings of a generator. The black terminal on each coil represents the reference end of the coil.

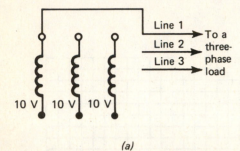

(a)

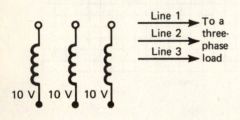

(b)

Fig. 8-3 Making wye and delta connections.

    a. Connect the windings in Fig. 8-3(*a*) in a wye configuration. (The line 1 connection has been made as an example.)

    b. What is the value of the voltage between line 1 and line 2? _____

    c. What is the value of the voltage between line 1 and line 3? _____

    d. What is the value of the voltage between the star connection and any of the three lines? _____

2. Refer to Fig. 8-3(*b*).

    a. Connect these phase windings in a delta configuration.

    b. What is the line voltage of this generator? _____

8-3 LAB EXPERIMENT: VIEWING AND MEASURING WAVEFORMS

PURPOSE

This experiment will acquaint you with the use of an oscilloscope to view and measure waveforms. It will introduce you to the audio signal generator. Finally, it will allow you to compare the voltage-measuring capabilities of the DMM and the oscilloscope.

MATERIALS

Qty.

1 oscilloscope with calibrated vertical input and time base
1 DMM

Qty.

1 signal generator, sinusoidal output, audio range

INTRODUCTION

An oscilloscope displays a voltage waveform when properly adjusted. That is, it plots a graph with voltage amplitude on the vertical axis and time on the horizontal axis. All oscilloscopes perform this same basic function. However, the details and specific names of the operating controls vary from oscilloscope to oscilloscope. An example of an oscilloscope is given in Fig. 8-4.

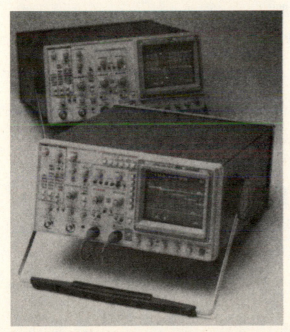

Fig. 8-4 Oscilloscope. (*Courtesy of Tektronix, Inc.*)

The common operating controls, and their functions, for a typical oscilloscope are listed and discussed below. After your teacher has demonstrated the operation of your oscilloscope, you can refer to this list to refresh your memory.

Oscilloscope Operating Controls

INTENSITY Controls the brightness of the waveform. Keep the brightness as low as possible while still displaying a waveform that is easily viewed.

POSITION   Controls the location of the waveform. There are two position controls. One controls the location of the waveform on the horizontal axis. The other controls the location of the waveform on the vertical axis. Adjust these controls to center the waveform both vertically and horizontally.

FOCUS   Determines the sharpness of the waveform. Adjust this control to obtain the minimum width of the trace line. The focus control and the intensity control often interact. Readjust the focus control after changing the intensity control.

ASTIGMATISM   Works together with the focus control in determining the sharpness of the waveform. Adjust this control whenever the focus control is changed. You may have to adjust the astigmatism and the focus controls several times to obtain the best focus. Not all oscilloscopes have this control.

VOLTS/DIVISION   Controls the height (vertical size) of the waveform. (The control is sometimes called "volts/centimeter" because the divisions on the screen are usually 1-cm squares.) This control has two control knobs. One is a rotary switch which makes coarse (step) adjustments. The other is a potentiometer which makes fine adjustments; it is often labeled "variable." The position of these two knobs determines how much voltage is needed to fill the screen of the oscilloscope.

The volts/division control is used to measure the voltage applied to the input (vertical input) of the oscilloscope. To measure the input voltage, the variable (fine adjustment) knob must be in the "calibrate" position. Then the coarse (step) adjustment indicates how much voltage is required to produce a waveform one division in height. Assume that a waveform is 4.6 divisions in height, the volts/division switch is on the 0.2 volts/division position, and the variable control is in the "calibrate" position. Therefore, the waveform has a peak-to-peak value of

$$V_{p-p} = 4.6 \text{ divisions} \times 0.2 \text{ V/division} = 0.92 \text{ V}$$

TIME/DIVISION   The time/division control determines how many cycles of the waveform are displayed on the screen. It, like the volts/division, has two control knobs. One operates a switch which is the coarse adjustment. The other operates a potentiometer for the fine (variable) adjustment.

The time/division control can be used to measure the period of a waveform. Again, the variable adjustment must be in the "calibrate" position in order to measure the period. For example, assume that the length of one cycle is approximately 2.8 divisions, the time/division switch is in the 1 millisecond/division (ms/div) position, and the variable knob is in the calibrate position. The period of the waveform, therefore, is:

$$\text{Period } (T) = 2.8 \text{ divisions} \times 1 \text{ ms/div} = 2.8 \text{ ms}$$

TRIGGERING   The triggering control (or controls) keeps the waveform stationary. The trigger level control is adjusted to the left or right of its center position until the waveform pattern stops moving. The other trigger controls should be in the "internal," "automatic," and "ac" positions for general use of the oscilloscope.

Most audio signal generators have controls that do the following:

1. *Select the desired frequency:* This is usually accomplished by two separate control knobs. One is a variable control which has a dial or dial indicator attached to it. The other is the band or range switch. Unless the generator has a digital readout, the frequency is determined by multiplying the dial reading by the range setting.

2. *Select the type of waveform:* Most generators provide a choice of at least a sine wave or a square wave.

3. *Adjust the output level:* Most generators have two output controls. One, which is a switch type of control, provides coarse (step) control. The other, which is continuously variable, provides the fine adjustment within each step. These controls are adjusted to obtain the desired peak-to-peak voltage from the signal generator.

Again, each manufacturer may use different types of controls and different names for the controls. However, all generators provide controls for the three functions listed above.

PROCEDURE

1. Apply power to both the signal generator and the oscilloscope. Set the oscilloscope for 0.5 V/div and 0.5 ms/div. Increase the intensity control until a horizontal line appears. Adjust the focus and astigmatism controls. Adjust the positioning controls to center the line on the screen, both horizontally and vertically.

   Now connect the output of the signal generator to the input of the oscilloscope. Set the frequency controls of the generator to provide a 400-Hz signal. Set the function switch to the sine wave position. Now adjust the output controls so that the waveform on the oscilloscope screen is four divisions high.

   Finally, adjust the trigger control to obtain a stationary waveform.

   a. What is the peak-to-peak value of the waveform you are viewing? _____

   b. What is the period of the waveform you are viewing? _____

   c. Change the volts/division switch to the 1-V/div position. Did the waveform increase or decrease in height? _____

   d. Does the oscilloscope indicate approximately the same voltage as it did in step 1a? _____

   e. Change the time/division switch to the 1-ms/div position. Did the number of cycles displayed increase or decrease? _____

   f. Does the oscilloscope now indicate the same period (within 5 percent) as it did in step 1b? _____

   g. If you were to decrease the frequency of the generator, would the number of cycles displayed increase or decrease? Check your answer by decreasing the frequency. _____

2. We are now going to compare the ac voltages measured with the DMM and the oscilloscope. The ac voltage function of any DMM is calibrated for measuring the rms value of sine waves. Some DMMs will provide the rms value of any type of ac waveform. The oscilloscope is calibrated to measure peak-to-peak values of any type of waveform. It will measure the voltage of waveforms that range in frequency from less than 1 Hz to many megahertz.

   Set the signal generator's frequency controls to 200 Hz. Adjust its output controls for a 10-V peak-to-peak reading on the screen of the oscilloscope. Leave the oscilloscope connected to the generator. Now, measure the output voltage of the generator with the DMM. (The DMM should be on the ac voltage function and the 10-V range.)

   a. How much voltage does the DMM indicate? _____

   b. Convert the peak-to-peak voltage indicated on the oscilloscope to rms voltage. Does it give approximately (± 10 percent) the same value you recorded in step 2a? _____

c. Increase the frequency of the generator to 100 kHz (100,000 Hz). Adjust its output so that it again indicates 10 V peak to peak on the oscilloscope. Now measure the output of the generator with the DMM. Does the DMM indicate the same voltage as it did in step 2a? _____

d. Change the generator frequency back to 200 Hz. Set the function switch to the square wave position. Adjust the output voltage to 10 V peak to peak (as indicated on the oscilloscope). Now measure the output voltage of the generator with the DMM. Does it indicate the same voltage as it did in step 2a? _____ Why?

_____

_____

3. Turn off the signal generator and the oscilloscope. This section will test your ability to interpret waveforms displayed on an oscilloscope. Refer to Fig. 8-5.

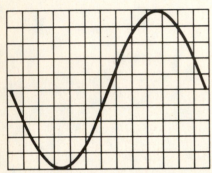

Oscilloscope controls are set for
5 V/div and 0.5 ms/div

Fig. 8-5 Oscilloscope display for experiment 8-3, step 3.

a. What is the period of the waveform? _____
b. What is the frequency of the waveform? _____
c. What is the peak voltage of the waveform? _____
d. How much voltage would the DMM indicate when measuring this waveform? _____

8-4 LAB EXPERIMENT: FREQUENCY AND VOLTAGE

PURPOSE

This simulation experiment will provide more experience with making measurements with an oscilloscope. Also, it will reemphasize the importance of specifying the correct amplitude values of voltage and current.

MATERIALS

Qty.

1 electronics-circuit simulation software
1 simulation-circuit file for Fig. 8-6 (available from your instructor)

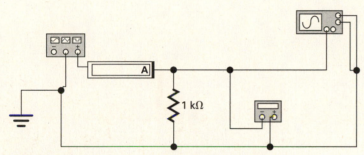

Fig. 8-6 Simulation circuit for experiment 8-4.

PROCEDURE

1. After opening the file Fig. 8-6.ewb, activate the circuit.
   a. Using the oscilloscope display, determine and record the period of the waveform. _____
   b. Calculate and record the frequency of the waveform. _____
   c. Does the calculated frequency agree with the value specified on the function generator? _____
   d. Record the voltage measured with the oscilloscope. _____
   e. Using the voltage measured with the oscilloscope and the specified value of R, calculate and record the current. _____
   f. Does the calculated current agree with the measured current? _____ Should it? _____
   g. Which voltage (V_{p-p}, V_p, V_{av}, or V) is specified on the function generator? _____
   h. Which voltage (V_{p-p}, V_p, V_{av}, or V) is specified on the oscilloscope? _____
   i. Which voltage (V_{p-p}, V_p, V_{av}, or V) is specified on the multimeter? _____
   j. Does the ammeter indicate I_{rms}? _____
   k. Would the oscilloscope frequency or amplitude indications change if the function of the generator were changed to square wave? _____
   l. Would the voltage indicated by the multimeter change if the function of the generator were changed to square wave? _____
   m. Check your answers to steps k and l by clicking on the square wave shown on the generator.

Power in AC Circuits

TEST: POWER IN AC CIRCUITS

For questions 1 to 18, determine whether each statement is true or false.

1. Angle θ will be 45° when the resistance and reactance in a circuit are equal. 1. _____
2. Current and voltage are 90° out of phase in a pure resistive circuit. 2. _____
3. A load which contains both resistance and reactance uses power. 3. _____
4. A circuit has reactance when the current and voltage are out of phase. 4. _____
5. A circuit has no resistance if the phase shift between current and voltage is exactly 90°. 5. _____
6. Power factor can be between zero and 1. 6. _____
7. Phasors rotate in a clockwise direction. 7. _____
8. Most electric motors can be considered inductive devices. 8. _____
9. Capacitance possesses reactance. 9. _____
10. Apparent power can be measured with a wattmeter. 10. _____
11. The current leads the voltage in an ac motor. 11. _____
12. All current phasors in a phasor diagram must use the same scale. 12. _____
13. In Fig. 9-1(*a*) the current is lagging the voltage. 13. _____
14. In Fig. 9-1(*b*) the voltage is leading the current. 14. _____
15. True power is always less than apparent power in circuits that have some reactance. 15. _____
16. The power factor is equal to the sine of angle θ. 16. _____
17. The angle between the total voltage and the total current is called θ. 17. _____
18. When the power factor is 1, the most efficient use of distribution lines and equipment occurs. 18. _____

For questions 19 to 22, choose the letter that best completes each statement.

19. Unless otherwise stated, ac power is specified in 19. _____
    a. Instantaneous value
    b. Average value
    c. Effective value
    d. Peak value
20. The form of opposition to alternating current that uses no power is called 20. _____
    a. Reluctance
    b. Reactance
    c. Resistance
    d. Resistivity

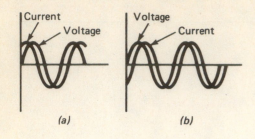

(a)　　　　(b)

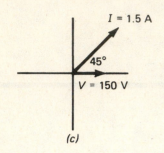

(c)

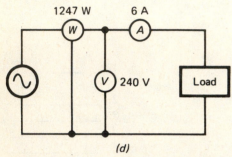

(d)

Fig. 9-1 Illustrations for test questions.

21. The base unit for apparent power is
  a. Ampere-turn
  b. Voltampere
  c. Watthour
  d. Ohmwatt

21. _____

22. The cosine of angle θ can be found by dividing
  a. Resistive voltage by total voltage
  b. The hypotenuse by the adjacent side
  c. The adjacent side by the opposite side
  d. Total current by reactive current

22. _____

For questions 23 to 31, solve each problem. Be sure to include units (watts, degrees, etc.) in your answer when appropriate.

23. How much power is used by a 120-V heater that draws 18 A?

23. _____

24. Does the phasor diagram in Fig. 9-1(*c*) represent the waveforms in Fig. 9-1(*a*) or those in Fig. 9-1(*b*)?

24. _____

25. What is the tangent of 65°? (Use your calculator or refer to Fig. 9-2.)

25. _____

26. How much power is used by the circuit represented by the phasors in Fig. 9-1(*c*)?

26. _____

27. What is the apparent power of the load in Fig. 9-1(*d*)?

27. _____

28. What is the power factor in the load in Fig. 9-1(*d*)?

28. _____

29. What is the phase relationship between the current and the voltage in Fig. 9-1(*d*)?

29. _____

Trigonometric functions

Angle	Sin	Cos	Tan
5	0.087	0.996	0.088
10	0.174	0.985	0.176
15	0.259	0.966	0.268
20	0.342	0.940	0.364
25	0.423	0.906	0.466
30	0.500	0.866	0.577
35	0.574	0.819	0.700
40	0.643	0.766	0.839
45	0.707	0.707	1.000
50	0.766	0.643	1.192
55	0.819	0.574	1.428
60	0.866	0.500	1.732
65	0.906	0.423	2.145
70	0.940	0.342	2.748
75	0.966	0.259	3.732
80	0.985	0.174	5.671
85	0.996	0.087	11.429
90	1.000	0.000	---------

Fig. 9-2 Trigonometric function table.

30. A current of 12 A is 40° out of phase with the voltage. What is the value of the resistive current?

30. _____

31. What is the power factor for a circuit in which I lags V by 60°?

31. _____

9-1 LAB EXPERIMENT: TRUE POWER AND APPARENT POWER

PURPOSE

This experiment will provide experience in measuring true and apparent power in several types of loads. You will gain experience in using an ac ammeter, voltmeter, and wattmeter. The results of this activity will verify that the power in an inductive circuit is not equal to current times voltage.

MATERIALS

Qty.

1 ac ammeter, 10-A range
1 ac wattmeter, 1000-W range, 300 V, 7 A
1 ac voltmeter, 150-V range

Qty.

1 heater or hair dryer, 500 W
1 ac motor, ⅓ or ½ hp
1 variable transformer, 0- to 120-V ac, 7 A

CAUTION The circuits in this experiment are powered from a 120-V ac outlet. A shock from such a circuit can be fatal. Make all connections in the circuit before connecting the variable transformer to the 120-V outlet. Do not touch any part of the circuit after it is connected to the 120-V source.

PROCEDURE

1. Connect the circuit shown in Fig. 9-3(a). Notice that the ammeter and the voltmeter have no polarity markings because ac changes polarity every half cycle. Set the variable transformer control for minimum output voltage. Then plug the transformer into a 120-V outlet. Now, rotate the variable transformer control until the voltmeter indicates 120 V.

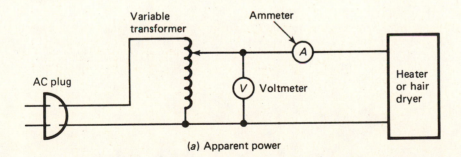

(a) Apparent power

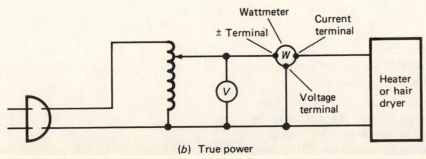

(b) True power

Fig. 9-3 Measuring the power of the hair dryer.

a. Read and record the current indicated by the ammeter. _____

b. Return the variable transformer to minimum setting and unplug it from the 120-V outlet. Using the measured current and voltage, calculate and record the apparent power of the heater. _____

c. Change the ammeter of Fig. 9-3(a) to a wattmeter as shown in Fig. 9-3(b). Notice that the wattmeter symbol shows three leads. However, many wattmeters have four terminals. Two terminals are for the current coil and two for the voltage coil. One terminal of each coil is marked with a ± sign. Connect the two terminals with the ± signs together and treat them as if they were a single terminal. Be sure the current and voltage terminals are connected as shown in Fig. 9-3(b). Now plug the transformer in and adjust it for 120 V as indicated on the voltmeter. Read and record the power indicated by the wattmeter.

_____

d. Reset the transformer for minimum voltage and unplug it. Compare the apparent power and the true power for this resistive load. Are they the same? _____ Why?

_____

_____

e. What is the power factor of this circuit? _____

2. Connect the circuit of Fig. 9-4(a). Check to be sure the variable transformer is set for minimum voltage. Plug in the transformer and slowly increase the voltage while watching the ammeter. Increase the voltage slowly so that the ammeter pointer moves smoothly. Continue increasing the voltage until the voltmeter indicates 120 V.

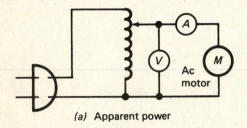

(a) Apparent power

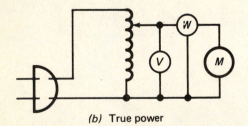

(b) True power

Fig. 9-4 Measuring the input to a motor.

a. Read and record the current. _____

b. Reduce the voltage to minimum value and unplug the transformer. Calculate and record the apparent power. _____

c. Connect the circuit of Fig. 9-4(b). Again, be sure the variable transformer control is set for minimum voltage before plugging it into the 120-V outlet. Now increase the transformer output voltage slowly so as not to damage the wattmeter. Adjust the transformer for 120 V. Read and record the power. _____

d. Again reduce the voltage to minimum and unplug the transformer. Are the apparent power and the true power the same for an ac motor? _____ Why?

_____

_____

e. Determine and record the power factor for this circuit. _____

f. Determine and record angle θ for this circuit. _____

9-2 ADVANCED PROBLEMS

9-1. Refer to Fig. 9-5 and answer the following:

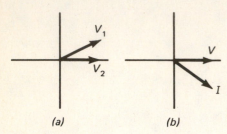

(a)   *(b)*

Fig. 9-5 Phasors.

    a. In Fig. 9-5(*b*), which phasor is leading? _____
    b. In Fig. 9-5(*a*), must V_2 be numerically smaller than V_1? _____
    c. In Fig. 9-5(*b*), is *I* leading or lagging *V*? _____
    d. In Fig. 9-5(*b*), must *V* be numerically larger than *I*? _____
    e. Are the phasors in Fig. 9-5(*b*) representing an inductive or a capacitive circuit? _____

9-2. A circuit has 4 V of resistive voltage and 3 V of inductive voltage. In the margin of this page, draw a phasor diagram showing the total voltage. Use a scale of 1 cm = 1 V.

9-3. A motor draws 7 A from a 240-V source at a power factor of 70 percent. Find the following:
    a. The apparent power _____
    b. The actual (true) power _____
    c. Angle θ _____
    d. The resistive current _____
    e. The reactive current _____

9-4. The apparent power in a circuit is 690 W and the actual power is 550 W. The source voltage is 115 V. Find the following:
    a. Total current _____
    b. Cosine θ _____
    c. Angle θ _____
    d. Resistive current _____

104

9-3 LAB EXPERIMENT: PHASE SHIFT

PURPOSE

As you vary the relative amounts of resistive and reactive loads on a circuit, the phase angle between I and V will vary. This simulation experiment allows you to observe the phase shift of the current and voltage waveforms as the combination load is varied.

MATERIALS

Qty.

1 electronics-circuit simulation software
1 simulation-circuit file for Fig. 9-6 (available from your instructor)

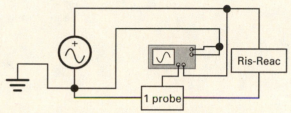

Fig. 9-6 Simulation circuit for experiment 9-3.

PROCEDURE

1. After opening the file Fig. 9-6.ewb, activate the circuit.
   a. Click the pause button to lock the waveforms. (You may have to click the button several times to get a locked waveform.) Measure and record the phase shift. _____
   b. Restart the circuit and make the load more resistive. Does this increase or decrease angle theta? _____
   c. Measure and record the minimum angle theta available with this load. _____
   d. Measure and record the maximum angle theta available with this load. _____

9-4 LAB EXPERIMENT: THETA AND POWER FACTOR

PURPOSE

This simulation experiment provides practice in measuring ac voltages and current to be used in determining other circuit quantities.

MATERIALS

Qty.

1   electronics-circuit simulation software
1   simulation-circuit file for Fig. 9-7 (available from your instructor)

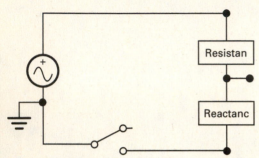

Fig. 9-7 Simulation circuit for experiment 9-4.

PROCEDURE

1. After opening the file Fig. 9-7.ewb, activate the circuit.
    a. Measure and record the voltage across the resistive part of the circuit.
    _____

    b. Measure and record the voltage across the reactive part of the circuit.
    _____

    c. From the results obtained in steps a and b, is theta greater than or less than 45°? _____

    d. Measure and record the total voltage and the total current.
    _____   _____

    e. Using your measured data, calculate and record the following:

    $P = $ _____

    $P_{app} = $ _____

    $\theta = $ _____

    $PF = $ _____

Chapter 10

Capacitance

TEST: CAPACITANCE

For questions 1 to 24, determine whether each statement is true or false.

1. Insulating material is used to make the dielectric in a capacitor. 1. _____
2. Electrons readily flow through the dielectric of a capacitor. 2. _____
3. The voltage between the plates of a capacitor decreases as energy is stored in the capacitor. 3. _____
4. For its weight and size, a capacitor stores more energy than a battery. 4. _____
5. Air has a larger dielectric constant than mica does. 5. _____
6. All capacitors have a positive temperature coefficient. 6. _____
7. Doubling the plate area of a capacitor doubles its capacitance if all other factors remain unchanged. 7. _____
8. For a given size and weight, an electrolytic capacitor has more capacitance than a ceramic capacitor. 8. _____
9. The outside foil of a tubular capacitor is identified by the curved line on a capacitor symbol. 9. _____
10. Most foil capacitors are self-healing. 10. _____
11. Ceramic capacitors are often used to filter pulsating direct current. 11. _____
12. Bypass capacitors are used in electronic photoflash equipment. 12. _____
13. The color band on the end of a film capacitor identifies the outside foil. 13. _____
14. Direct current continuously flows through a capacitor. 14. _____
15. The voltage leads the current by 90° in an ideal capacitor. 15. _____
16. A nonelectrolytic capacitor usually has more than 1 percent energy loss. 16. _____
17. Capacitance uses no power in either an ac or a dc circuit. 17. _____
18. Capacitors block alternating current in a circuit. 18. _____
19. A capacitor returns energy to the main energy source twice each cycle. 19. _____
20. The quality of a capacitor can be indicated by its power factor. 20. _____
21. The larger of two series capacitors in an ac circuit drops more voltage. 21. _____
22. The larger of two parallel capacitors in an ac circuit passes more current. 22. _____
23. A capacitor changes its voltage by 36.8 percent during one time constant. 23. _____
24. A ceramic capacitor that is not defective should indicate about midscale on the highest range of an ohmmeter. 24. _____

For questions 25 to 32, choose the letter that best completes each statement.

25. The dielectric material of a capacitor 25. _____
    a. Seals the capacitor from moisture
    b. Is a conductor
    c. Is an insulator
    d. Connects to the leads

26. Capacitors have a voltage rating because the
    a. Plates can store only a limited number of electrons
    b. Dielectric can store only a limited number of electrons
    c. Dielectric can withstand the force of only a limited electric field
    d. Plates can withstand the force of only a limited electric field
27. The voltage rating of a capacitor is referred to as its
    a. ESR rating
    b. DCWV rating
    c. DFV rating
    d. PFV rating
28. The capacitance of a capacitor is not determined by the
    a. Thickness of the dielectric
    b. Temperature
    c. Plate area
    d. Frequency
29. The dielectric constant of a material indicates its ability to
    a. Resist current
    b. Conduct current
    c. Store energy
    d. Withstand voltage
30. A film capacitor could have a dielectric composed of
    a. Polystyrene
    b. Ceramic
    c. Mica
    d. Metal oxide
31. If two capacitors of unequal value are series-connected to a dc source,
    a. Each capacitor will develop all the source voltage
    b. Each capacitor will develop half the source voltage
    c. The smaller capacitor will develop more voltage
    d. The larger capacitor will develop more voltage
32. Minimum specifications for ordering ceramic capacitors need not include
    a. Voltage rating
    b. Current rating
    c. Tolerance
    d. Capacitance

26. _____

27. _____

28. _____

29. _____

30. _____

31. _____

32. _____

For questions 33 to 44, supply the missing word or phrase in each statement.

33. An _____ capacitor is polarized.
34. The opposition of a capacitor is called _____.
35. A capacitor is over 99 percent charged after _____ time constants.
36. A capacitor's opposition is _____ proportional to frequency.
37. _____ capacitors generally have a lower Q than other types of capacitors.
38. The dielectric in an electrolytic capacitor is _____.
39. The symbol for capacitive reactance is _____.
40. The base unit of capacitance is the _____.
41. The abbreviation or symbol for capacitance is _____.
42. Physical devices that store energy in an electric field are called _____.
43. In terms of other base units, the base unit of capacitance equals a _____.
44. Aluminum or _____ is used for the plates of an electrolytic capacitor.

33. _____
34. _____
35. _____
36. _____
37. _____
38. _____
39. _____
40. _____
41. _____
42. _____
43. _____
44. _____

108

For questions 45 to 52, solve each problem. Be sure to include units in your answer when appropriate.

45. How much energy can a capacitor store if it is rated at 560 μF and 400 V?

46. How many picofarads are there in 0.0015 μF?

47. What is the reactance of a 0.22-μF, 250-V capacitor at 400 Hz?

48. What is the equivalent capacitance of a 220-pF capacitor and a 100-pF capacitor connected in parallel?

49. What is the equivalent capacitance of the capacitors in question 48 when connected in series?

50. What is the time constant of a 470-kΩ resistor and a 0.33-μF capacitor series-connected to a 40-V dc source?

51. For the circuit in Fig. 10-1, determine the following:
  a. The voltage across the 0.8-μF capacitor
  b. The total opposition

45. _____

46. _____

47. _____

48. _____

49. _____

50. _____

51. *Place answers below.*
  a. _____
  b. _____

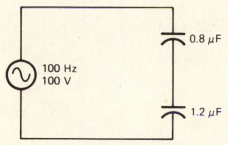

Fig. 10-1 Circuit for question 51.

52. For the circuit in Fig. 10-2, determine the following:
  a. The current through the 0.001-μF capacitor
  b. The total current

52. *Place answers below.*
  a. _____
  b. _____

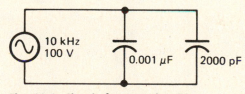

Fig. 10-2 Circuit for question 52.

10-1 LAB EXPERIMENT: CAPACITORS IN AC AND DC CIRCUITS

PURPOSE

This experiment will provide visual evidence of the major characteristics of capacitors in ac and dc circuits. It will provide experience in correctly connecting electrolytic capacitors in ac and dc circuits.

MATERIALS

Qty.

1 power supply, 6 V ac, 60 Hz (a 6-V transformer)
1 power supply, 10 V dc
2 capacitors, electrolytic, 1000 μF, 50 WV dc (minimum)
1 capacitor, nonelectrolytic, 1 μF, 50 WV dc (minimum)

Qty.

1 capacitor, nonelectrolytic, 0.47 μF, 50 WV dc (minimum)
1 lamp, no 47 (6.3 V, 0.15 A)
1 holder for no. 47 lamp
1 DMM, 10 MΩ minimum input resistance
1 switch, SPST, 1 A, 125 V

PROCEDURE

1. Construct the circuit of Fig. 10-3. Recheck the circuit to be sure you have the correct polarity on C_1. Open S_1. Discharge C_1 by momentarily connecting a jumper lead from one lead of the capacitor to the other lead. Remove the jumper. Now, while watching the lamp, close S_1.

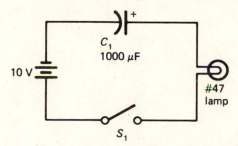

Fig. 10-3 Circuit for experiment 10-1, step 1.

   a. Did the lamp flash? _____
   b. Is current still flowing in the circuit? _____ Why?

        _____

        _____

   c. Check your answer to step 1b by measuring the voltage drop across the lamp. (Remember that a voltage drop across the lamp indicates a current flow.) What is the voltage across the lamp? _____
   d. Now open S_1. Is the capacitor now charged? If it is, it should provide a voltage even though S_1 is open. _____
   e. What value of voltage should the capacitor provide? _____
   f. Check your answer to step 1e by measuring the voltage across capacitor C_1.
   g. Further evidence that a capacitor stores energy can be obtained by rapidly discharging the capacitor. Close S_1 to recharge the capacitor. Open S_1. Now short out the capacitor with a jumper lead. What happened?

        _____

        _____

2. The two electrolytic capacitors in Fig. 10-4 are connected positive terminal to positive terminal. This arrangement provides the equivalent of one nonpolarized 500-μF capacitor. Construct the circuit shown in Fig. 10-4 (be sure the capacitors are connected as indicated on the schematic). Close the switch and observe the lamp.

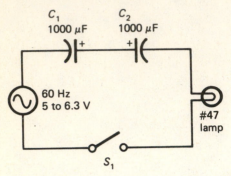

Fig. 10-4 Circuit for experiment 10-1, step 2.

    a. Does the lamp light? _____

    b. Will the lamp light at this brightness for an extended period of time?

_____

    c. Measure and record the voltage across the lamp. _____

    d. Measure and record the voltage across the combination of C_1 and C_2 (negative lead of C_1 to negative lead of C_2). _____

    e. Does the lamp or the capacitor offer more opposition to the alternating current? _____

3. Construct the circuit shown in Fig. 10-5. Open S_1 and discharge C_1 with a jumper lead. Then discharge C_2 with the jumper lead (and remove the jumper lead). This procedure ensures that both capacitors are fully discharged before power is applied to the circuit. Now close S_1 and allow the capacitors to charge.

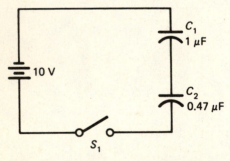

Fig. 10-5 Circuit for experiment 10-1, step 3.

    a. How much voltage should be across C_1? _____

    b. How much voltage should be across C_2? Open S_1. _____
    In making the following measurements, be prepared to read your voltmeter as quickly as possible. Quick reading is necessary to achieve accurate results because the capacitor's voltage will be discharged through the meter.

    c. Measure and record the voltage across C_1. _____

    d. Does your measured voltage agree (within 10 percent) with the voltage you predicted in step 3a? _____

112

e. Measure the voltage across C_2 and compare it with the value predicted in step 3b. Do the two values agree within 10 percent of each other?
_____

4. As a review, answer the following questions:
   a. Does current flow in a dc circuit while a capacitor is charging?
   b. Does current flow in a dc circuit after a capacitor has charged?
   c. Does a capacitor block alternating current? _____
   d. Does a capacitor block direct current? _____
   e. How does dc voltage distribute in a series capacitor circuit?

   _____

   _____

10-2 LAB EXPERIMENT: RESISTOR-CAPACITOR TIME CONSTANTS

PURPOSE

The purpose of this experiment is to measure RC time constants of both charging and discharging circuits. These measurements will verify that $T = RC$.

MATERIALS

Qty.

1 power supply, 10 V dc
1 capacitor, nonelectrolytic,
    1 μF, 50 WV dc (minimum)
    $\pm$10%

Qty.

1 capacitor, nonelectrolytic,
    0.47 μF, 50 WV dc
    (minimum) $\pm$10%
1 switch, SPST, 1 A, 125 V ac
1 DMM, 11 MΩ input resistance

INTRODUCTION

In this experiment we will be using the internal resistance of the voltmeter as the resistance in our RC circuits. Thus, the meter will serve a dual function. First, it serves as the resistor in the circuit, and second, it measures the voltage across itself [Fig. 10-6(a)]. The net effect is like having a voltmeter with infinite input resistance measuring the voltage across an 11-MΩ resistor, as in Fig. 10-6(b).

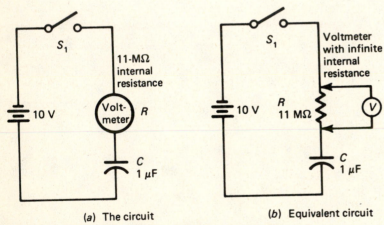

(a) The circuit   (b) Equivalent circuit

Fig. 10-6 Circuit for experiment 10-2, step 1.

In Fig. 10-6(a) we will be measuring the voltage across R. However, we really want to know the voltage across C. Then we will know when it has charged to 63.2 percent of the available voltage (one time constant). This is really no problem. Since we know V_T and are measuring V_R, we can use Kirchhoff's voltage law to find V_C:

$$V_T = V_R + V_C$$

Therefore,

$$V_C = V_T - V_R$$

We can use this last expression to find the instantaneous value of V_C at any instant we know V_R. For instance, if after 11 s the meter indicates 3.7 V, the capacitor will have

$$\text{Voltage across } C = 10 \text{ V} - 3.7 \text{ V} = 6.3 \text{ V}$$

114

PROCEDURE

1. **a.** How many seconds are there in one time constant for the circuit in Fig. 10-6(*a*)? _____

   b. At the end of one time constant, how many volts should be across the capacitor? _____

   c. At the end of one time constant, how many volts should be across the resistor (meter)? _____

   d. Construct the circuit shown in Fig. 10-6(*a*). Open the switch and discharge the capacitor by connecting a jumper lead across it. Remove the jumper. Now close the switch and read the voltmeter at the end of one time constant (11 s). Does the reading agree (within 15 percent) with the value you predicted in step 1c? (If not, repeat your calculations and measurements.) Record your results in the first row of the data table in Fig. 10-7(*a*). _____

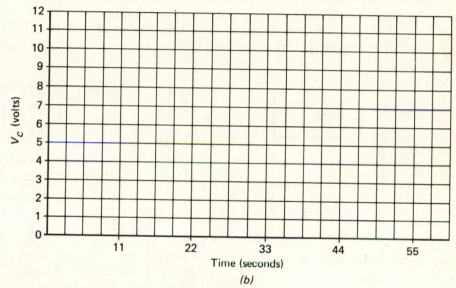

Time (seconds)	V_R (volts)	V_C $(V_T - V_R)$ (volts)
11		
22		
33		
44		
55		

(a)

Fig. 10-7 Plotting a charge curve. (*a*) Data table for recording charging voltages. (*b*) Graph paper for plotting a charge curve.

   e. How much voltage would you expect across the resistor at the end of two time constants? _____ Check your answer by opening S_1, discharging C, closing S_1, and reading the meter at the end of 22 s. (You may switch ranges on the meter as the capacitor charges to obtain more accurate readings.) Record your results in the second row of the data table. Repeat this process until you have completed the data table in Fig. 10-7(*a*).

   f. Now, using the data collected in Fig. 10-7(*a*), plot five points (time versus V_C) on the graph paper in Fig. 10-7(*b*). Then connect the five points together to form an approximate charge curve for a capacitor. Does this curve resemble the universal charge curve for a capacitor?

   _____

2. When the switch in Fig. 10-8 is closed, the capacitor will charge. When the switch is open, the capacitor will discharge through the resistance of the meter.

   a. What is the time constant of the circuit in Fig. 10-8? _____

   b. After one time constant, how much voltage will the voltmeter indicate?

   _____

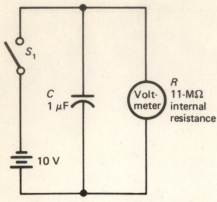

Fig. 10-8 Circuit for experiment 10-2, steps 2 and 3.

c. Construct the circuit of Fig. 10-8 and check your answer to step 2b. Record your answer in the first row of the data table of Fig. 10-9(a).

d. Now close S_1 to recharge the capacitor. Open S_1 and measure V_C at the end of two time constants. Record your reading in the data table of Fig. 10-9(a). Repeat this procedure for three, four, and five time constants.

Time (seconds)	V_C (volts)
11	
22	
33	
44	
55	

(a)

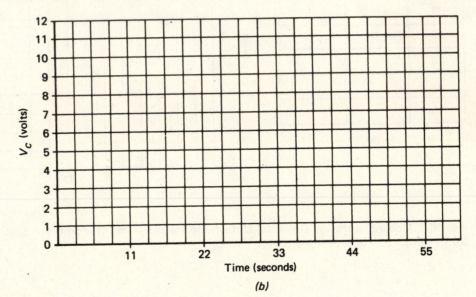

(b)

Fig. 10-9 Plotting a discharge curve. (a) Data table for recording discharging voltages. (b) Graph paper for plotting a discharge curve.

e. Now, use this data to plot and draw a discharge curve on the graph paper in Fig. 10-9(b).

f. Is there any difference between the time constant of a charging capacitor and a discharging capacitor? _____

g. Are the curves you constructed in Figs. 10-7(b) and 10-9(b) mirror images of each other? _____

3. a. If the capacitance in Fig. 10-8 were decreased, would the time constant increase or decrease? _____

b. Check your answer by changing the capacitor in Fig. 10-8 from 1 μF to 0.47 μF. Then measure and record how long it takes the 0.47-μF capacitor to discharge to 3.68 V. _____

c. Would changing the source voltage in Fig. 10-8 change the time constant of the circuit? _____

d. Would paralleling the voltmeter with a resistor change the time constant in Fig. 10-8? _____

116

10-3 LAB EXPERIMENT: RELATIONSHIPS BETWEEN FREQUENCY, CAPACITANCE, AND REACTANCE

PURPOSE

This experiment will allow you to verify the relationships between f, C, and X_C. The data collected will lead to the conclusion that X_C is inversely proportional to C and f. This experiment will also verify the capacitive reactance formula.

MATERIALS

Qty.

1 ammeter, ac, 0 to 5 mA, 148-Ω (or less) internal resistance, ±3% (or less) accuracy
1 DMM or VOM, 10-V ac range
1 capacitor, nonelectrolytic, 1 μF, 50 WV dc (minimum), ±10%

Qty.

1 capacitor, nonelectrolytic, 0.47 μF, 50 WV dc (minimum), ±10%
1 signal generator, sinusoidal, 20- to 1000-Hz range

PROCEDURE

1. **a.** Construct the circuit shown in Fig. 10-10 using a 1-μF capacitor for C_1. Set the generator frequency for 100 Hz. Adjust the output control for 3 V across the capacitor. Record the current flowing through the capacitor. _____

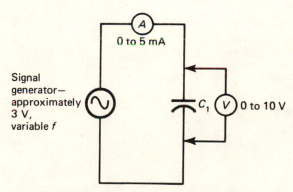

Fig. 10-10 Circuit for experiment 10-3.

   b. Using your measured current and voltage, compute and record the reactance of the capacitor using $X_C = V_C/I_C$. _____
   c. Calculate and record the reactance using the reactance formula.

   _____

$$X_C = \frac{1}{6.28fC}$$

   d. Are the values computed in steps 1b and 1c within 10 percent of each other? (If not, repeat steps 1b and 1c.) _____
   e. Do your results confirm the reactance formula (within the tolerances of the meter, the generator, and the capacitor)? _____

2. **a.** Suppose the generator frequency is changed to 50 Hz while the voltage remains at 3 V. What will happen to the reactance?

_____

_____

b. What will happen to the circuit current?

_____

_____

c. Change the generator frequency to 50 Hz and record the new current.

_____

d. Does your answer to step 2c support your answer to step 2b?

_____

e. How much current would you expect if the frequency were changed to 200 Hz and V_C remained at 3 V? _____

f. Change the frequency to 200 Hz and adjust the generator for 3 V across the capacitor. Record the current. _____

g. Is capacitive reactance inversely proportional to frequency?

_____

h. If the frequency were changed to 400 Hz, how much current would you expect through C? _____

3. **a.** Change the capacitor in Fig. 10-10 to 0.47 μF. Leave the frequency at 200 Hz and adjust the output voltage until V_C equals 3 V. How does the new circuit current compare with the current measured in step 2f? _____ Why?

_____

_____

b. If the frequency is reduced to 100 Hz and V_C remains at 3 V, how much current should flow in the circuit? Check your answer by reducing the frequency to 100 Hz and measuring the current. _____

c. What relationship exists between capacitance and capacitive reactance?

_____

_____

4. As a review, answer the following questions:
   a. If both f and C double, how much will X_C change? _____
   b. If f doubles and C is reduced to half, how much will X_C change?

   _____

   c. If both f and C are reduced to half, how much will X_C change?

   _____

10-4 LAB EXPERIMENT: SERIES AND PARALLEL CAPACITORS

PURPOSE

This experiment will illustrate voltage drops and current distribution in series and parallel capacitor ac circuits. You will calculate equivalent capacitance and reactance of series and parallel circuits.

MATERIALS

Qty.

1 ammeter, ac, 0 to 5 mA, 148-Ω (or less) internal resistance, ±3% (or less) accuracy
1 DMM or VOM, 10-V ac range
1 capacitor, nonelectrolytic, 1 μF, 50 WV dc (minimum), ±10%

Qty.

1 capacitor, nonelectrolytic, 0.47 μF, 50 WV dc (minimum), ±10%
1 signal generator, sinusoidal, 20- to 1000-Hz range

PROCEDURE

1. Refer to the series circuit in Fig. 10-11.

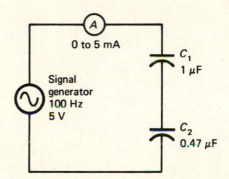

Fig. 10-11 Circuit for experiment 10-4, step 1.

  a. What is the equivalent capacitance of the circuit? (*Note:* Since the capacitors have 10 percent tolerances, consider C_2 to be 0.5 μF for all calculations.) _____
  b. What is the total reactance of the circuit? _____
  c. How much current should flow in the circuit? _____
  d. Construct the circuit of Fig. 10-11 and measure the current. Does the measured current agree (within 10 percent) with the predicted current in step 1c? _____
  e. How much voltage would you expect across C_1? _____
  f. How much voltage would you expect across C_2? _____
  g. To check your answers to steps 1e and 1f, measure and record these voltages. _____ _____
  h. In a series capacitor circuit, does the smallest or largest capacitor drop the most voltage? _____
  i. Is the total reactance of the series circuit greater than or less than the reactance of either capacitor? _____
2. Refer to the parallel circuit in Fig. 10-12.
  a. What is the equivalent (total) capacitance of the circuit?

  _____
  b. What is the total reactance of the circuit? _____

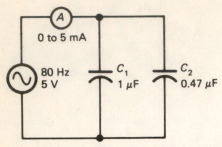

Fig. 10-12 Circuit for experiment 10-4, step 2.

    c. What is the total current in the circuit? _____

    d. Construct the circuit shown in Fig. 10-12. Measure and record the total current. _____

    e. Do your answers to steps 2c and d agree within 10 percent? _____

    f. If they do, does it indicate that you used the correct procedures in answering steps 2a and b? _____

    g. Will C_1 or C_2 carry more current? _____

    h. Measure and record I_{C_1} and I_{C_2}.
_____ _____

    i. Does your answer to step 2h confirm your answer to step 2g? _____

    j. Do your answers to steps 2d and h confirm Kirchhoff's current law? _____

3. As a review, answer the following questions:

    a. Should two capacitors be connected in series or parallel to provide the most capacitance? _____

    b. Should two capacitors be connected in series or parallel to provide the most reactance? _____

    c. Should two capacitors be connected in series or parallel to draw the most current from the source? _____

    d. Does the larger or smaller of two parallel capacitors draw more current? _____

10-5 ADVANCED PROBLEMS

10-1. A series-parallel capacitor circuit is shown in Fig. 10-13. Determine the following for the circuit:
  a. C_T (total capacitance across source) _____
  b. X_{C_T} _____
  c. I_{C_4} _____
  d. V_{C_3} _____

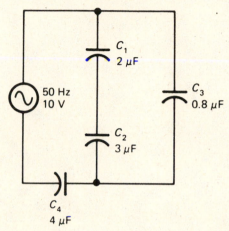

Fig. 10-13 Circuit for experiment 10-5, problem 10-1.

10-2. Refer to Fig. 10-14 and determine the following:
  a. X_{C_1} _____
  b. X_{C_2} _____
  c. C_1 _____
  d. I_T _____

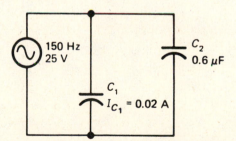

Fig. 10-14 Circuit for experiment 10-5, problem 10-2.

10-3. How much capacitance and charge are required to store 180 J of energy at 450 V? _____   _____
10-4. A capacitor is charged to 400 V by 5 C.
  a. Determine the capacitance of the capacitor. _____
  b. How much energy is stored in the capacitor? _____

10-6 LAB EXPERIMENT: TROUBLESHOOTING 1

PURPOSE

This experiment provides experience in troubleshooting an *RC* circuit powered by a dc source (see Fig. 10-15). The simulated circuit makes it possible for the test instrument to be connected only to the test points (dots) provided; thus, it simulates a circuit that is soldered in place.

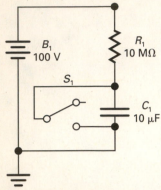

Fig. 10-15 Circuit for experiment 10-6.

MATERIALS

Qty.

1 electronic-circuit simulation program
1 Fig. 10-15.ewb (provided by your instructor)

PROCEDURE

1. **a.** Using your simulation program, open the file Fig. 10-15.ewb. S_1 is provided so that you can short out C_1 to discharge it when you want to remeasure charging time and/or voltage. (When S_1 is opened, C_1 starts to charge.) The multimeter has 10 MΩ of internal resistance on its dc voltage function.
    b. Calculate and record the time constant for the circuit. _____
    c. Record the expected voltage across R_1 after one time constant. _____
    d. When the multimeter (dc voltage function) is connected to R_1, what is the time constant? _____
2. Activate the circuit and determine which component or components are faulty and what is wrong with the component(s). Submit a report that details how you arrived at your conclusions.

10-7 LAB EXPERIMENT: TROUBLESHOOTING 2

PURPOSE

This experiment involves troubleshooting the circuit shown in Fig. 10-16. The simulated circuit makes it possible for the test instrument to be connected only to the test points (dots) provided; thus, it simulates a circuit that is soldered in place.

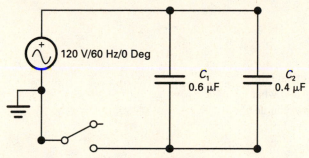

Fig. 10-16 Circuit for experiment 10-7.

MATERIALS

Qty.

1   electronic-circuit simulation program
1   Fig. 10-16.ewb (provided by your instructor)

PROCEDURE

1. Using your simulation program, open the file Fig. 10-16.ewb. Activate the circuit and determine which component or components are faulty and what is wrong with the component(s). Submit a report that details how you arrived at your conclusions.

10-8 LAB EXPERIMENT: TROUBLESHOOTING 3

PURPOSE

This experiment involves troubleshooting the circuit shown in Fig. 10-17. The simulated circuit makes it possible for the test instrument to be connected only to the test points (dots) provided; thus, it simulates a circuit that is soldered in place.

MATERIALS

Qty.

1   electronic-circuit simulation program
1   Fig. 10-17.ewb (provided by your instructor)

PROCEDURE

1. Using your simulation program, open the file Fig. 10-17.ewb. Activate the circuit and determine which component or components are faulty and what is wrong with the component(s). Submit a report that details how you arrived at your conclusions.

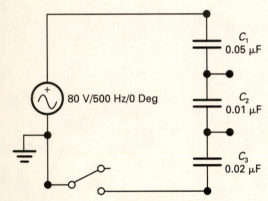

Fig. 10-17 Circuit for experiment 10-8.

Chapter 11

Inductance

TEST: INDUCTANCE

For questions 1 to 23, determine whether each statement is true or false.

1. Ohmmeters cannot measure the reactance of an inductor.
2. The polarity of the cemf always opposes the action that created the cemf.
3. Inductance resists a change in current in an inductive circuit.
4. A straight length of conductor has both resistance and reactance.
5. An inductor has mutual inductance between its turns.
6. An inductor stores energy in its magnetic field.
7. Inductance converts electric energy into heat energy.
8. The cemf of an inductor opposes the source voltage when the current in the circuit is decreasing.
9. Adding turns to an inductor increases its inductance.
10. Increasing the space between the turns of an inductor increases its inductance.
11. Other factors being equal, a small-diameter coil will have less inductance than a large-diameter coil.
12. The inductance of a laminated-iron-core inductor decreases when its current increases.
13. The air-core symbol is used to represent a coil wound on a phenolic core.
14. Toroid cores are made from magnetic materials.
15. RF chokes usually have less than one base unit of inductance.
16. Mutual inductance can be reduced by magnetic shielding.
17. The dc resistance of an inductor can be measured with an ohmmeter.
18. The quality of an inductor depends on the frequency at which it is used.
19. Current decays more slowly in a resistor than it does in an inductor.
20. Inductive kick occurs when an inductive circuit is closed.
21. It is impossible for the cemf of an inductor to exceed the source voltage under any conditions.
22. At any frequency, a small inductance produces more reactance than a large inductance.
23. Current induced in the iron core of an inductor causes the inductance to increase.

1. _____
2. _____
3. _____
4. _____
5. _____
6. _____
7. _____
8. _____
9. _____
10. _____
11. _____
12. _____
13. _____
14. _____
15. _____
16. _____
17. _____
18. _____
19. _____
20. _____
21. _____
22. _____
23. _____

For questions 24 to 30, supply the missing word or phrase in each statement.

24. The resistance of a coil is greater than its ohmic resistance because of the _____.

24. _____

25. The induced voltage in an inductor is called _____.

25. _____

26. Movable slug-type cores are used in _____ inductors.

26. _____

27. Filter chokes for power-frequency circuits usually use _____ cores.

27. _____

28. _____-core inductors usually have a voltage rating as well as an inductance rating.

28. _____

29. Inductive current _____ inductive voltage by _____ degrees.

29. _____

30. Litz wire is used to reduce the _____.

30. _____

For questions 31 to 42, choose the letter that best completes each statement.

31. The symbol for inductance is
   a. *H*
   b. *L*
   c. *I*
   d. *Q*

31. _____

32. An inductor should not be called a
   a. Choke
   b. Coil
   c. Reactor
   d. Turn

32. _____

33. The opposition of inductance to alternating current is called
   a. Reactance
   b. Reluctance
   c. Permeability
   d. Impedance

33. _____

34. Inductance is that electrical property that
   a. Converts electric energy into heat energy
   b. Converts heat energy into electric energy
   c. Opposes changes in current
   d. Opposes changes in resistance

34. _____

35. Flux from one turn of an inductor cutting the adjacent turns of the same inductor is an example of
   a. Impedance
   b. Reactance
   c. Self-inductance
   d. Mutual inductance

35. _____

36. The symbol for reactance is
   a. *X*
   b. *H*
   c. *L*
   d. *Q*

36. _____

37. The base unit of inductance is the
   a. Henry
   b. Ohm
   c. Tesla
   d. Lenz

37. _____

38. The base unit of reactance is the
   a. Henry
   b. Ohm
   c. Tesla
   d. Lenz

38. _____

39. An inductor is wound on a paper tube. Its inductance is greatest when the tube contains
   a. Air   c. Phenolic
   b. Brass   d. Ferrite

39. _____

40. An inductor is wound on a paper tube. Its inductance is least when the tube contains
   a. Air   c. Silicon steel
   b. Brass   d. Ferrite

40. _____

126

41. An inductor used to help smooth a pulsating direct current is
    a. An RF coil
    b. A filter choke
    c. An RF choke
    d. A molded choke

41. _____

42. Iron-core inductors are not rated for
    a. Power
    b. Quality
    c. Current
    d. Voltage

42. _____

For questions 43 to 51, solve each problem. Be sure to include units (watts, degrees, etc.) in your answer when appropriate.

43. What is the reactance of an inductor that draws 0.25 A from a 60-V, 200-Hz source?

43. _____

44. What is the reactance of a 2.5-mH inductor connected to a 100-kHz, 20-V source?

44. _____

45. What is the quality of a 0.01-H inductor that has a resistance of 40 Ω at 50 kHz?

45. _____

46. What is the equivalent inductance of a 4-H inductor and a 6-H inductor connected in parallel?

46. _____

47. Suppose the parallel inductors in question 46 were connected to an ac source. Which inductor would draw more current?

47. _____

48. Refer to Fig. 11-1. Which inductor will drop the most voltage?

48. _____

49. Refer to Fig. 11-1. What is the total inductance of the circuit?

49. _____

50. Refer to Fig. 11-1. What is the current in the circuit?

50. _____

51. Determine the frequency that is needed to produce a reactance of 2500 Ω with a 3.3-mH inductor.

51. _____

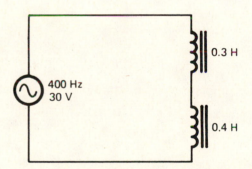

Fig. 11-1 Circuit for questions 48 through 50.

11-1 LAB EXPERIMENT: INDUCTORS IN AC AND DC CIRCUITS

PURPOSE

This experiment will visually demonstrate the major characteristics of inductors in both ac and dc circuits.

MATERIALS

Qty.

1   choke, 0.4 H, 275 mA dc,
    22-Ω dc resistance
1   choke, 2.5 mH, 125 mA,
    38-Ω dc resistance
1   resistor, 22 Ω, 1 W, 10%

Qty.

1   lamp, no. 47, 6.3 V, 0.15 A
1   lamp holder for no. 47 lamp
1   power supply, 6 to 7 V dc
1   power supply, 6 to 7 V ac
1   VOM or DMM

PROCEDURE

1. Construct the circuit shown in Fig. 11-2(*a*). Note that the lamp is not at full brightness. This is because of the dc, or ohmic, resistance of the inductor. Remove the inductor from the circuit.

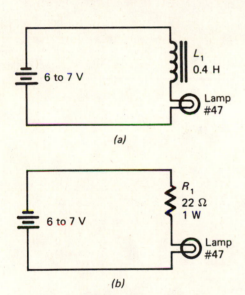

Fig. 11-2 Circuits for experiment 11-1, steps 1 and 3.

    a. Measure and record the (ohmic) resistance between the inductor's terminals. _____

    b. Now construct the circuit in Fig. 11-2(*b*). This replaces the inductor with a 22-Ω, 1-W resistor. Does the lamp have about the same brightness with the resistor in the circuit as it did with the inductor in the circuit? _____

    c. Do the results above indicate that the only opposition an inductor has to pure direct current is its ohmic (dc) resistance? _____

2. Construct the circuit of Fig. 11-3(*a*) by changing from a dc to an ac supply.

    a. Does the lamp have the same brightness as it did with the dc supply?

    _____

    b. Does the result in step 2a indicate that a resistor behaves the same in dc circuits as it does in ac circuits? _____

    c. Now replace the resistor with the 0.4-H inductor to provide the circuit

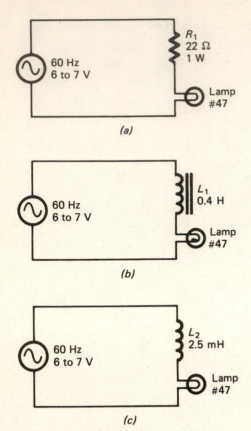

Fig. 11-3 Circuits for experiment 11-1, steps 2 and 4.

shown in Fig. 11-3(*b*). Does the lamp now light? _____
Why?

_____

_____

d. Do the results in steps 2a and c indicate that an inductor offers more opposition to alternating current than just its ohmic resistance?
_____

e. What is this additional opposition called? _____

f. Is there any current flowing through the lamp in Fig. 11-3(*b*)? _____ Check your answer by measuring the ac voltage across the lamp. (If current is flowing, there must be a voltage drop.)

g. Would a smaller inductance allow more current to flow through the lamp? _____

h. Replace the 0.4-H inductor with a 2.5-mH inductor, as in Fig. 11-3(*c*). Does the lamp light now? _____ Why?

_____

_____

i. Does a 0.4-H inductor or a 2.5-mH inductor have the greater reactance? _____

3. This section is concerned with observing inductive kick. Reconnect the circuit of Fig. 11-2(*b*). Quickly make and break (close and open) the circuit by interrupting the connection at one end of the resistor. Note the size of the spark which occurs as the circuit is interrupted. Now, reconnect the circuit of Fig. 11-2(*a*) and observe the spark when this circuit is interrupted. Which circuit provided the larger spark? _____ Why?

_____

_____

4. As a review, answer the following questions:

    a. Does an ohmmeter measure the reactance of an inductor?

    _____

    b. How much reactance does the inductor in Fig. 11-3(*b*) have?

    _____

    c. How much reactance does the inductor in Fig. 11-3(*c*) have?

    _____

    d. What type of core does L_1 in Fig. 11-3(*b*) have? _____

11-2 LAB EXPERIMENT: INDUCTIVE KICK

PURPOSE

This experiment will show visual evidence of inductive kick. It will provide proof that a cemf can far exceed the source voltage which created it when the circuit is opened.

MATERIALS

Qty.   **Qty.**

1   choke, 0.4 H, 275 mA dc,   1   dry cell, 1.5 V, size D
    22-Ω dc resistance   1   switch, SPST, 1 A, 125 V
3   neon lamps, NE-2

INTRODUCTION

NE-2 lamps will be used to indicate the magnitude of the inductive kick (cemf) of an inductor. It requires about 80 V (see Fig. 11-4) to fire (ionize) an NE-2. Once the lamp fires, it requires about 70 V to maintain ionization. The current through the lamp, once it fires, rises very high unless it is limited by the source or by a series resistor. In this activity the source will be the energy stored in the inductor's magnetic field. This source can provide only a small current at the 70 V required to keep the NE-2 ionized.

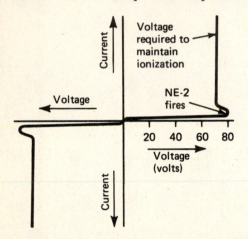

Fig. 11-4 Characteristic curve of an NE-2 neon lamp.

Throughout this experiment, S_1 in Fig. 11-5 should be closed only when called for in the procedure. Leaving S_1 closed for extended periods will only shorten the useful life of the dry cell.

PROCEDURE

1. Construct the circuit shown in Fig. 11-5(a); have S_1 open. While observing the NE-2 lamp, close S_1 for a moment and then open S_1.
   a. Did the NE-2 fire when S_1 first closed? _____
   b. Did the NE-2 fire while S_1 remained closed? _____
   c. How much voltage must have been across the NE-2 while S_1 was closed? _____
   d. Did the lamp ionize when the switch was opened? _____
   e. How much voltage appeared across the inductor and the NE-2 when the switch was open? (Fig. 11-4) _____
   f. What caused this relatively high voltage to appear across the NE-2?
   _____

132

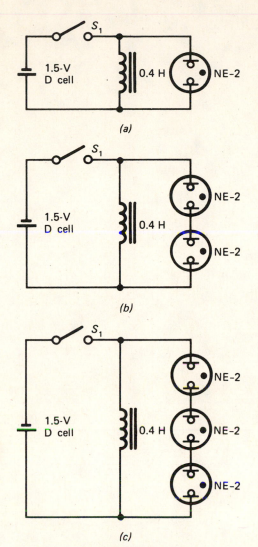

(a)

(b)

(c)

Fig. 11-5 Circuits for experiment 11-2.

2. The NE-2 in Fig. 11-5(a) uses up the inductor's stored energy once it fires. It also limits the inductor's cemf to the 80 V required for ionization. Do you think that the inductor's cemf can rise high enough to fire two NE-2 lamps connected in series? (This will require about 160 V.) Construct the circuit of Fig. 11-5(b) and see if it will. Does the inductive kick fire both lamps? _____

3. **a.** How much voltage will be required to fire the three NE-2 lamps in Fig. 11-5(c)? _____
   b. Construct the circuit and see if the cemf will fire the three lamps. Did it? _____
   c. The main source voltage for this circuit is the 1.5-V cell. How many times larger is the inductor's cemf than the source voltage when S_1 is opened?

   _____

   _____

11-3 LAB EXPERIMENT: RELATIONSHIP BETWEEN f AND X_L

PURPOSE

This experiment will demonstrate the effect of frequency on inductive reactance. It will also provide experience in calculating reactance by the reactance formula and by Ohm's law.

MATERIALS

Qty.

1 choke, 2.5 mH, 125 mA, 38-Ω dc resistance
1 VOM or DMM

Qty.

1 signal generator, 5 V, 25- to 100-kHz sinusoidal output
1 resistor, 100 Ω, 5%, ½ W

INTRODUCTION

Ammeters that will measure 25-kHz currents are not common. The circuit in this experiment operates at 25 kHz and above. Therefore, we are going to indirectly determine the circuit current. That is, we will measure the voltage across a known resistance and then use Ohm's law to calculate the current ($I_R = V_R/R$). The circuit (Fig. 11-6) used in this experiment is a series circuit. Thus, the current through the resistor is also the current through the inductor ($I_R = I_L$). [The resistor in the circuit has little effect (less than 4 percent) on the circuit current.]

Fig. 11-6 Circuit for experiment 11-3.

The inductive reactance X_L can now be experimentally determined by using the measured voltage across the inductor and Ohm's law ($X_L = V_L/I_L$).

You may notice in this experiment that the arithmetic sum of V_R and V_L is greater than the supply voltage. Do not be concerned; the arithmetic sum should be greater. Resistive voltage and inductive voltage must be treated as phasors. Phasors are covered in more detail in Chap. 13.

PROCEDURE

1. Construct the circuit shown in Fig. 11-6. Be sure the generator is set for 25 kHz and the output voltage is 5 V. Measure the output voltage with the DMM. Measure the voltage across R_1 and record it in the data table of Fig. 11-7. Now calculate the current through the resistor and enter it in the data table. Next measure and record the voltage across the inductor. Finally, calculate the reactance and enter it in the table (remember $I_R = I_L$).

   Check to see if the reactance determined above agrees with the value calculated by the reactance formula. Calculate and record the reactance using the formula $X_L = 6.28fL$. _____

   The reactance calculated here should be within 15 percent of the reactance you listed in the data table. If it is not, recheck your measurements and your calculations.

134

Frequency f	Voltage across R_1 V_{R_1} (measured)	Current through R_1 I_{R_1}	Voltage across L_1 V_{L_1} (measured)	Inductive reactance X_{L_1}
25 kHz				
50 kHz				
100 kHz				

Fig. 11-7 Data table for experiment 11-3.

2. Change the frequency of the generator to 50 kHz. Measure the output voltage of the generator. Readjust the output control (if necessary) to obtain exactly 5 V. You have doubled the frequency of the generator and held the voltage constant.

   a. What do you predict will happen to the reactance?

   _____

   _____

   b. What do you predict will happen to the current?

   _____

   _____

   c. Make the measurements and calculation necessary to complete the second row of the data table. Does your data table support your predictions in steps 2a and b? _____

3. Change the generator frequency to 100 kHz. Readjust the output for 5 V if necessary. From the reactance you determined in the first two rows of the data table, predict and record the reactance you will have at 100 kHz. _____ Complete the third row of the data table of Fig. 11-7 to check your prediction.

11-4 LAB EXPERIMENT: SERIES AND PARALLEL INDUCTORS

PURPOSE

This experiment will illustrate the current and voltage distribution in series and parallel inductance circuits. It will also verify the series and parallel formulas used for determining total inductance and total reactance.

MATERIALS

Qty.

2 chokes, 2.5 mH, 125 mA,
   38-Ω dc resistance
1 VOM or DMM

Qty.

1 signal generator, 5 V,
   50-kHz sinusoidal output
1 resistor, 51 Ω, 5%, ½ W
2 resistors, 100 Ω, 5%, ½ W

INTRODUCTION

The circuits in this experiment are all operated at 50 kHz. Ammeters which measure current at 50 kHz are not common. Therefore, the current in these circuits will be indirectly determined by using Ohm's law. A small resistor is put in the circuit in which we wish to measure current. The resistor is kept so small that it has little (less than 2 percent) effect on the current. Then the voltage across the resistor is measured and Ohm's law ($I_R = V_R/R$) is used to calculate the current.

Once we have determined the current in a circuit, we can again use Ohm's law to determine the inductive reactance. The formula is

$$X_L = \frac{V_L}{I_L}$$

Of course, I_L will be the same as I_R when the resistor is in series with the inductor.

You may notice that the arithmetic sum of V_R and V_L is greater than the source voltage. Resistive voltage and inductive voltage must be treated as phasors. Phasors are covered in Chap. 13.

PROCEDURE

1. **a.** The reactance of a 2.5-mH inductor at 50 kHz is 785.4 Ω. How much reactance would you expect from two 2.5-mH inductors connected in parallel? _____

    b. Check your response by constructing the circuit in Fig. 11-8(a) and determining its total reactance. First measure and record the voltage across the resistor. _____

    c. Then calculate and record the current through the resistor ($I_{R_1} = V_{R_1}/R_1$). This is the total current. _____

    d. The total current splits at the junction of L_1 and L_2 and goes through the parallel inductors. Therefore, the total inductive reactance can be found

    $$X_{L_x} = \frac{V_L}{I_T}$$

    Measure and record the voltage across either inductor. _____

    e. Calculate and record the total reactance. Is your answer within 15 percent of your answer to step 1a? _____ If not, check your work!

    f. Calculate and record the total inductance of L_1 and L_2 in parallel:
    _____

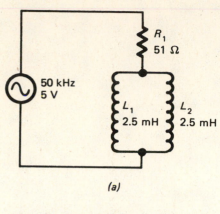

(a)

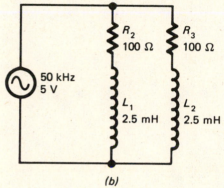

(b)

Fig. 11-8 Circuits for experiment 11-4, steps 1 and 2.

$$L_T = \frac{L_1 \times L_2}{L_1 + L_2}$$

    g. Now calculate and record the inductive reactance of this total induc-
tance by using the reactance formula. This value of X_{L_T} should be the
same (within 15 percent) as you found in step 1e. _____

2. a. To check the current distribution in a parallel inductor circuit, set up
the circuit shown in Fig. 11-8(b). Measure and record the voltage across
R_2 and then across R_3. _____   _____

    b. Since $R_2 = R_3$, do your results show that $I_{L_1} = I_{L_2}$ (within component
tolerances, ± 15 percent)? _____

    c. If L_1 were a 5-mH inductor, would $I_{L_1} = I_{L_2}$? _____

3. a. Refer to the circuit in Fig. 11-9. Would you expect V_{L_1} to be equal to
V_{L_2}? _____ Why?

_____

_____

    b. What should the total reactance of the circuit be? _____

    c. Construct the circuit in Fig. 11-9 and check your answers to steps 3a
and b. Measure and record V_{L_1}. _____

    d. Measure and record V_{L_2}. _____

    e. Measure and record V_{R_1}. _____

    f. Calculate and record I_T ($I_T = I_{R_1} = V_{R_1}/R_1$). _____

    g. Calculate and record X_{L_T}. _____ Note:

$$X_{L_T} = \frac{V_{L_T}}{} \text{ and } V_{L_T} = V_{L_1} + V_{L_2}$$

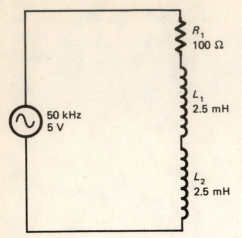

Fig. 11-9 Circuit for experiment 11-4, step 3.

h. Do your results show that both inductance and inductive reactance are additive when in series? _____

11-5 ADVANCED PROBLEMS

11-1. Refer to the circuit in Fig. 11-10(a) and calculate and record the following:

    a. L_T _____   **d.** I_{L_1} _____

    b. X_{L_T} _____   **e.** I_{L_2} _____

    c. X_{L_1} _____

11.2. Refer to the circuit in Fig. 11-10(b) and calculate and record the following:

    a. X_{L_2} _____   **c.** V_{L_1} _____

    b. X_{L_T} _____   **d.** L_1 _____

11-3. Refer to the circuit in Fig. 11-10(c) and calculate and record the following:

    a. X_{L_1} _____   **d.** X_{L_3} _____

    b. X_{L_2} _____   **e.** L_3 _____

    c. I_{L_2} _____

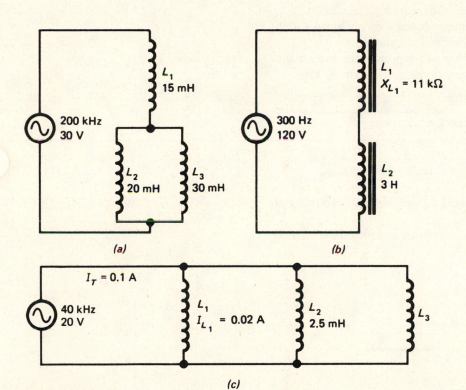

(a)   **(b)**

(c)

Fig. 11-10 Circuits.

11-6 LAB SIMULATION: *L, f,* AND X_L RELATIONSHIPS

PURPOSE

This experiment is a repeat of experiment 11-3 except that it is written for electronic-circuit simulation software.

MATERIALS

Qty.

1   electronic-circuit simulation program

PROCEDURE

1. Using a simulation program, construct the circuit shown in Fig. 11-11. Activate the circuit.
   a. Measure and record the voltage across and the current through the inductor. _____   _____
   b. Using the above measured values, calculate and record X_L.
      _____
   c. Using the reactance formula, calculate and record X_L. _____
   d. If the values of X_L determined in steps 1b and c do not agree within ±2 percent, check your measurements and calculation.
2. Predict (and record your prediction) what will happen to the current and reactance when you change the frequency of the generator to 50 kHz.
   I: _____
   X_L: _____
3. Change the frequency to 50 kHz and check predictions.
   a. Measure and record the voltage _____
   b. Measure and record the current. _____
   c. Using the measured value, calculate and record the reactance.
      _____
4. What value of current would you expect if L_1 were changed to 5 mH and *f* were changed back to 25 kHz? _____
5. Make the changes specified in step 4 and measure and record the current.
   _____

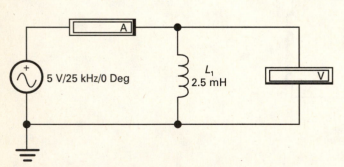

Fig. 11-11 Circuit for experiment 11-6.

11-7 LAB SIMULATION: *L* IN SERIES AND PARALLEL

PURPOSE

This experiment is a repeat of experiment 11-4 except that it is written for electronic-circuit simulation software.

MATERIALS

Qty.

1 electronic-circuit simulation program.

PROCEDURE

1. **a.** Calculate and record the reactance of a 2.5-mH inductor at 50 kHz.
    _____

    b. From the above calculation, predict the total reactance of the circuit in Fig. 11-12. _____

    c. Calculate and record the total inductance for the circuit in Fig. 11-12.
    _____

    d. Using your answer to step 1c, calculate and record the total reactance for the circuit in Fig. 11-12. _____

    e. Do the values of steps 1b and d agree? _____ (If not, re-think your answers!)

    f. Calculate and record the total current for the circuit in Fig. 11-12.
    _____

    g. Should $I_{L_1} = I_{L_2}$ in the circuit in Fig. 11-12? _____

    h. If L_1 were a 5-mH inductor would $I_{L_1} = I_{L_2}$? _____

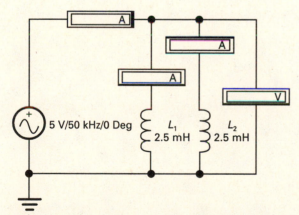

Fig. 11-12 Simulation circuit for experiment 11-7, steps 1 and 2.

2. Using a circuit simulation program, construct and activate the circuit shown in Fig. 11-12.

    a. Record the measured total voltage. _____

    b. Record the measured total current. _____

    c. Using measured values, calculate and record the total reactance. _____ (Check your answer against that given in step 1d.)

    d. Do the measured values of I_{L_1} and I_{L_2} support your answer given in step 1g? _____

    e. What value of I_T would you expect if L_1 were changed to 5 mH? _____

f. Change L_1 to a 5-mH inductor and then measure and record I_T.

_____

3. a. For the circuit shown in Fig. 11-13, calculate and record values for the following:

X_{L_1} _____ I_T _____

X_{L_T} _____ V_{L_1} _____

  b. Should $V_{L_1} = V_{L_2}$ in this circuit? _____

4. Using a simulation program, construct and activate the circuit shown in Fig. 11-13.

  a. Record the following measured values:

V_T _____ V_{L_1} _____

I_T _____ V_{L_2} _____

  b. Using measured values, calculate and record the following quantities:

X_{L_T} _____ X_{L_1} _____

  c. Do the values you measured and calculated in steps 4a and b agree (within 2 percent) with your answers in steps 3a and b? _____ (If not, there is a problem!)

  d. If L_2 in Fig. 11-13 were changed to 10 mH, predict the following:

V_{L_1} _____ I_T _____

  e. Change L_2 to 10 mH. Do the measured values support your answers to step d above? _____

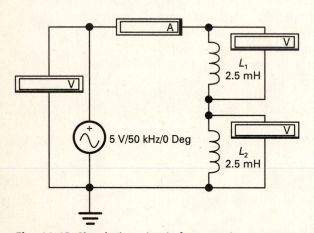

Fig. 11-13 Simulation circuit for experiment 11-7, steps 3 and 4.

11-8 LAB EXPERIMENT: TROUBLESHOOTING 1

PURPOSE

Troubleshooting this inductor circuit will give you more experience and practice in both measuring quantities and predicting and/or calculating expected values. Predicting and measuring values are the essence of troubleshooting.

Qty.

1 electronic-circuit simulation program.
1 Fig. 11-14.ewb (provided by your instructor)

PROCEDURE

1. For the circuit shown in Fig. 11-14, calculate and record the following:

   X_{L_1} _____ X_{L_2} _____
   I_T _____ V_{L_1} _____

2. Using your simulation program, open file Fig. 11-14.ewb and activate the circuit. Determine which component or components are faulty and what is wrong with the component(s). Submit a report detailing how you found the faulty component(s).

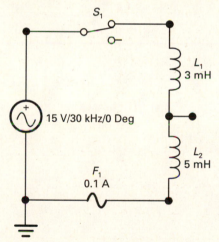

Fig. 11-14 Circuit for experiment 11-8.

11-9 LAB EXPERIMENT: TROUBLESHOOTING 2

PURPOSE

Troubleshooting this inductor circuit will give you more experience and practice in both measuring quantities and predicting and/or calculating expected values. Predicting and measuring values are the essence of troubleshooting.

Qty.

1   electronic-circuit simulation program
1   Fig. 11-15.ewb (provided by your instructor)

PROCEDURE

1. For the circuit shown in Fig. 11-15, calculate and record the following:

   X_{L_1} _____ I_T _____
   X_{L_2} _____ V_{L_1} _____
   X_{L_3} _____ I_{L_2} _____

2. Using your simulation program, open file Fig. 11-15.ewb and activate the circuit. Determine which component or components are faulty and what is wrong with the component(s). Submit a report detailing how you found the faulty component(s).

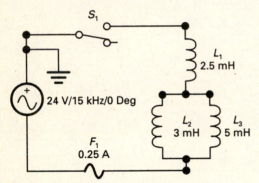

Fig. 11-15 Circuit for experiment 11-9.

Chapter 12

Transformers

TEST: TRANSFORMERS

For questions 1 to 27, determine whether each statement is true or false.

1. The same base unit is used for both mutual inductance and self-inductance.

2. Transformers sometimes have a nonmagnetic shield around the coil.

3. The primary of a transformer converts electric energy into magnetic energy.

4. The designated primary of a transformer can be used as a secondary.

5. Air-core transformers have a higher coefficient of coupling than laminated-iron-core transformers do.

6. Leakage flux reduces the coefficient of coupling.

7. The voltage ratio of a transformer must be greater than the turns ratio.

8. The turns-per-volt ratio of the secondary is usually smaller than the turns-per-volt ratio of the primary.

9. On a multisecondary transformer, each secondary has the same turns-per-volt ratio.

10. A 400-W transformer has fewer turns per volt than a 30-W transformer.

11. A coefficient of coupling that is less than 1 means that some of the primary flux does not cut the secondary coil.

12. Both the core and the coils in a magnetic-core transformer cause the transformer to heat up when operating.

13. A core material with a narrow hysteresis loop should be used to reduce transformer losses.

14. Eddy currents are induced in the secondary of a transformer.

15. The I^2R loss in a transformer is also called copper loss.

16. The primary and secondary currents in a transformer create magnetizing forces that aid each other.

17. Autotransformers provide electrical isolation between the primary and the secondary.

18. From the primary side of a step-down transformer, the secondary load appears to be greater than its actual value.

19. Impedance matching provides maximum efficiency as power is transferred from source to load.

20. The turns ratio and the impedance ratio of a transformer are numerically equal.

21. If the current ratings of a transformer are not exceeded, other transformer ratings will not be exceeded.

22. Rated secondary voltage is the voltage provided by the secondary before it is loaded.

1. _____
2. _____
3. _____
4. _____
5. _____
6. _____
7. _____
8. _____
9. _____
10. _____
11. _____
12. _____
13. _____
14. _____
15. _____
16. _____
17. _____
18. _____
19. _____
20. _____
21. _____
22. _____

23. Operating a transformer with less than rated voltage on the primary doesn't harm the transformer.

24. Dual primary windings are connected in parallel for operation on the lowest-rated primary voltage.

25. If a primary is wye-connected, the secondary must be delta-connected.

26. The transformer in Fig. 12-1(*a*) has a wye primary.

27. The transformer in Fig. 12-1(*b*) is a step-down autotransformer.

23. _____

24. _____

25. _____

26. _____

27. _____

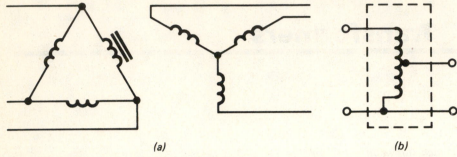

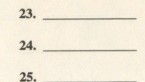

(a)   (b)

Fig. 12-1 Symbols for questions 26 and 27.

For questions 28 to 33, supply the missing word or phrase in each statement.

28. The primary and secondary of a transformer are coupled together by _____.

29. For a given primary voltage, the secondary voltage will increase if the coefficient of coupling is _____.

30. A _____ transformer has less secondary voltage than it has primary voltage.

31. Before going to the power lines, the voltage from the power plant generator is _____.

32. If a transformer steps up voltage, it will _____ current.

33. Hysteresis is caused by the _____ in the magnetic core material.

28. _____

29. _____

30. _____

31. _____

32. _____

33. _____

For questions 34 to 47, choose the letter that best completes each statement.

34. Transformers operate on the principle of
    a. Reactance
    b. Reluctance
    c. Mutual inductance
    d. Self-inductance

34. _____

35. A transformer always
    a. Changes voltage levels
    b. Matches impedances
    c. Electrically isolates two circuits
    d. Converts some electric energy to heat energy

35. _____

36. Power loss in the core of a transformer is caused by
    a. Reactance of the coils
    b. Reluctance of the core
    c. Permeability of the core
    d. Eddy currents

36. _____

37. Iron-core laminations are made from
    a. Silicon steel
    b. Hysteresis iron
    c. Pure iron
    d. Reluctance steel

37. _____

38. Eddy currents are reduced by
   a. Laminating the core
   b. Using a silicon-steel core
   c. Using large-diameter wire in the secondary
   d. Using large-diameter wire in the primary

39. Transformers have minimum efficiency when they are
   a. Overloaded
   b. Fully loaded
   c. Half loaded
   d. Unloaded

40. Decreasing the load on a transformer causes
   a. The primary current to increase
   b. The transformer to become less inductive
   c. The power factor to increase
   d. Angle θ to increase

41. Energizing current refers to the
   a. Sum of the loaded primary and secondary currents
   b. Fully loaded primary current
   c. Unloaded primary current
   d. Fully loaded secondary current

42. A rectifier transformer is a type of
   a. Power transformer
   b. Isolation transformer
   c. Audio transformer
   d. Constant-voltage transformer

43. In Fig. 12-2(*a*), if terminals 4 and 2 were connected, the two windings would be series-aiding. To connect the secondaries in parallel, the correct connections would be
   a. 2 to 3 and 1 to 4
   b. 3 to 4 and 2 to 1
   c. 3 to 1 and 2 to 4

38. _____

39. _____

40. _____

41. _____

42. _____

43. _____

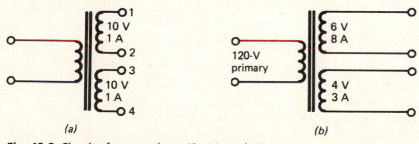

Fig. 12-2 Circuits for questions 43, 44, and 45.

44. Refer to Fig. 12-2(*b*). When connected series-opposing, the secondaries could provide
   a. 10 V and 8 A
   b. 10 V and 3 A
   c. 10 V and 5 A
   d. 2 V and 3 A

45. Refer to Fig. 12-2(*b*). When connected series-aiding, the secondaries could provide
   a. 10 V and 8 V
   b. 10 V and 3 A
   c. 10 V and 5 A
   d. 2 V and 3 A

44. _____

45. _____

46. Refer to Fig. 12-3. To form a wye primary, the terminals that could be connected together are
   a. 1 to 3, 4 to 5, and 2 to 6
   b. 1 to 4 to 6 and 2 to 3 to 5
   c. 1 to 3 to 5
   d. 2 to 3, 4 to 5, and 6 to 1

46. _____

47. Refer to Fig. 12-3. For a delta secondary, the terminals that could be connected together are
   a. 8 to 10 to 12
   b. 8 to 10 to 12 and 7 to 9 to 12
   c. 8 to 9, 10 to 11, and 12 to 7
   d. 12 to 10, 7 to 9, and 8 to 11

47. _____

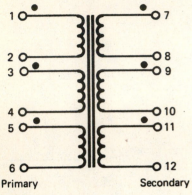

Fig. 12-3 Transformer for questions 46 and 47.

For questions 48 to 54, solve each problem. Be sure to include units (watts, degrees, etc.) in your answer when appropriate.

48. How much primary power is required by a transformer that is 92 percent efficient and provides 600 W of secondary power?

48. _____

49. What is the impedance ratio of a transformer that has 750 turns in the primary and 50 turns in the secondary?

49. _____

50. If the secondary load in question 49 is 14 Ω, what will the primary impedance be?

50. _____

51. The 208-V primary of a transformer has 1040 turns. How many turns does its 230-V secondary have?

51. _____

52. A multiple-secondary transformer has four turns per volt in its 20-V secondary. How many volts does its 50-turn secondary produce?

52. _____

53. What is the turns-per-volt ratio of the transformer in question 51?

53. _____

54. A transformer requires 850 W from its primary source to deliver 720 W to its load. What is its efficiency?

54. _____

12-1 LAB EXPERIMENT: TRANSFORMER EFFICIENCY AND POWER FACTOR

PURPOSE

This experiment will show you how to determine some of the characteristics of a transformer under load. You will gain additional experience in using a wattmeter and in constructing ac circuits.

MATERIALS

Qty.

1 transformer, 115/230-V primary, two 6-V, 2-A secondaries (Triad F-106Z or Stancor P-6376 or equivalent)
1 wattmeter, 50- or 100-W range, 150 V, 1 A
1 ammeter, ac, 300- or 500-mA range

Qty.

1 VOM or DMM with ac voltage ranges
1 resistor, 6 Ω, 50 W (Dale RH-50)
1 resistor, 25 Ω, 12 W
1 0.5-A fuse (with holder)

CAUTION The resistor in this experiment can get very warm if the circuit is operated for extended periods of time. This circuit is powered from a 115-V ac outlet. Make all circuit connections before connecting to the 115-V outlet. After the circuit is connected to the outlet, do not touch any part of it with your fingers (or your body). When making voltage measurements, be certain that you touch only the insulated part of the test probes.

PROCEDURE

1. Construct the circuit shown in Fig. 12-4, but do not connect it to the 115-V source at this time. Refer back to experiment 9-1 if you have forgotten how to connect a wattmeter. Notice that the primary is parallel-connected and it operates from 115 V.

   a. If the primary were series-connected, how much voltage should it operate from to give rated values of output voltage? _____

   b. Would the transformer operate equally well if terminals 1 and 4 and terminals 2 and 3 were connected to the 115-V source? _____ Why?

   _____

   _____

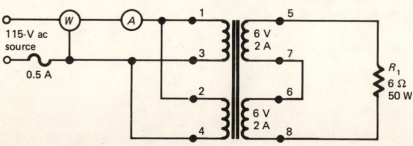

Fig. 12-4 Circuit for experiment 12-1.

2. Recheck your circuit to be certain the transformer terminals are connected as specified in Fig. 12-4. Now connect the circuit to the 115-V source.
   a. Record the power measured by the wattmeter. _____
   b. Record the current measured by the anmeter. _____
   c. Using your multimeter on the 15-V ac range, measure and record the voltage across the 6-Ω resistor. Disconnect (unplug) the circuit from the 115-V source. You now have the data needed to determine efficiency, power factor, and angle θ. (This assumes that the outlet voltage in your laboratory is actually 115 V. If this point is in doubt, measure and record the actual value for use in all the calculations to follow.) _____

3. a. Calculate and record the apparent power drawn from the primary source. (Use your measured value of current and the source voltage.) _____
   b. Next, use the apparent power just calculated and the true power (measured) to determine the power factor (cos θ). _____
   c. From the calculated power factor (cos θ), determine the angle θ by which primary current and voltage are out of phase. _____
   d. Do your results in this section indicate that a loaded transformer appears to the source to be mostly inductive or resistive? _____

4. a. To determine efficiency, you must first calculate the power delivered by the secondary. You can do this in two steps with

$$I = \frac{V}{R} \text{ and } P = VI$$

Or, you can do it in one step with

$$P = \frac{V^2}{R}$$

(Use the voltage you measured across R_1 and the value of R_1 shown in Fig. 12-4.) P_{load} = _____
   b. Using this calculated value of secondary power and the measured value of primary power from step 2a, determine and record the transformer's efficiency. _____

5. Change the 6-Ω resistor in Fig. 12-4 to a 25-Ω resistor. This decreases the load on the transformer to about 25 percent of its former value. Connect the circuit to the 115-V source and record the new current and power indicated by the meters. Measure and record the voltage across R_1. Disconnect the power from the 115-V source. Compare the current and power just recorded with the values recorded in steps 2a and b.

P_{pri} = _____
I_{pri} = _____
V_{R_1} = _____

   a. Did the primary current drop as much, proportionately, as the power? _____
   b. Did the apparent power decrease as much, proportionately, as the true power? _____
   c. Did the power factor increase or decrease? _____
   d. Did the primary power decrease as much, proportionately, as the secondary power? _____
   e. Did the efficiency increase or decrease? _____

12-2 LAB EXPERIMENT: SERIES AND PARALLEL WINDINGS

PURPOSE

This experiment will provide experience in proper phasing of windings for both series and parallel connections. It will show you how to adjust secondary voltage by aiding or bucking a small part of the primary winding.

MATERIALS

Qty.

1 transformer, 115/230-V primary, two 6-V, 2-A secondaries (Triad F-106Z or Stancor P-6376 or equivalent)

Qty.

1 fuse, 0.5 A (with holder)
1 VOM or DMM

CAUTION This circuit is powered from a 115-V ac outlet. Make all circuit connections before connecting to the 115-V outlet. After the circuit is connected to the outlet, do not touch any part of it with your fingers (or your body). When making voltage measurements, be certain you touch only the insulated part of the test probes.

PROCEDURE

1. The start end of each winding of the transformer is indicated in Fig. 12-5.

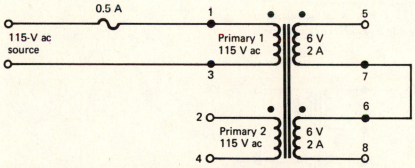

Fig. 12-5 Circuit for experiment 12-2, steps 1 through 4.

   a. Will connecting terminals 7 and 6 (7–6) together produce series-aiding or series-opposing secondaries? _____

   b. Will the output voltage be approximately 0, 6, or 12 V?

   _____

   c. Construct the circuit in Fig. 12-5 to see whether your answers to the questions in steps 1a and b are correct. We are using only one of the primary windings. Since we will not be loading the secondaries, one primary can easily carry the required primary current. (There is no need to connect the primaries in parallel and complicate the circuit wiring.) Now connect the circuit of Fig. 12-5 to the 115-V source. Measure and record the voltage available from the series-connected secondaries (measure between terminals 5 and 8). _____

d. Disconnect the circuit from the 115-V source. Does the measured secondary voltage verify your answers to questions in steps 1a and b? _____

2. a. Remove the connection between terminals 6 and 7 in Fig. 12-5 and connect terminals 5 and 8 together. What type (series-aiding or series-opposing) of connection will this provide? _____

b. Check your answer by applying power (connecting to 115-V source) and measuring the output voltage (voltage between terminals 6 and 7). _____

c. Remove power from the circuit. Does the measured voltage support your answer to step 2a? _____

3. a. Remove the connection between terminals 5 and 8 and connect terminals 5 and 6 together. How much output voltage do you anticipate now? _____

b. Apply power to the circuit and measure the voltage between terminals 7 and 8. Remove power from the circuit. Are the secondaries now connected series-aiding or series-opposing? _____

4. When terminals 5 and 6 are connected together, there is no voltage between terminals 7 and 8. (This was shown in step 3.) Therefore, it is safe to connect terminals 7 and 8 together while 5 and 6 are still connected.

a. Make the connection between 7 and 8 and apply power to the circuit. Measure and record the output voltage between terminals 5 and 8. _____

b. Remove power from the circuit. Are the secondary windings now connected in series or in parallel? _____

c. Are there any other combinations of terminals that yield correctly phased parallel secondaries? _____

5. a. Refer to Fig. 12-6(*a*). Are the primaries connected series-aiding or series-opposing? _____

b. If they are series-aiding and the primary source voltage has not been doubled, what will happen to the secondary voltage? _____

c. Construct the circuit of Fig. 12-6(*a*) and apply power. Measure and record the voltage of either secondary. _____

d. Now, disconnect the primary from the 115-V source. Is the turns-per-volt ratio of the transformer as connected in Fig. 12-6(*a*) the same as it was in Fig. 12-5? _____

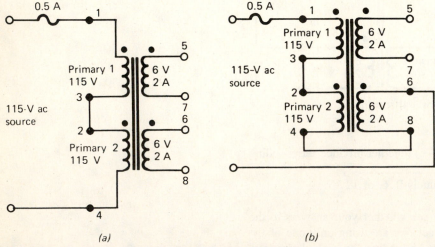

(a)   (b)

Fig. 12-6 Circuits for experiment 12-2, steps 5 and 6.

6. In this part of the experiment we will use one of the 6-V secondaries as part of the primary. The turns of the 6-V winding (between terminals 6 and 8) can be connected either aiding or opposing the rest of the primary.

a. Construct the circuit shown in Fig. 12-6(*b*) and apply power. Measure and record the secondary voltage (between terminals 5 and 7). Remove the power from the circuit. _____

b. Is the voltage found in step 6a less or more than that measured in step 5c? _____

c. Therefore, is the additional primary aiding or opposing the two original primaries? _____

d. Be sure the circuit is disconnected from the 115-V source. Now reverse the connections to terminals 6 and 8. Will this new connection increase or decrease the secondary voltage? _____

e. Apply power to the circuit and check your answer by measuring and recording the secondary voltage. Remove power from the circuit. _____

12-3 LAB EXPERIMENT: IMPEDANCE MATCHING

PURPOSE

This experiment has two objectives. The first objective is to verify that maximum power is transferred when impedances are matched. The second objective is to show that a transformer can match a small load impedance to a large source impedance (or vice versa).

MATERIALS

Qty.

1 transformer, 115/230-V primary, two 6-V, 2-A secondaries (Triad F-106Z or Stancor P-6376 or equivalent)
1 0.5-A fuse (with holder)
1 transformer, approximately 10:1 turns ratio (Triad F-106Z or Stancor P-6376 or equivalent)
1 resistor, 2.2 Ω, ½ W, 5%
1 resistor, 4.7 Ω, ½ W, 5%

Qty.

1 resistor, 10 Ω, ½ W, 5%
1 resistor, 22 Ω, ½ W, 5%
1 resistor, 47 Ω, ½ W, 5%
1 resistor, 220 Ω, ½ W, 5%
1 resistor, 470 Ω, ½ W, 5%
2 resistors, 1000 Ω, ½ W, 5%
1 resistor, 4700 Ω, ½ W, 5%
1 DMM or VOM with a low (less than 2 V) ac voltage range

INTRODUCTION

In this experiment we will use the power from a transformer secondary as the source. The transformer used has a very low internal impedance, so we will add a series resistor and consider it part of the internal resistance. For this experiment then, consider the source to be everything inside the broken lines in Fig. 12-7(a). The 1000 Ω of resistance [R_1 in Fig. 12-7(a)] is very high compared with the rest of the impedance of the transformer. Therefore, for this experiment, we can consider the source impedance to be 1000 Ω. Figure 12-7(b) shows the equivalent circuit for Fig. 12-7(a). The load impedances will consist of a number of resistors.

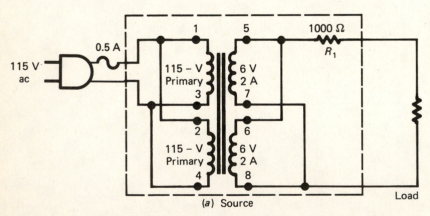 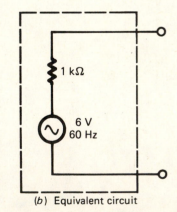

Fig. 12-7 An ac source with 1000 Ω of internal resistance.

In an electronic circuit the high-impedance source could be the output of an amplifier or a microphone. The load might be a speaker or the low input impedance of another amplifier.

If you are using electronic-circuit simulation software for this experiment, you will be using the equivalent circuit of Fig. 12-7(b) for step 1 and Fig. 12-9(a) for step 2. These circuits are found in the files labeled Fig. 12-7(b).ewb and Fig. 12-9(a).ewb. The files are available from your instructor.

CAUTION This circuit is powered from a 115-V ac outlet. Make all circuit connections before connecting to the 115-V outlet. After the circuit is connected to the outlet, do not touch any part of it with your fingers (or your body). When making voltage measurements, be certain that you touch only the insulated part of the test probes.

PROCEDURE

1. Using a 220-Ω resistor as the load, construct the circuit of Fig. 12-7. Apply power to the circuit. Measure the load voltage and record it in the table in Fig. 12-8(a). Now calculate the power used by the load and record it in Fig. 12-8(a).

Without impedance-matching transformer

Load resistance (ohms)	Load voltage measured (volts)	Load power calculated (watts) $P = V^2/R$
220		
470		
1000		
2200		
4700		

(a)

With impedance-matching transformer

Load resistance (ohms)	Load voltage measured (volts)	Load power calculated (watts) $P = V^2/R$
2.2		
4.7		
10		
22		
47		

(b)

Fig. 12-8 Data tables for experiment 12-3.

   a. Disconnect the power, change the load to 470 Ω, and reapply the power. Measure and record the new load voltage. Also, calculate and record the new load power. Did the load power increase with the high resistance? _____

   b. With which of the load resistances listed in Fig. 12-8(a) do you expect the greatest load power? _____

   c. Repeat the procedure outlined in step 1a until the table in Fig. 12-8(a) is completed. Do your results support your answer to step 1b? _____

   d. Do your results support the statement "Maximum power is transferred when the source and the load impedances are matched"? _____

2. Look at Fig. 12-9. It is like Fig. 12-7 except that it has an impedance-matching transformer between the source and the load. The secondaries are connected series-aiding. Thus, the voltage ratio of the transformer is 115 to 12, or approximately 10:1.

   a. What is the turns ratio of the transformer? _____

   b. What is the impedance ratio of the transformer? _____

   c. Which of the resistances listed in Fig. 12-8(b) should provide the correct reflected impedance to match the source impedance? _____

   d. Construct the circuit shown in Fig. 12-9 (start with the 2.2-Ω load) and apply power to the circuit. Since the matching transformer steps down the voltage, the load voltage will be quite small (less than 1 V). Using the lowest ac voltage range of your VOM, measure and record in the

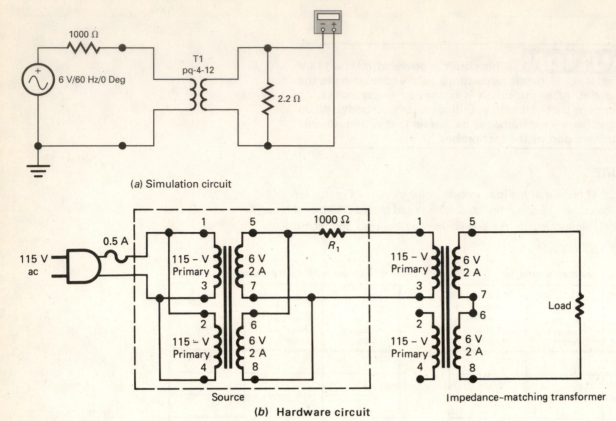

(a) Simulation circuit

(b) Hardware circuit

Fig. 12-9 Using an impedance-matching transformer.

table the load voltage of Fig. 12-9. Then calculate the load power and record it in the data table of Fig. 12-8(b). Change the load resistor to the next higher value and again measure load voltage and calculate load power. Continue this process until the table is completed. Do your results support your answer to the question in step 2c? _____

e. Did the matching transformer make the load resistors appear to the source to be higher or lower than their true value? _____ How much higher or lower?

_____

_____

f. Notice that the maximum power reaching the load was less in Fig. 12-8(b) than in Fig. 12-8(a). What do you think would cause this?

_____

_____

g. What value of load resistance would match the source if we used only one secondary of the matching transformer? _____

h. What value of load resistance would match the source if we used both primaries (series-aiding) and both secondaries (series-aiding) of the matching transformer? _____

12-4 LAB EXPERIMENT: THREE-PHASE TRANSFORMER CONNECTIONS

PURPOSE

This experiment provides experience in connecting three single-phase transformers for transforming three-phase voltages. It will illustrate the differences between wye and delta connections and between balanced and unbalanced loads.

MATERIALS

Qty.

3 transformers, single-phase, 230-V primary, 6-V, 2-A secondary (Triad F-106Z or Stancor P-6376 or equivalent)

3 0.5-A fuses (with holders)

Qty.

3 no. 47 lamps, 6.3 V, 150 mA, with holders

2 ammeters, ac, 300- or 500-mA range

1 VOM or DMM

CAUTION A shock received from a 208-V circuit is very dangerous. It can be fatal. Make all circuit connections before applying power (connecting to the three-phase source). Once power is applied, do not touch any part of the primary circuit.

PROCEDURE

1. Study the circuit in Fig. 12-10. It uses three transformers to make the equivalent of a single three-phase transformer. Notice that the two primary windings of each transformer are connected series-aiding so they can operate on 208 V (although rated at 230 V). One secondary (terminals 6 and 8) of each transformer is not used. They have been left off the schematic diagram to keep the diagram from getting too cluttered.

   Construct the circuit in Fig. 12-10. Check your circuit to be sure that the terminal connections are as shown on the diagram. Then apply power.

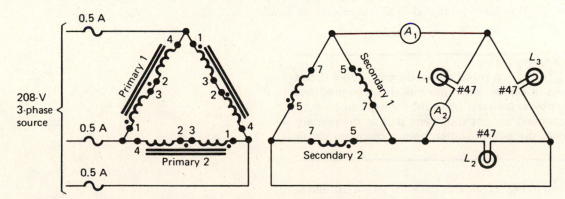

Fig. 12-10 Delta-delta connection connected to a balanced load.

    a. Do all three lamps light with equal brightness? _____

    b. Is the line current (meter A_1) or the load current (meter A_2) the higher?

    c. Is the higher current approximately 1.73 times as high as the lower current? _____

d. Remove L_3 from its socket. Do the other two lamps still light with full brightness? _____

e. Did the current through A_1 increase, decrease, or stay the same? _____

f. Did the current through A_2 increase, decrease, or stay the same? _____

Now you are going to check the phasing of the delta-connected secondary. **Disconnect the circuit from the power source.** Remove the loads and ammeters. Interrupt the delta and insert the VOM (20-V ac range) as shown in Fig. 12-11(*a*). (The primary connections are not shown in Fig. 12-11. They are the same as before.) Apply power to the circuit.

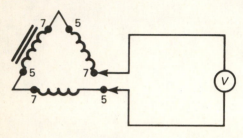

(a) Correct phasing

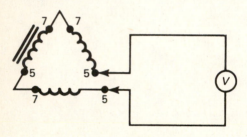

(b) Incorrect phasing
(do not complete the delta)

Fig. 12-11 Checking delta phasing on a transformer secondary.

g. How much voltage does the meter indicate? _____

h. Remove power from the circuit and reverse the leads to one of the secondaries [Figure 12-11(*b*)] to provide incorrect phasing. Again apply power to the circuit. How much voltage does the meter indicate now? Remove power from the circuit. _____

CAUTION A shock received from a 208-V circuit is very dangerous. It can be fatal. Make all circuit connections before applying power (connecting to the three-phase source). Once power is applied, do not touch any part of the primary circuit. Disconnect the power source before changing circuit connections.

2. Notice that the circuit in Fig. 12-12 uses the same primary connections as you have been using. However, it has a wye-connected secondary with a balanced load. Construct the circuit in Fig. 12-12 and apply power.

a. Do all the lamps light with equal brightness? _____

b. Measure the line voltages (line 1 to line 2, line 2 to line 3, and line 1 to line 3). Are all the line voltages the same? _____

c. Measure the load voltages across the individual lamps. Are they all equal? _____

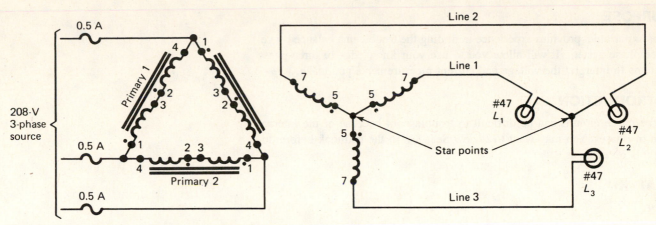

Fig. 12-12 Delta-wye connection connected to a balanced load.

    d. Is the line voltage approximately 1.73 times the load voltage? _____

    e. The circuit in Fig. 12-12 has a balanced load. Should there be any voltage between the star point of the load and the star point of the secondaries? _____

    f. Connect a 300-mA ac meter between the star points. How much current flow does the meter indicate? _____

    g. If the loads are perfectly balanced and the secondaries are identical, should there be any current indicated on the meter? Remove the ammeter from between the star points. _____

    h. Now remove any one of the three lamps from its socket. The wye now has an unbalanced load. Do the two remaining lamps light as brightly as they did when all three lamps were present? _____

    i. Connect a conductor (called a neutral wire) between the two star points. Do the two remaining lamps light to full brightness now? _____

    j. Remove the neutral wire and connect the ammeter between the star points. How much current does it indicate? _____

    k. Disconnect power from the circuit. Does a neutral wire in a three-phase wye carry current when the loads are unbalanced? _____

3. Be sure the power is removed from the circuit. Remove all loads and the ammeter from the circuit. Now reverse the secondary terminal connections on one transformer to provide the secondary configuration in Fig. 12-13. Figure 12-13 is an improperly phased wye connection (the primary connections, not shown, are the same as in Figs. 12-10 and 12-12). Apply power to the incorrectly phased circuit.

    a. Measure all three of the phase voltages (star point to terminal 5 or 7). Are they all equal? _____

    b. Measure the three line voltages (terminals 7 to 7, 7 to 5, and 5 to 7). Are they all equal? _____

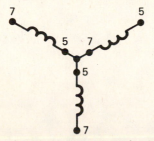

Fig. 12-13 Incorrect phasing of a wye-connected transformer secondary.

12-5 LAB EXPERIMENT: TROUBLESHOOTING 1

PURPOSE

This experiment provides experience in finding the trouble in a balanced-wye, three-phase system. It will allow you to use your knowledge of three-phase systems to interpret the voltage and current measurements you make.

INTRODUCTION

Three-phase circuits can be difficult to troubleshoot because of the interaction of phases. You may want to review Sec. 8-8 in the textbook before doing this experiment.

MATERIALS

Qty.

1 electronic-circuit simulation software
1 Fig. 12-14.ewb (provided by your instructor)

PROCEDURE

1. Calculate the following for Fig. 12-14:
   $V_{R_1} =$ _____
   $I_{R_1} =$ _____
   $V_{\text{line 1 to line 2}} =$ _____
   $V_{\text{load star point to source star point}} =$ _____
2. Should the other load voltages and currents have the same value calculated in step 1? _____
3. With your simulation program, open and activate the file Fig. 12-14.ewb. Submit a report detailing how you determined the fault in this circuit.

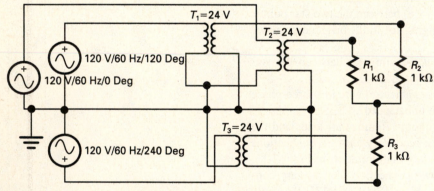

Fig. 12-14 Circuit for experiments 12-5 and 12-6.

12-6 LAB EXPERIMENT: TROUBLESHOOTING 2

PURPOSE

This experiment provides experience in finding the trouble in a balanced-wye, three-phase system. It will allow you to use your knowledge of three-phase systems to interpret the voltage and current measurements you make.

INTRODUCTION

Three-phase circuits can be difficult to troubleshoot because of the interaction of phases. You may want to review Sec. 8-8 in the textbook before doing this experiment.

MATERIALS

Qty.

1 electronic-circuit simulation software
1 Fig. 12-15.ewb (provided by your instructor)

PROCEDURE

1. Calculate the following for Fig. 12-14:

   $V_{R_1} =$ _____

   $I_{R_1} =$ _____

   $V_{\text{line 1 to line 2}} =$ _____

   $V_{\text{load star point to source star point}} =$ _____

2. Should the other load voltages and currents have the same value calculated in step 1? _____

3. With your simulation program, open and activate the file Fig. 12-15.ewb. Submit a report detailing how you determined the fault in this circuit.

Chapter 13

R, C, and L Circuits

TEST: *R, C,* AND *L* CIRCUITS

For questions 1 to 27, determine whether each statement is true or false.

1. Current and voltage are always out of phase in a circuit which has only resistance and inductance.

2. Current leads voltage in an *RC* circuit.

3. The Pythagorean theorem can be used to find the resultant of a series-connected resistance and reactance.

4. Impedance and reactance are never 90° out of phase.

5. Impedance has no base unit.

6. A resistance of 6 Ω in series with 8 Ω of reactance results in an impedance of 14 Ω.

7. In a series circuit, if the value of R is one-half that of X, then V_R is one-half of V_X.

8. Increasing the resistance of a series *RC* circuit causes angle θ to increase.

9. In a parallel *RL* circuit, both R and X_L must be larger than the impedance.

10. In a phasor diagram for a series circuit, the current phasor is the reference phasor.

11. The capacitive voltage can be higher than the source voltage in a series *RCL* circuit.

12. The impedance may be lower than the resistance in a series *RCL* circuit.

13. The impedance of a parallel resonant circuit is higher than the impedance of a series resonant circuit.

14. A series *RCL* circuit is inductive when X_L is greater than X_C.

15. A parallel *RCL* circuit is capacitive when X_C is greater than X_L.

16. Inductive reactance equals capacitive reactance for both series and parallel resonance.

17. Decreasing C increases the resonant frequency of a parallel *LC* circuit.

18. Increasing L increases the resonant frequency of a series *LC* circuit.

19. A 0.01-μF and a 1-mH inductor produce parallel resonance at more than one frequency.

20. For both parallel and series resonant circuits, angle θ is zero.

21. For a parallel *RC* circuit, cos θ is equal to the resistive current divided by the source voltage.

22. A parallel resonant circuit is commonly referred to as a tank circuit.

23. The quality Q of a resonant circuit is determined primarily by the Q of the capacitor.

24. A series resonant *LC* circuit draws a high current from its source.

25. A high-Q circuit has a wider bandwidth than a low-Q circuit does.

26. A high-pass filter passes high frequencies around the load.

1. _____
2. _____
3. _____
4. _____
5. _____
6. _____
7. _____
8. _____
9. _____
10. _____
11. _____
12. _____
13. _____
14. _____
15. _____
16. _____
17. _____
18. _____
19. _____
20. _____
21. _____
22. _____
23. _____
24. _____
25. _____
26. _____

27. A series resonant circuit can be used in either a band-pass or a band-reject filter.

27. _____

For questions 28 to 35, choose the letter that best completes each statement.

28. The symbol or abbreviation for impedance is
    a. I
    b. Q
    c. X
    d. Z

28. _____

29. The formula that would not be used to determine the power factor in a series *RC* circuit is

    a. $\cos \theta = \dfrac{V_R}{V_T}$

    b. $\cos \theta = \dfrac{I_R}{I_T}$

    c. $\cos \theta = \dfrac{P}{P_{app}}$

    d. $\cos \theta = \dfrac{X_C}{Z}$

29. _____

30. Impedance is always greater than resistance in
    a. Parallel *RC* circuits
    b. Parallel *RL* circuits
    c. Series *RL* circuits
    d. Series *RCL* circuits

30. _____

31. Increasing the frequency decreases the power in a
    a. Parallel *RC* circuit
    b. Parallel *RL* circuit
    c. Series *RC* circuit
    d. Series *RL* circuit

31. _____

32. Reactive voltage can be greater than source voltage in a
    a. Series *RL* circuit
    b. Series *RCL* circuit
    c. Parallel *RC* circuit
    d. Parallel *RCL* circuit

32. _____

33. Reactive current can be greater than source current in a
    a. Series *RL* circuit
    b. Series *RCL* circuit
    c. Parallel *RC* circuit
    d. Parallel *RCL* circuit

33. _____

34. When a circuit is resonant,
    a. $L = C$
    b. $X_L = X_C$
    c. $\theta = 45°$
    d. $Q = Z$

34. _____

35. To be most selective, a parallel resonant *LC* circuit should have a
    a. High-quality inductor
    b. Low-quality capacitor
    c. Cos θ equal to zero
    d. Large bandwidth

35. _____

For questions 36 to 43, solve each problem. Be sure to include units (watts, degrees, etc.) when appropriate.

36. A parallel *LC* circuit is resonant at 150 kHz. It uses a 2.5-mH inductor with 25 Ω of resistance. What is the quality of the circuit?

36. _____

37. What is the quality of a circuit that is resonant at 4 MHz and has a bandwidth of 30 kHz?

37. _____

38. What is the bandwidth of the circuit in question 36?

38. _____

164

NAME _____ DATE _____

39. A 1800-Ω resistor is in series with a 0.15-μF capacitor. They are connected to a 20-V, 350-Hz source. Determine the following:
  a. Impedance
  b. Source current
  c. Power
  d. Power factor

40. What is the resonant frequency of a 0.1-mH inductor and a 560-pF capacitor?

41. Suppose the components in question 39 were connected in parallel rather than in series. Determine the following:
  a. Impedance
  b. Capacitive current
  c. Theta
  d. Source current

42. For the circuit in Fig. 13-1, do the following:
  a. Determine the impedance.
  b. Determine the power factor (cos θ).
  c. Determine the voltage across C.
  d. Determine whether the circuit is inductive or capacitive.

39. *Place answers below.*
  a. _____
  b. _____
  c. _____
  d. _____

40. _____

41. *Place answers below.*
  a. _____
  b. _____
  c. _____
  d. _____

42. *Place answers below.*
  a. _____
  b. _____
  c. _____
  d. _____

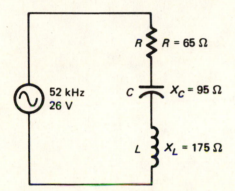

Fig. 13-1 Circuit for question 42.

43. For the circuit in Fig. 13-2, do the following:
  a. Compute the current through L.
  b. Compute the impedance.
  c. Determine whether the circuit is inductive or capacitive.
  d. Compute the power factor.

43. *Place answers below.*
  a. _____
  b. _____
  c. _____
  d. _____

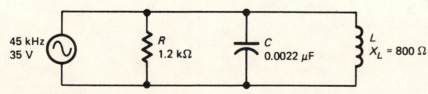

Fig. 13-2 Circuit for question 43.

Copyright © by Glencoe/McGraw-Hill.

165

13-1 LAB EXPERIMENT: IMPEDANCE

PURPOSE

This experiment will provide experience in making and interpreting measurements in R, C, and L combination circuits. It will also verify many of the formulas used in solving impedance problems.

MATERIALS

Qty.   **Qty.**

1   signal generator, sinusoidal,   1   resistor, 1000 Ω, ½ W,
    audio range   ±10%
1   VOM or DMM   1   resistor, 2200 Ω, ½ W,
1   ammeter, ac, 0 to 5 mA,   ±10%
    ± 3% accuracy or equivalent   1   capacitor, 1500 pF, 100 WV
1   choke, 2.5 mH, 125 mA,   dc (minimum), ±10%
    38 Ω dc resistance   1   capacitor, 0.47 μF, 100 WV
1   resistor, 470 Ω, ½ W,   dc (minimum), ±10%
    ±10 %   1   capacitor, 1 μF, 100 WV dc
                                               (minimum), ±10%

PROCEDURE

1. The circuit in Fig. 13-3 is a series RC circuit operating at 160 Hz. You will determine its impedance, current, and voltage drops both mathematically and by measurement. First, solve the circuit mathematically (assume the meter has zero internal resistance).

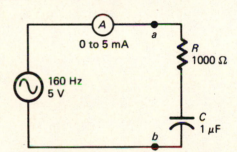

Fig. 13-3 Circuit for experiment 13-1, steps 1, 2, and 3.

    a. What is X_C? _____
    b. What is Z? _____
    c. What is I_T? _____
    d. What is V_R? _____
    e. What is V_C? _____
    f. Now construct the circuit in Fig. 13-3. Be sure the generator is set for 160 Hz. Connect the DMM (ac voltage range) between points *a* and *b* and adjust the generator's voltage output until the DMM indicates 5 V. How much current does the milliammeter indicate?
    g. Does the measured current agree, within 10 percent, with the calculated current? _____
    h. Next, using the DMM, measure and record the voltages across the resistor and the capacitor.
      V_R _____
      V_C _____
    i. Do these voltages agree, within 10 percent, with the calculated values in steps 1d and e? _____

j. Using the current measured in step 1f and the 5-V source voltage between points *a* and *b*, calculate and record the impedance.

_____

k. Does this value of impedance agree, within 10 percent, with the value determined in step 1b? _____

2. If the frequency in Fig. 13-3 is decreased to 100 Hz, will the following quantities increase or decrease:

    a. I_T _____

    b. V_R _____

    c. V_C _____

    Change the frequency of the generator to 100 Hz and adjust the output for 5 V between points *a* and *b*. Now measure and record the following current and voltages at this new frequency:

    d. I_T _____

    e. V_R _____

    f. V_C _____

    g. Compare the current recorded in step 2d with that in step 1f. Was your response to step 2a correct? _____

    Check your response to steps 2b and c by comparing the voltages measured in step 1 with those measured in step 2. Reset the generator frequency control for 160 Hz.

3. Suppose the capacitor in Fig. 13-3 were changed to 0.47 μF. Would the following quantities increase or decrease?

    a. I_T _____

    b. V_R _____

    c. V_C _____

    Change the capacitor in Fig. 13-3 to a 0.47-μF capacitor. Adjust the voltage output for 5 V between points *a* and *b* (be sure the frequency is set for 160 Hz). Now measure and record the following current and voltages:

    d. I_T _____

    e. V_R _____

    f. V_C _____

    g. Compare these voltages and currents with those measured in step 1. Were your predictions in steps 3a, b, and c correct? _____

4. Refer to the parallel *RC* circuit in Fig. 13-4(*a*). Calculate and record the following reactance, currents, and impedance for the circuit:

    a. X_C _____

    b. I_C _____

    c. I_R _____

    d. I_T _____

    e. Z _____

    f. Now construct the circuit shown in Fig. 13-4(*a*). Adjust the generator's voltage control to provide 4 V between points *a* and *b*. Record the current indicated on the meter. _____

    g. With this measured current and the 4 V of the source, determine the impedance. _____

    h. Are the values determined in steps 4f and g within 10 percent of the values calculated for steps 4d and e? _____

    i. Now change the location of the ammeter to that in Fig. 13-4(*b*). Measure and record I_C. _____

    j. Next change the ammeter to the location shown in Fig. 13-4(*c*). Measure and record I_R. _____

    k. Do these measured currents agree, within 10 percent, with the currents recorded in steps 4b and c? _____ They should!

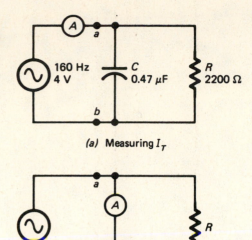

(a) Measuring I_T

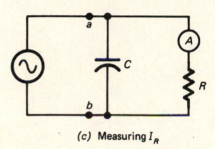

(b) Measuring I_C

(c) Measuring I_R

Fig. 13-4 Circuits for experiment 13-1, steps 4 and 5.

5. If you decrease the frequency in the three circuits in Fig. 13-4, what will happen to each of the following (answer "increase," "decrease," or "no change"):
   a. I_R _____
   b. I_C _____
   c. I_T _____

   Check your responses by changing the frequency to 100 Hz and measuring these three currents:
   d. I_R _____
   e. I_C _____
   f. I_T _____
   g. What happened to the phase angle (angle θ) when the frequency was decreased from 160 to 100 Hz? _____

6. Construct the circuit shown in Fig. 13-5. Be sure the generator controls are set for 100 kHz. Adjust the voltage controls for 5 V across the circuit. Measure and record the following voltages:
   a. V_L _____
   b. V_C _____
   c. V_R _____

   Recall two things about series circuits. One is that the current throughout the circuit is the same. The other is that the individual voltage drops are proportional to the individual oppositions. From your measured voltages,

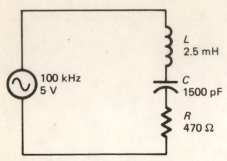

Fig. 13-5 Circuit for experiment 13-1, steps 6 and 7.

    d. Is X_L greater or less than X_C? _____

    e. Is X_C greater or less than R? _____

    f. Is X_C greater or less than Z? _____

    g. Is R greater or less than Z? _____

    h. Now, using Ohm's law and the measured resistive voltage, calculate the current in the circuit ($I_T = I_R = V_R/R$). _____

    i. Using this current and the source voltage (5 V), calculate the impedance of the circuit. _____

    j. Finally, using $X_C = V_C/I_C$, calculate the reactance of the capacitor. Do your answers to steps 6i and j support your answers to steps 6f and g? If not, you have made an error. _____

7. If the frequency in Fig. 13-5 is increased, will the following increase or decrease:

    a. V_L _____

    b. V_C _____

    c. V_R _____

    d. I_T _____

    Check your answers by changing the frequency and making the appropriate measurements.

13-2 LAB EXPERIMENT: RESONANCE, QUALITY, AND BANDWIDTH

PURPOSE

The purpose of this experiment is to provide experience in measuring and determining the characteristics of resonant circuits.

MATERIALS

Qty.

1 signal generator, sinusoidal, audio to 150-kHz range
1 choke, 2.5 mH, 125 mA, 38-Ω dc resistance

Qty.

1 capacitor, 1000 pF, 100 WV dc (minimum), ±10%
1 resistor, 1 kΩ, ½ W, ±10%
1 multimeter, 10-MΩ minimum input resistance

INTRODUCTION

The resistor and voltmeter in Fig. 13-6 are used to indicate the current in the circuit. The impedance of the parallel resonant *LC* is very high compared with the resistance of the resistor. Therefore, the current of the total circuit will be essentially determined by the resonant *LC* circuit. At resonance, the current in the circuit (and thus the voltage across *R*) will be at its minimum value.

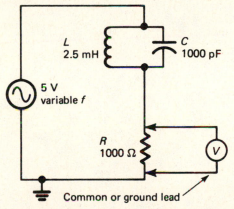

Fig. 13-6 Circuit for experiment 13-2, steps 1 and 2.

When the generator's frequency is at the edge of the bandwidth of the *LC* circuit, the current will be 1.414 times greater than at resonance. (This is because the impedance of the *LC* circuit is only 0.707 times as great as it was at resonance.) Therefore, the edge of the bandwidth of the *LC* circuit occurs when the voltage across *R* is 1.414 times as great as it was at resonance.

PROCEDURE

1. **a.** Calculate and record the resonant frequency of the circuit in Fig. 13-6.

    _____

    b. Construct the circuit in Fig. 13-6 and adjust the generator for 5-V output at the calculated resonant frequency. (Be sure to keep the ground terminal of the voltmeter connected to the ground terminal of the generator for all voltage measurements.) Now connect the voltmeter across the resistor. Carefully adjust the generator frequency to obtain the lowest possible voltage across the resistor. Record this voltage.

c. Determine and record the circuit current by the formula

$$I_T = I_R = \frac{V_R}{R} = \frac{V_R}{1000} = \underline{\hspace{2cm}}$$

d. Now determine and record the circuit impedance by the formula

$$Z = \frac{V_T}{I_T} = \frac{5}{I_T} = \underline{\hspace{2cm}}$$

e. Since Z is so high compared with R, you can assume that this calculated Z is the impedance of the LC part of the circuit. Does a parallel resonant circuit offer minimum or maximum opposition at its resonant frequency? _____

2. a. Slowly decrease the generator frequency until the voltmeter indicates 1.414 times as much voltage as it did in step 1b. This is the lowest frequency of the bandwidth; record it. _____

b. Now increase the frequency of the generator until V_R is again 1.414 times as great as it was in step 1b. Record the highest frequency of the bandwidth. _____

c. What is the bandwidth of the circuit? _____

d. Now determine and record the quality of the circuit by the formula

$$Q = \frac{f_r}{BW} = \underline{\hspace{2cm}}$$

3. Construct the series LC circuit of Fig. 13-7(a). Notice that the L and C are the same values you used in the parallel circuit.

a. What should the resonant frequency of the circuit be? _____

b. The resonant frequency of the circuit in Fig. 13-7(a) is that frequency which produces maximum indication on the voltmeter. Adjust the generator frequency for maximum voltage across the capacitor in Fig. 13-7(a). Record this voltage. _____

c. Now measure the voltage output from the generator. The generator voltage should be at its minimum value when the circuit is at resonance. Since the voltmeter has a small amount of internal capacitance, it may change the resonant frequency when measuring the total voltage. Therefore, readjust the generator's frequency to obtain the lowest possible indication on the voltmeter. Record this value. _____

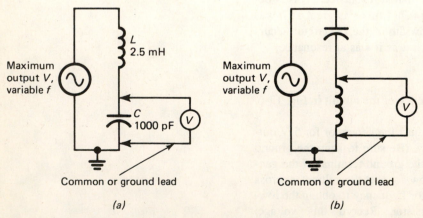

(a)   (b)

Fig. 13-7 Circuit for experiment 13-2, step 3.

d. Now you can calculate and record the quality of the circuit with the formula

$$Q = \frac{V_C}{V_T} = \underline{\hspace{3cm}}$$

e. Should this value of Q be the same as the value you calculated in step 2d? _____

f. At resonance, should $V_C = V_L$? _____

g. Check your response to step 3f by reversing L and C as shown in Fig. 13-7(b). Again adjust the frequency of the generator for maximum voltage across the inductor. Does $V_L = V_C$ at resonance? _____

4. a. Calculate and record the reactance of the inductor in Fig. 13-7 at the resonant frequency of the circuit ($X_L = 6.28fL$). _____

b. Now, using the value of Q from step 3d, calculate the effective resistance of the circuit ($R = X_L/Q$) _____.

c. How does this calculated value of R compare with the dc resistance of the inductor? _____

d. Do your results indicate that the quality of a circuit is determined primarily by the resistance of the inductor? _____

13-3 LAB EXPERIMENT: FILTERS

PURPOSE

The purpose of this experiment is to determine the characteristics of various filters. The experiment will also provide experience in plotting frequency response curves.

MATERIALS

Qty.

1   signal generator, audio to 150-kHz range
1   capacitor, 0.47 μF, 100 WV dc, $\pm$10%

Qty.

1   resistor, 220 Ω, $\frac{1}{2}$ W, $\pm$10%
1   VOM or DMM

INTRODUCTION

Frequency response curves are usually plotted on graph paper which has a nonlinear scale on the horizontal axis. The nonlinear scale is called a logarithmic scale or a "log" scale. We will use this type of graph so that we can get a wide frequency range on a relative small graph.

PROCEDURE

1. **a.** What type of filter circuit is shown in Fig. 13-8(a)? _____
    b. Should the output voltage of the filter be greater at 100 or 600 Hz?

    _____

    c. Construct the circuit in Fig. 13-8(a) and adjust the generator frequency for 30 Hz. Adjust the generator's output voltage control to provide 5 V at the input terminals of the filter. Record the output voltage in the data table of Fig. 13-8(b). Does your answer to step 1a appear to be correct?

    _____

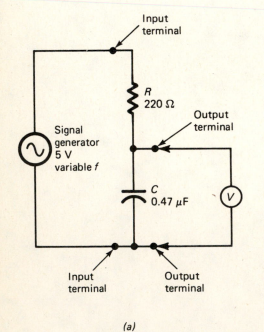

(a)

Data table

Frequency (hertz)	Output voltage (volts)
30	
60	
100	
300	
600	
1000	
3000	
6000	
10,000	
30,000	
60,000	
100,000	

(b)

Fig. 13-8 Circuit and data table for experiment 13-3, step 1.

Now change the generator frequency to 60 Hz and adjust the generator output voltage (if necessary) to maintain 5 V input to the filter. Record the output voltage of the filter in the data table. Continue to change the frequency, adjust the generator output voltage, and record the filter output voltage until the data table is completed.

d. Use the data from Fig. 13-8(*b*) to plot frequency-voltage points on the semilogarithmic graph paper in Fig. 13-9(*a*). After you have plotted all 12 frequency-voltage points on the graph, connect them together to form a frequency response curve. From your completed curve, determine and record the filter output voltage at 800 Hz when the input is 5 V.

_____

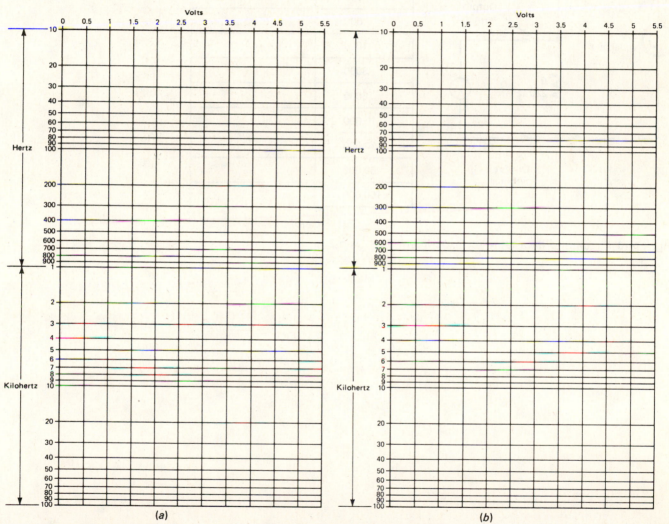

Fig. 13-9 Semilogarithmic graph paper for experiment 13-3, steps 1d and 2d.

2. a. Refer to Fig. 13-10(*a*). Is this a high-pass or a low-pass filter?

_____

b. Should the filter output be smaller at 100 or 10,000 Hz?

_____

c. Construct the circuit of Fig. 13-10(*a*). Following the procedure used in step 1, complete the data table [Fig. 13-10(*b*)]. Does your data support your answers to steps 2a and b? _____

d. Using the data collected in Fig. 13-10(*b*), construct a response curve on the semilogarithmic graph paper in Fig. 13-9(*b*). Compare the curves from steps 1d and 2d. What is the approximate frequency at which the two filters have the same output voltage? _____

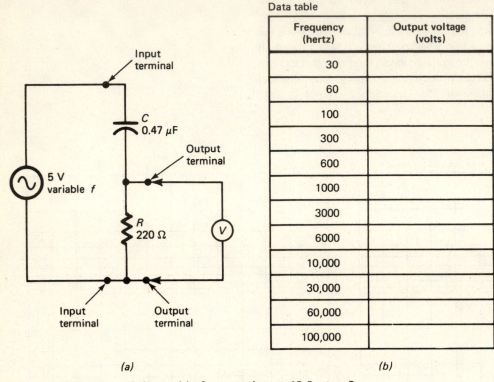

Data table

Frequency (hertz)	Output voltage (volts)
30	
60	
100	
300	
600	
1000	
3000	
6000	
10,000	
30,000	
60,000	
100,000	

(a)   (b)

Fig. 13-10 Circuit and data table for experiment 13-3, step 2.

13-4 LAB EXPERIMENT: MEASURING PHASE RELATIONSHIPS

PURPOSE

The purpose of this experiment is to provide experience in measuring phase shift in an ac circuit. This experiment will provide further experience in using an oscilloscope.

MATERIALS

Qty.

1   oscilloscope with external trigger (or sync)
1   resistor, 2200 Ω, ½ W, ±10%
1   capacitor, 0.47 μF, 100 WV dc, ±10%

Qty.

1   signal generator, sinusoidal output, audio range
1   grease pencil for drawing on the graticule (face of the screen) of the oscilloscope

INTRODUCTION

In experiment 8-3 you learned how to measure voltage (V) and frequency (f) with an oscilloscope. This experiment will use the oscilloscope in the same way as in experiment 8-3 except that you will use external triggering. To reacquaint yourself with the oscilloscope, reread the introduction to experiment 8-3. Then continue on with the next paragraph.

By using the external trigger (or sync) function of an oscilloscope, we can measure phase relationships of voltages in a circuit. External triggering causes the oscilloscope to respond to the time differences between the signals at the normal input (vertical) and the external trigger input. The signal applied to the external trigger input becomes the reference signal. The phase angle of any signal applied to the main (vertical) input is referenced to the external trigger signal. This idea is illustrated in Fig. 13-11. In Fig. 13-11(*a*) three out-of-phase voltages are shown. They are all the same frequency. Suppose V_2 is applied to the external trigger input. Now, suppose we also apply V_2 to the

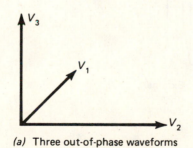

(a) Three out-of-phase waveforms

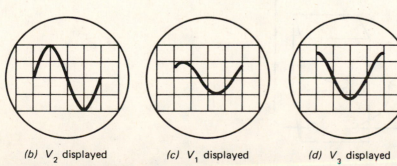

(b) V_2 displayed   *(c)* V_1 displayed   *(d)* V_3 displayed

Fig. 13-11 Phase relationships shown on oscilloscope.

main input. The result would be a waveform on the screen of the oscilloscope as in Fig. 13-11(b). The waveform would be the reference waveform because it is a display of the voltage applied to the external trigger input. Notice in Fig. 13-11(b) that each division on the horizontal axis represents 90 electrical degrees.

Now suppose we remove V_2 from the main input and apply V_1 to the main input. (V_2, the reference signal, is still applied to the external trigger input.) V_1 will produce the waveform shown in Fig. 13-11(c). This waveform is clearly out of phase with the waveform in Fig. 13-11(b). Its peak value occurs 45° before the peak value of the waveform in Fig. 13-11(b). Also, notice that the waveform in Fig. 13-11(c) has less amplitude than the one in Fig. 13-11(b). In other words, the oscilloscope has, in two steps, displayed the voltage and phase relationships between V_1 and V_2 that are indicated in Fig. 13-11(a).

You can see from Fig. 13-11(d) what happens when V_3 replaces V_1 as the signal applied to the normal input. As expected from Fig 13-11(a), the waveform in Fig. 13-11(d) leads the waveform in Fig. 13-11(b) by exactly 90°.

PROCEDURE

1. Construct the circuit shown in Fig. 13-12(a). Connect the main lead to the top of R (test point 1). Notice that V_T will be the reference voltage for this circuit as it is applied to the external trigger input.

   Put the trigger selection control on the external trigger position. Adjust the trigger level control until you have a stable waveform. Then adjust the time/division controls until you have a single cycle displayed. Now adjust the output voltage of the generator for 10 V peak to peak (as measured by the oscilloscope). You now have one cycle of the 10-V peak-to-peak reference signal displayed. Center the waveform in the middle of the screen. Now, using a *soft* grease pencil, carefully draw this waveform on the screen

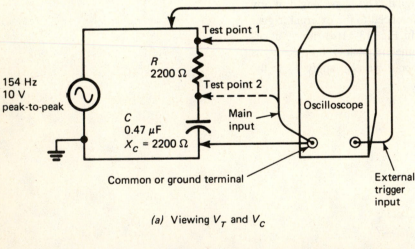

(a) Viewing V_T and V_C

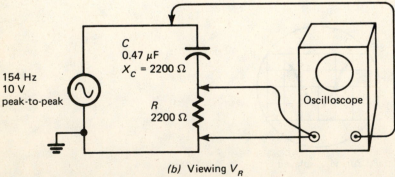

(b) Viewing V_R

Fig. 13-12 Circuit for experiment 13-4.

178

of the oscilloscope. This drawing can be used as a reference when the other signals are displayed on the screen.

Change the main input connection from the top of R to the bottom of R (test point 2). This is shown by the dotted line connection in Fig. 13-12(a). (Do not adjust any of the controls on the oscilloscope.) The voltage V_C is now being displayed.

a. What is the peak-to-peak voltage across the capacitor? _____

b. Does the capacitor voltage lead or lag the generator (reference) voltage? _____

c. Now, using the soft grease pencil, trace the waveform of the capacitor voltage on the screen of the oscilloscope. By what angle does the capacitor voltage lead or lag the reference voltage? _____

d. Next, reverse the position of R and C in the circuit as shown in Fig. 13-12(b). You are now viewing the waveform of the resistor's voltage. What is the peak-to-peak voltage across the resistor? _____

e. Does the resistor voltage lead or lag the capacitor voltage? _____

f. By how many degrees does the resistor voltage lead or lag the capacitor voltage? _____

g. Does the resistor voltage lead or lag the source voltage? _____

h. By how many degrees does it lead or lag? _____

2. **a.** Notice in Fig. 13-12 that R and X_C are equal. Therefore, their voltages should also be equal. Were the voltages measured in steps 1a and 1d within 10 percent of each other? _____

b. According to Kirchhoff's voltage law, the instantaneous voltage of $V_C + V_R$ should equal V_T. Do the three voltages indicated by the waveforms on the screen of the oscilloscope verify this law? _____

13-5 LAB EXPERIMENT: *LC* RESPONSE CURVES

PURPOSE

This experiment provides experience in using a response curve to determine f_r, BW, and Q. It also demonstrates how resistance determines the shape of the response curve and the Q of the circuit when C and L are unchanged.

MATERIALS

Qty.

1   electronic-circuit simulation software
1   simulation-circuit file for Fig. 13-13

INTRODUCTION

This experiment uses simulation software to display a series *LC* response curve (see Fig. 13-13) for a wide range of frequencies. By positioning the vertical cursor on the Bode plotter, you can determine the portion of the source voltage that develops across the current-sensing resistor at any frequency. The cursor can be moved by dragging it with the mouse or by using the direction arrows on the Bode plotter. The circuit, with the Bode plotter connected, is contained in the file labeled Fig. 13-13.ewb. This file is available from your instructor.

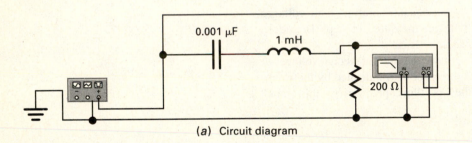

(*a*)   Circuit diagram

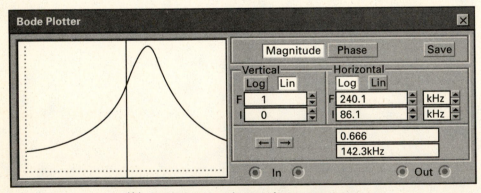

(*b*)   Bode plotter settings and response curves

Fig. 13-13 Circuit for experiment 13-5.

PROCEDURE

1. Using simulation software, open the file labeled Fig. 13-13.ewb and activate the circuit. Use the mouse to drag the vertical cursor to the approximate desired location. Then use the direction arrows for fine adjustment of the cursor location.

a. Determine and record the resonant frequency of the circuit by positioning the cursor in the center of the curve. _____

b. Using the L and C values on the diagram, calculate and record the resonant frequency. _____

c. Do the values obtained in steps 1a and 1b agree within 5 percent?

_____

d. Using the cursor, determine (and record) the upper and lower frequencies of the bandwidth.

Upper f _____   Lower f _____

e. Record the BW of the circuit. _____

f. Calculate and record the Q of the circuit. _____

g. If the resistance in the circuit is changed to 100 Ω, what value of Q and BW would you expect? Q _____   BW _____

h. Change R to 100 Ω. Now determine and record the new Q and BW.

Q _____   BW _____

i. Do Q and R appear to be directly or inversely proportional?

_____

j. Predict, and record your prediction for, the values of Q and BW when R is 20 Ω. Q _____   BW _____

k. Change R to 20 Ω and determine the new values for Q and BW.

Q _____   BW _____

l. What happened to the shape of the response curve as R was reduced?

_____

_____

13-6 LAB EXPERIMENT: TROUBLESHOOTING

PURPOSE

This experiment provides experience in analyzing and troubleshooting an *LCR* circuit. The simulation used in this experiment resembles a "soldered in place" circuit in that the components cannot be removed from the circuit.

MATERIALS

Qty.

1   electronic-circuit simulation software
1   Fig. 13-14.ewb (provided by your instructor)

PROCEDURE

1. For the circuit in Fig. 13-14, calculate and record the following:

   X_C _____
   X_L _____
   Z _____
   I _____
   V_C _____
   V_L _____
   V_R _____

2. Open and activate the file labeled Fig. 13-14.ewb. Determine the faulty component. Submit a report detailing how you determined which component was faulty and the nature of the fault.

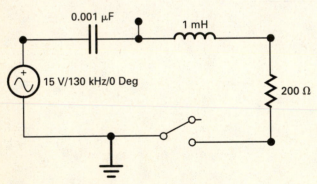

Fig. 13-14 Circuit for experiment 13-6.

Chapter 14

Electric Motors

TEST: ELECTRIC MOTORS

For questions 1 to 13, determine whether each statement is true or false.

1. A split-phase motor develops maximum torque at its rated speed.
2. A typical 240-V motor can safely operate on a nominal 230-V line that has long-term variations of ± 10 percent.
3. The wire in the start winding of a capacitor-start motor is larger than that in an equivalent hp split-phase motor.
4. Most permanent-capacitor motors use a salient-pole stator.
5. Split-phase motors are commonly available in ihp sizes.
6. "Pull-out torque" is another name for "locked-rotor torque."
7. The current and voltage which cause rotational torque in a squirrel-cage rotor are induced by generator action.
8. Slot insulators are used in the squirrel-cage rotor.
9. To optimize efficiency and PF, an induction motor should be operated at rated hp.
10. A waterproof motor prevents water from entering the motor enclosure under any operating conditions.
11. For optimum starting torque, the run-winding current should be 45° out of phase with the start-winding current.
12. All reluctance-start motors are synchronous motors.
13. A rheostat in the field winding of one type of dc motor can control the motor's speed.

1. _____
2. _____
3. _____
4. _____
5. _____
6. _____
7. _____
8. _____
9. _____
10. _____
11. _____
12. _____
13. _____

For questions 14 to 18, choose the letter that best completes each statement.

14. The motor with the lower full-load current is the
    a. Permanent-capacitor
    b. Split-capacitor
    c. Split-phase
    d. Shaded-pole
15. Which of these motors uses a start switch:
    a. Permanent-capacitor
    b. Capacitor-start
    c. Shaded-pole
    d. Reluctance-start
16. The motor that has the greater starting torque is the
    a. Reluctance-start
    b. Shaded-pole
    c. Permanent-capacitor
    d. Capacitor-start
17. Which of these motors is synchronous:
    a. Shaded-pole
    b. Reluctance
    c. Permanent-capacitor
    d. Capacitor-start
18. Which of these motors is not easily reversible:
    a. Two-value capacitor
    b. Split-phase
    c. Shaded-pole
    d. Capacitor-start

14. _____

15. _____

16. _____

17. _____

18. _____

For questions 19 to 35, solve each problem. Be sure to include units (hp, rpm, etc.) in your answer when appropriate.

19. A motor has a rated speed of 1140 rpm and develops a torque of 2.88 lb-ft at rated speed. Determine its hp.

20. A 240-V, 60-Hz, 1725-rpm, ¾-hp motor has a service factor rating of 1.15. With a constant load, how much hp can it continuously deliver?

21. How much torque will a 120-V, 50-Hz, 1725-rpm, ½-hp motor develop at rated speed?

22. Determine the percentage of slip of a 120-V, 60-Hz, 4-pole, ¼-hp motor that operates at 1710 rpm.

23. What is the PF of a motor that is 70 percent efficient and draws 15 A from a 240-V source while delivering 2.5 hp?

24. What is the synchronous speed of an eight-pole, 100-V, 80-Hz motor?

25. A 440-V motor draws a full-load current of 12 A. It is to be connected to a source that provides a minimum of 400 V. What is the maximum distance the motor can be from the source if the resistance of the connecting conductors is 2.525 Ω/1000 ft?

26. Which type of dc motor has the better speed regulation?

27. Which type of dc motor has the greater starting torque?

28. Which type of dc motor should be used for a variable-speed operation?

29. Which type of compound winding (differential or cumulative) is usually used in a dc motor?

30. Which type of dc motor has electrical characteristics that are equivalent to those of the universal motor?

31. What are the names of the windings in dc and universal motors?

32. What type of dc motor provides good starting torque but doesn't reach a destructive speed when its load is disconnected?

33. At what percentage of rated speed does a start switch usually open?

34. A motor is rated for a 65°C temperature rise. What is its maximum operating temperature?

35. What is the efficiency of a motor that produces 0.75 hp when drawing 7.6 A at a PF of 0.8 from a 120-V source?

19. _____

20. _____

21. _____

22. _____

23. _____

24. _____

25. _____

26. _____

27. _____

28. _____

29. _____

30. _____

31. _____

32. _____

33. _____

34. _____

35. _____

14-1 LAB EXPERIMENT: REVERSING ROTOR ROTATION

PURPOSE

This experiment will provide experience in reversing the direction of rotation in a split-phase motor. In the process, you will see the construction details of a motor and learn to identify the run-winding and start-winding leads of a motor.

MATERIALS

Qty.   **Qty.**

1   split-phase, four-pole,   •   hand tools needed to
    115-V, ⅓- or ½-hp,   disassemble and assemble
    reversible motor   the motor
1   multimeter

CAUTION   Before connecting the motor to a 120-V outlet, be certain that (1) the motor is securely mounted on a stable base, (2) the motor is electrically grounded, and (3) there are no exposed electrical terminals or connections. Do not touch, or allow loose clothing or hair to touch, the rotating shaft of the motor.

PROCEDURE

1. Apply power to the motor. Note, and record, whether the shaft rotates clockwise or counterclockwise. Remove power from the motor.

2. Before disassembling a motor, remove, with a file, any imperfections on the shaft that may mar the bearing surface when the motor is disassembled. Also, check the end shields and stator housing for alignment marks. If none are found, make alignment marks on these parts with a center punch. These marks are used in reassembling the motor so that parts will have their original mechanical alignment.

3. Following the procedure demonstrated by your instructor, disassemble the motor. Examine the centrifugal mechanism and locate the spring-retained weights. Pull out on these weights and note that the bobbin, which would normally be in contact with the start switch located in the end shield, moves back on the shaft toward the rotor. This is the action which opens the start switch.

4. Next, look at the start switch.

    a. Is it open or closed when the motor is disassembled? _____

    b. Are the start windings connected in parallel with the run windings at this time? _____ Why?

        _____

        _____

    c. Measure and record the resistance between the power terminals on the terminal board. _____

    d. Is the resistance measured in step 4c the resistance of the run winding, the start winding, or the combination of the two windings? Note: The run winding, or both the run and the start winding, may be connected in series with a thermal cutout device, but the resistance of this device is very small compared with the resistance of the windings. Its resistance can be ignored in this activity._____

e. Examine the stator of the motor and notice three things: the start winding is on the top of the run winding, the start-winding wire is much smaller than the run-winding wire, and the stator has four leads leaving it.

One of the four leads from the stator goes to the start switch, so it must be connected to one end of the start winding. Connect one lead of an ohmmeter (lowest range) to this lead. Two of the three remaining leads from the stator will be electrically connected together either by terminating on the same point (a terminal post) or by terminating on two points that are connected together by a jumper wire. Temporarily disconnect these two leads by removing one of them from a terminal post. Now, with the other lead from the ohmmeter, measure the resistance to each of the three isolated leads. The lead that yields the smallest resistance will, of course, be the other end of the start winding. (The resistance to the other two leads should be too great to measure with an ohmmeter.) Record the start-winding resistance. _____

f. How does the start-winding resistance compare with the run-winding resistance? _____

g. Finally, determine how you can reverse the leads to one of the windings without reversing the leads to both windings. On a motor that is made to be reversed, this can always be done by switching lead connections at the terminal board or at a junction box. Make the required lead changes and reassemble the motor.

Use the ohmmeter to check for shorts between the frame and the power leads. Of course, if there is a short, the cause must be determined and corrected.

Observing the caution (motor mounted, grounded, and insulated) at the beginning of this experiment, prepare to apply power but remember to *immediately* remove power if the motor does not operate properly. Does the motor now turn in the opposite direction from that recorded at the beginning of this experiment? _____

14-2 LAB EXPERIMENT: MEASURING MOTOR CHARACTERISTICS

PURPOSE

This experiment will provide experience in using a clamp-on ammeter to measure and compare locked-rotor and no-load currents on two types of single-phase motors. Also, the locked-rotor torque of these two motors will be measured and compared.

MATERIALS

Qty.

1   clamp-on ammeter, multirange with a 100-A range
1   split-phase, four-pole, 115-V, ⅓- or ½-hp motor

Qty.

1   capacitor-start, four-pole, 115-V, ⅓- or ½-hp motor
1   locked-rotor torque-measuring apparatus

CAUTION   Before applying power from the 120-V outlet, be certain that (1) the motor is securely mounted on a stable base, (2) the motor is electrically grounded, and (3) there are no exposed electrical terminals or connections. Do not touch the rotating shaft of a motor or let loose clothing or hair come in contact with the rotating shaft. Put the ammeter clamp around one of the current-carrying cord conductors before connecting the motor cord to the 120-V outlet.

PROCEDURE

1. With the split-phase motor disconnected from the torque-measuring apparatus, measure and record in Fig. 14-1 its no-load current. Also, determine if the motor is rotating in the direction needed to measure its locked-rotor torque. If not, reverse the direction of rotation.

Type of Motor	Current			Torque	
	No-load	Locked-rotor	Rated	Locked-rotor	Rated
Split-phase					
Capacitor-start					

Fig. 14-1 Table for experiment 14-2, steps, 1, 2, and 3.

2. Connect the split-phase motor to the starting-torque-measuring apparatus. Also, connect the ammeter (100-A range). Have your instructor check your setup before applying power. To minimize the time that power is applied to the motor with a locked rotor, have one person read the ammeter while another person reads the force scale. *Do not* apply power for more than the second that it takes to read the instruments.
   a. Apply power; read the instruments; turn off power. Record the measured current and the torque in Fig. 14-1. (Torque is the force in pounds times the length in feet of the torque arm.)

b. Why is the locked-rotor current so much larger than the no-load current?

_____

_____

c. From the motor nameplate, obtain and record in Fig. 14-1 the rated current for the motor. Why is there such a small difference between the no-load and full-load (rated) currents?

_____

_____

d. From the nameplate data, determine and record in Fig. 14-1 the rated (full-load) torque of this motor (torque = 5252 hp/rpm). Is the locked-rotor torque greater than the rated torque? _____ Should it be? _____

3. Repeat steps 1 and 2 using the capacitor-start motor. Figure 14-1 should now be complete.

4. **a.** Which of the two motors you tested has the larger starting current? _____ Why?

_____

_____

b. Which of the two motors has the larger starting torque? _____ Why?

_____

_____

c. What difference, if any, does there appear to be in the run windings of these two motors?

_____

_____

d. Why were the motors operated for only a short period of time with locked rotors?

_____

_____

e. Would you expect the locked-rotor current to increase or decrease if power were applied for several seconds? _____ Why?

_____

_____

14-3 LAB EXPERIMENT: SHUNT MOTOR CHARACTERISTICS

PURPOSE

This simulation experiment demonstrates the major characteristics of a dc shunt motor. You will gain experience in determining I^2R loss, P_{out}, and efficiency using measured data gathered under a variety of load conditions.

MATERIALS

Qty.

1   electronic-circuit simulation program
1   Fig. 14-2.ewb (provided by your instructor)
1   Fig. 14-3.ewb (provided by your instructor)

	Load Torque in Nm							
	N.L.	1.0	2.0	3.0	4.0	4.917	6.0	7.0
I_{arm}, A								
I_{field}, A								
S, rpm								
P_{in}, W								
I^2R_{field}, W								
I^2R_{arm}, W								
P_{out}, W								
eff, %								

Fig. 14-2 Data table for experiment 14-3.

INTRODUCTION

In the motor simulation circuit provided in the file labeled Fig. 14-2.ewb, the voltmeter connected to the shaft of the motor is acting as a tachometer. Each volt registered on the meter represents one revolution per minute. Thus, a reading of 1.428 kV represents a shaft speed of 1428 rpm.

The torque load on the motor is expressed in newton-meters (Nm). One newton-meter of torque equals 0.7376 lb-ft.

The motor model used in this simulation assumes that core loss is negligible. The bearing friction is set so low that it is also negligible. Thus, the only losses to account for are the I^2R losses of the windings.

PROCEDURE

1. Using your simulation software, open the file labeled Fig. 14-2.ewb. If a "Models clash" window appears, click on the "Use circuit model" button. Double-click on the motor symbol. Click on "Edit" and then click on "Sheet 1." Sheet 1 shows the characteristics of the motor used in this simulation experiment.
   a. Notice, and record, the following:
      Rated speed   = _____
      Rated armature I = _____

Rated source V = _____

b. Also record the specified resistances for the armature and field coils.

R_{arm} _____

R_{field} _____

c. Now, click on Sheet 2, which is where you will enter different load torques to check the behavior of the motor under different load conditions. Enter zero for load torque. Click "OK" on Sheet 2. Click "OK" on Models. Finally, activate the circuit and record measured values in the first three rows of the N.L. column of the table in Fig. 14-2. Why is the value of I_{arm} so very small?

_____

_____

d. Change the torque load to the next value called for in Fig. 14-2 by doing the following:

- Double-click on the motor symbol
- Click on Edit
- Click on Sheet 2
- Enter the desired load
- Click "OK" on Sheet 2
- Click "OK" on Models

Fill in the first three rows of the next column in Fig. 14-2.

e. Repeat step d until the first three rows of Fig. 14-2 are completed.

f. What happens to the speed when the load is increased?

_____

_____

g. Does the field current change as the load is changed? _____
Why?

_____

_____

h. When the load torque is doubled, what happens to the armature current?

_____

_____

i. When the load torque is doubled, does the output power also double?
_____ Why?

_____

_____

j. Using your measured and recorded data, complete the table in Fig. 14-2. P_{out} in watts can be calculated with the formula $P = 0.1048\ TS$, where T is in newton-meters and S is in revolutions per minute.

k. When does maximum efficiency occur for this motor?

_____

l. What is the rated horsepower of this motor? (Remember: 1 hp = 746 W.) _____

m. Do the data in the P_{out} row of Fig. 14-2 support your answer to step i?

_____

n. Do the power losses in the winding equal the difference between P_{in} and P_{out} for each load condition? _____ Why?

_____

_____

2. Open and activate the circuit in the file Fig. 14-3.ewb. This is the same motor as in Fig. 14-2.ewb. It has a 1-Nm load torque.

a. Note and record the speed and currents.

I_{arm} = _____

190

I_{field} = _____
Speed = _____

b. Should decreasing the resistance of the rheostat increase or decrease the speed? _____ Why?

_____

_____

c. Decrease the resistance (use the R key) to 250 Ω and record the following:

I_{arm} = _____
I_{field} = _____
Speed = _____

d. Decrease the resistance to 0 Ω. Do the meter readings now agree with those in column 2 of Fig. 14-2? _____

e. With this 1-Nm load torque, what speed range was achieved without exceeding rated I_{arm}? _____

f. Would you expect this same speed range with a 3-Nm load torque? _____Why?

_____

_____

g. Change the load torque to 3 Nm. Now determine and record the speed range obtainable without exceeding rated I_{arm}. _____

h. Adjust the resistance to 15 percent (75 Ω). For this resistance setting, and the 3-Nm load torque, determine the following:

I^2R_{field} = _____
I^2R_{arm} = _____
P_{in} = _____
P_{out} = _____

i. Do the I^2R losses account for the difference between P_{in} and P_{out}? _____

j. How much speed range would you expect with a 4.917-Nm load torque? _____ Why?

_____

_____

14-4 LAB EXPERIMENT: SERIES MOTOR CHARACTERISTICS

PURPOSE

This experiment uses simulation software to investigate the characteristics of a series dc motor. You will use measured data to determine efficiency and horsepower. Data collected at various loads will illustrate the relationships between load, efficiency, current, and speed.

MATERIALS

Qty.

1 electronic-circuit simulation program
1 Fig. 14-4.ewb (provided by your instructor)

INTRODUCTION

In the motor simulation circuit provided in the file labeled Fig. 14.4.ewb, the voltmeter connected to the shaft of the motor is acting as a tachometer. Each volt registered on the meter represents one revolution per minute. Thus, a reading of 1.428 kV represents a shaft speed of 1428 rpm.

The torque load on the motor is expressed in newton-meters (Nm). One newton-meter of torque equals 0.7376 lb-ft.

The motor model used in this simulation assumes that core loss is negligible. The bearing friction is set so low that it is also negligible. Thus, the only losses to account for are the I^2R losses of the windings.

PROCEDURE

1. Using your simulation software, open the file labeled Fig. 14-4.ewb. If a "Models clash" window appears, click on the "Use circuit model" button. Double-click on the motor symbol. Click on "Edit" and then click on "Sheet 1." Sheet 1 shows the characteristics of the motor used in this simulation experiment.
   a. Record the following for future reference:
   Rated speed = _____
   Rated I_{arm} = _____
   $R_{armature}$ = _____
   R_{field} = _____
   b. At the rated current, what is the I^2R loss for this motor? _____
   c. At the rated current, what is the input power? _____
   d. At the rated current, what is the output power of the motor? _____
   e. At the rated current, what is the efficiency of the motor? _____
   f. Using the motor power output formula $P = 0.1048\ TS$, where the units are watts, newton-meter, and revolutions per minute, determine and record the load torque needed to load the motor to its rated I and speed (S).
   g. Change the load torque setting to the value calculated in step f and activate the circuit. Is the motor operating at its rated values? _____ (If not, you have made an error in one or more of the previous steps.)
2. Complete the first two rows of the table in Fig. 14-3 by changing the load torque to each value specified and recording the measured I and speed (S).
   a. What is the ratio of the minimum-load speed to the rated-load speed of this motor? _____

	Load Torque in Nm							
	0.1	0.2	0.4	0.8	1.6	3.2	5.41	7
I, A								
S, rpm								
P_{in}, W								
P_{out}, W								
I^2R, W								
eff, %								

Fig. 14-3 Data table for experiment 14-4.

    b. How does the speed ratio of the series motor compare to the shunt motor used in experiment 14-3?

        _____

        _____

    c. Complete the rest of the table in Fig. 14-3 using the data you have collected.

    d. What happens to the efficiency of this motor as the load increases? _____ Why?

        _____

        _____

    e. Does the I^2R loss equal the difference between P_{in} and P_{out}? _____ Should it? _____

    f. What is the rated horsepower of this motor? _____

Chapter 15

Instruments and Measurements

TEST: INSTRUMENTS AND MEASUREMENTS

For questions 1 to 24, determine whether each statement is true or false.

1. Meter shunts and multipliers are usually constructed using 10 percent resistors.

2. Meter movements have both a current rating and a resistance rating.

3. External shunts have both a current and a voltage rating.

4. A d'Arsonval meter movement responds equally well to alternating and direct current.

5. An iron-vane meter responds to either alternating or direct current.

6. An electrodynamometer responds to either alternating or direct current.

7. The pointer on an electrodynamometer is rotated by the interaction of the magnetic fields of the stationary and moving coils.

8. A 100-μA meter movement makes a more sensitive voltmeter than a 50-μA meter movement.

9. A clamp-on ammeter uses the current transformer principle.

10. Use of a current transformer requires physical interruption of a circuit.

11. Alternating-current voltmeters usually have higher input resistance than dc voltmeters.

12. The internal resistance of the dc voltage function of a DMM is the same for all ranges.

13. Insulation testers use higher voltages than ohmmeters do.

14. A typical ohmmeter has an accuracy of ± 3 percent of full-scale value.

15. A bridge balances only when the resistance of the rheostat is the same as the unknown resistance.

16. Voltmeter loading is more common than ammeter loading.

17. Meter loading with ac meters is frequency-dependent.

18. The moving coil of a wattmeter is wound with smaller-diameter wire than the stationary coil is.

19. A wattmeter can be overloaded even if the meter indicates very little, or zero, power.

20. A wattmeter indicates apparent power.

21. Wattmeter polarity must be observed only when measuring three-phase power.

22. Vibrating-reed meters are used to measure frequencies in the radio-frequency range.

23. Alternating-current bridges can measure Q as well as L or C.

24. The current-voltage method of measuring impedance is especially useful at higher frequencies and impedances.

1. _____
2. _____
3. _____
4. _____

5. _____
6. _____
7. _____

8. _____

9. _____
10. _____
11. _____

12. _____

13. _____
14. _____
15. _____

16. _____
17. _____
18. _____

19. _____

20. _____
21. _____

22. _____

23. _____
24. _____

For questions 25 to 36, choose the letter that best completes each statement.

25. The meter movement that a rectifier-type meter uses is the   25. _____
    a. Electrodynamometer
    b. D'Arsonval
    c. Vibrating-reed
    d. Iron-vane

26. The thermocouple meter is used to measure   26. _____
    a. Resistance
    b. Current
    c. Inductance
    d. Capacitance

27. A multirange ammeter uses a switch that is   27. _____
    a. Normally closed
    b. Normally open
    c. Shorting
    d. Nonshorting

28. A multirange voltmeter uses a switch that is   28. _____
    a. Normally closed
    b. Normally open
    c. Shorting
    d. Nonshorting

29. To keep meter loading to less than 5 percent when measuring voltage   29. _____
    across a 5-kΩ series resistor, the voltmeter input resistance should be at
    least
    a. 50 kΩ c. 500 kΩ
    b. 100 kΩ d. 1 MΩ

30. The meter movement that uses a permanent magnet is the   30. _____
    a. Electrodynamometer
    b. D'Arsonval
    c. Vibrating-reed
    d. Iron-vane

31. The meter movement that uses more than one coil is the   31. _____
    a. Electrodynamometer
    b. D'Arsonval
    c. Vibrating-reed
    d. Iron-vane

32. The meter movement that is used in a wattmeter is the   32. _____
    a. Electrodynamometer
    b. D'Arsonval
    c. Vibrating-reed
    d. Iron-vane

33. The rheostat in an ohmmeter is used to   33. _____
    a. Adjust for zero current in the meter
    b. Adjust for the tolerance of the series resistor
    c. Adjust for full-scale current in the meter
    d. Adjust for infinity ohms

34. Increasing the voltage (and changing the series resistor) in an ohmmeter   34. _____
    will
    a. Raise the center-scale resistance of the ohmmeter
    b. Lower the center-scale resistance of the ohmmeter
    c. Cause more current to flow in the ohmmeter
    d. Cause less current to flow in the ohmmeter

35. Adding a shunt (and changing the series resistor) in an ohmmeter will   35. _____
    a. Not change the center-scale resistance of the ohmmeter
    b. Raise the center-scale resistance of the ohmmeter
    c. Lower the center-scale resistance of the ohmmeter
    d. Cause less current to flow in the ohmmeter

36. The meter used in a Wheatstone bridge is
    a. An ammeter
    b. A voltmeter
    c. A d'Arsonval
    d. A galvanometer

           36. _____

For questions 37 to 47, solve each problem. Be sure to include units when appropriate.

37. A meter movement is rated at 50 μA and 250 mV. What is its internal resistance?

           37. _____

38. The power in a balanced three-phase load is being measured. A wattmeter indicates 1100 W for phase 2. What is the power of the load?

           38. _____

39. Two wattmeters are connected to a three-phase load. One wattmeter, with reverse polarity, indicates 360 W. The other wattmeter, with normal polarity, indicates 3200 W. What power is being used by the load?

           39. _____

40. Refer to Fig. 15-1. Find the value of C_u if R_2 is 4.2 kΩ when the bridge is balanced.

           40. _____

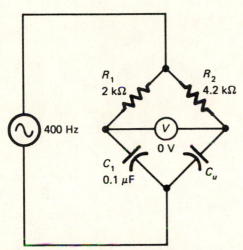

Fig. 15-1 Circuit for question 40.

41. What is the center-scale resistance of an ohmmeter that uses a 6-V battery and a 3-mA meter movement?

           41. _____

42. A bridge has a 2000-Ω resistor at R_1 and a 500-Ω resistor at R_2. It balances when the rheostat (replacing C_u in Fig. 15-1) is adjusted to 180 Ω. What is the value of the unknown resistor?

           42. _____

43. A 5000-Ω, 50-μA meter movement is used in a 1-mA ammeter. What is the resistance of the shunt?

           43. _____

44. What is the sensitivity (ohms-per-volt rating) of a voltmeter which uses a 60-μA meter movement?

           44. _____

45. What is the input resistance of a 20,000-Ω/V voltmeter on the 50-V range?

           45. _____

46. What value of multiplier resistance is needed to make a 25-V voltmeter from a 200-μA, 500-Ω meter movement?

           46. _____

47. What quantity is measured by a digital meter when measuring the value of each of the following components?
    a. Resistor
    b. Capacitor
    c. Inductor

           47. *Place answers below.*

           a. _____
           b. _____
           c. _____

15-1 LAB EXPERIMENT: EXTENDING THE RANGE OF A VOLTMETER

PURPOSE

This experiment is designed to provide experience in working with voltmeters and multipliers. It will show how to extend the range of a panel meter with an external multiplier. It will also provide practical experience in using series-circuit relationships and Ohm's law.

MATERIALS

Qty.   **Qty.**

1   dc panel meter, 5 V,   1   resistor, 20,000 Ω, 1%, ½ W
    1000 Ω/V   1   voltmeter (VOM or DMM),
1   dc power supply, variable,   25-V range
    0 to 20 V or 0 to 25 V

PROCEDURE

1. The range of the 5-V panel meter is to be extended to 25 V. To do this, you will need to add an external multiplier. The external multiplier's resistance is easy to find. The external multiplier's resistance will have to equal the difference between the input resistance of the 25-V meter and the input resistance of the 5-V meter.

2. Determine the total internal resistance (input resistance) of the 5-V panel meter. (This will include the meter-movement resistance plus the internal-multiplier resistance.)

   a. What is the internal resistance of the panel meter? _____

   b. Next, calculate the input resistance that the 25-V meter will have. Note that the 25-V meter will also have a sensitivity of 1000 Ω/V.
   _____

   c. Now, determine the resistance of the external multiplier needed to convert the 5-V meter to a 25-V meter. Connect this value of multiplier resistor in series with the 5-V panel meter and you have a 25-V meter.
   _____

3. Check the accuracy of your extended-range voltmeter by connecting the circuit shown in Fig. 15-2. Complete Table 15-1. The percentage of error is determined as follows:

$$\% \text{ error} = \frac{\text{VOM reading} - \text{extended range reading}}{\text{VOM reading}} \times 100$$

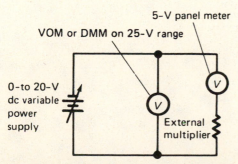

Fig. 15-2 Comparing voltmeter readings.

TABLE 15-1 Voltmeter Comparisons

VOM Reading	Extended-Range Voltmeter Reading	% Error
5 V		
10 V		
15 V		
20 V		
25 V		

15-2 LAB EXPERIMENT: VOLTMETER LOADING

PURPOSE

This experiment will illustrate voltmeter loading. It will show when it is necessary to use a DMM rather than a 20-kΩ/V VOM.

MATERIALS

Qty.   **Qty.**

2 resistors, 1 kΩ, 5%, ½ W   1 DMM, at least 10 MΩ input
2 resistors, 200 kΩ, 5%, ½ W   resistance
2 resistors, 10 MΩ, 5%, ½ W   1 VOM, 20-kΩ/V sensitivity
1 dc power supply, 0 to 20 V

PROCEDURE

1. Refer to the circuit in Fig. 15-3(a).

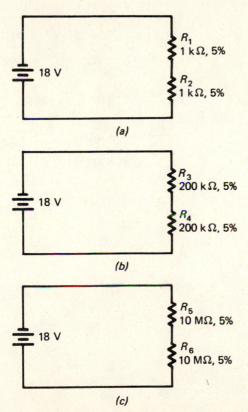

Fig. 15-3 Circuits for checking meter loading.

    a. How much voltage would you expect across R_1? _____
    b. How much voltage would you expect across R_2? _____
    c. Would you expect voltmeter loading to occur in this circuit when voltages are measured with the DMM? _____
    The VOM? _____ Why?

_____

_____

d. Construct the circuit in Fig. 15-3(*a*) and adjust the source voltage for exactly 18 V. Measure and record the voltages across R_1 and R_2 with the VOM on the 10-V range.

$V_{R_1} =$ _____ $V_{R_2} =$ _____

e. Next, measure and record these voltages with the DMM on the 10-V range.

$V_{R_1} =$ _____ $V_{R_2} =$ _____

f. Allowing for tolerances of the resistors and accuracy of the meters, do the measured voltages agree with the predicted voltages?

_____

g. Did voltmeter loading occur in this circuit? _____

2. Notice that the series resistors in Fig. 15-3(*b*) are equal, as they were in Fig. 15-3(*a*). Therefore, each resistor will still drop 9 V.

a. Do you predict voltmeter loading will occur in this circuit when using the DMM? _____ The VOM? _____ Why?

_____

_____

b. Construct the circuit in Fig. 15-3(*b*). Measure and record the voltages across the two resistors with the VOM and the DMM. With the VOM on the 10-V range, what were the voltages for V_{R_3} and V_{R_4}?

$V_{R_3} =$ _____ $V_{R_4} =$ _____

c. With the DMM, what were the readings for V_{R_3} and V_{R_4}?

$V_{R_3} =$ _____ $V_{R_4} =$ _____

d. Which meter, the VOM or the DMM, gave the more accurate measurements? _____

e. Using the voltages measured with the VOM, does $V_T = V_{R_3} + V_{R_4}$?

_____

f. Will the measured voltages in a circuit satisfy Kirchhoff's voltage law when meter loading occurs? _____

3. Construct the circuit of Fig. 15-3(*c*). If necessary, readjust the dc power supply for exactly 18 V. Measure and record V_{R_5} and V_{R_6} with each of the two meters. (Use the 10-V range on each meter.)

a. With the VOM, what were the measured voltages for V_{R_5} and V_{R_6}?

$V_{R_5} =$ _____ $V_{R_6} =$ _____

b. With the DMM, what were V_{R_5} and V_{R_6}?

$V_{R_5} =$ _____ $V_{R_6} =$ _____

c. Did meter loading occur with both meters? _____

d. Which meter yielded the more accurate results? _____

e. Knowing the input resistance of the DMM, could you have predicted the voltage indicated by the DMM across R_5? _____ How?

_____

_____

15-3 LAB EXPERIMENT: DC BRIDGE

PURPOSE

This experiment provides experience in using a Wheatstone bridge to measure a wide range of resistances. You will learn how to change the range of a bridge.

MATERIALS

Qty.

1 DMM
1 potentiometer, 0 to 10 kΩ,
2 W, 5%, linear taper
1 resistor, 220 Ω, ½ W, 10%
1 resistor, 470 Ω, ½ W, 10%
1 resistor, 1000 Ω, ½ W, 2%
1 resistor, 10 kΩ, ½ W, 2%
1 resistor, 20 kΩ, ½ W, 1%

Qty.

• Assorted test resistors between 10 Ω
   and 20 kΩ
1 6-V dc supply
1 switch SPST toggle
   or
1 electronic-circuit simulation
   software
1 Fig. 15-4.ewb

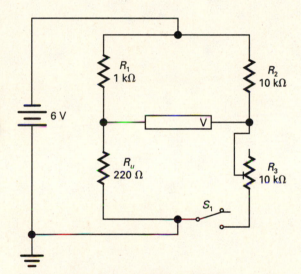

Fig. 15-4 Circuit for experiment 15-3.

PROCEDURE

Note: If you are using simulation software, S_1 is not necessary. You do not need to measure the value of R_1; its value can be figured from its percent setting when the bridge is nulled. The DMM is autoranging, so you need not take precautions to avoid overloading the meter. The circuit you will use is contained in the file labeled Fig. 15-4.ewb. The file is available from your instructor.

1. Construct the circuit shown in Fig. 15-4. Set the DMM on a range greater than 6 V. Close S_1 and apply power to the circuit.
   a. At what value of R_3 would you expect the bridge to be nulled?

   _____

   b. Adjust R_3 for null (lowest reading on the meter). If you reduce the range of the meter to obtain a more precise null, be sure to return it to a range greater than 6 V before opening S_1. Open S_1 and measure (and record) the value of R_3. _____

c. Assuming that R_3 can be accurately adjusted from 100 to 9800 Ω, calculate and record the minimum and maximum resistance that the bridge can measure with R_1=1 kΩ and R_2=10 kΩ.

$R_{min} =$ _____ $R_{max} =$ _____

d. Check your answers to step c by measuring available resistors that are as close as possible to the values you calculated in step c. Do your answers to step c seem reasonable? _____

e. Change R_1 to a 20-kΩ resistor. Assuming the same range for R_3 as in step c, calculate and record minimum and maximum values of R_u that can be measured.

$R_{min} =$ _____ $R_{max} =$ _____

f. Check your answers to step e by measuring available resistors that are as close as possible to the values you calculated in step e. Do your answers to step e seem reasonable? _____

g. Change R_2 to 1 kΩ and leave R_1 at 20 kΩ. If R_3 can be adjusted to 10 kΩ, how large can R_u be and still achieve bridge balance (null)?

_____

h. Change R_2 to 1 kΩ and check your answer to step g. Were you correct?

_____

15-4 LAB EXPERIMENT: AC BRIDGE

PURPOSE

The purpose of this experiment is to construct an ac bridge. With the bridge you will determine the capacitance of several capacitors.

MATERIALS

Qty.

1 VOM or DMM
1 potentiometer, 0 to 10 kΩ, 2 W, 5%, linear taper
1 resistor, 1 kΩ, 1 W, ±2%
1 resistor, 10 kΩ, 1 W, ±2%
1 capacitor, 1000 pF, 100 WV dc, ±10%
1 capacitor, 1500 pF, 100 WV dc, ±10%

Qty.

1 capacitor, 0.005 μF, 100 WV dc, ±10%
1 capacitor, 0.01 μF, 100 WV dc, ±10%
1 signal generator, audio range
1 switch, SPST, 1 A, 125 V

   or

1 electronic circuit simulation program
1 Fig. 15-5.ewb

PROCEDURE

Note: If you have a calibrated potentiometer, use it for R_1. Then when the directions call for measuring the value of R_1, you can just read the value of R_1 from the dial plate.

If you are using simulation software, S_1 is not necessary and you do not need to measure the value of R_1. Just figure its value from the percent setting when the bridge is nulled. The circuit you will use is constructed in the file labeled Fig. 15-5.ewb. This file is available from your instructor.

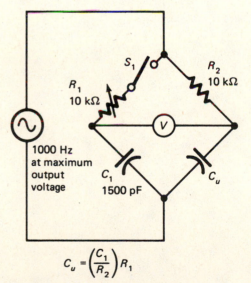

$$C_u = \left(\frac{C_1}{R_2}\right) R_1$$

Fig. 15-5 Circuit for experiment 15-4.

1. Construct the bridge circuit in Fig. 15-5, using a 1000-pF capacitor for C_u. Rearranging the bridge formula (Fig. 15-5) to solve for R_1 yields

$$R_1 = \frac{R_2 C_u}{C_1}$$

   a. What resistance value should R_1 be when the bridge is balanced?

   _____

b. With S_1 closed, adjust R_1 for bridge balance as indicated by the lowest reading of the voltmeter. (The lowest voltmeter reading is also referred to as the *null voltage*. The bridge is nulled, or it is adjusted for null.) Once the bridge is nulled, open S_1. Then measure and record the value of R_1. _____

c. Does your answer to step 1b agree (within 15 percent) with your answer to step 1a? You now know what value of R_1 represents 1000 pF (0.001 μF) of capacitance. _____

2. a. Suppose R_2 were changed to 1 kΩ. Then the multiplier in the bridge formula (C_1/R_2) would be 10 times larger. What value of C_u would be indicated if R_1 nulled the bridge with the same resistance as recorded in step 1b? _____

b. Change R_2 to 1 kΩ, and change C_u to the value you predicted in step 2a. Now close S_1 and null the bridge with R_1. Open S_1 and measure R_1. Is R_1 the same value it was in step 1b? _____

c. Suppose C_u were changed to a 0.005-μF capacitor (R_2 remains at 1 kΩ). What value of R_1 would balance the bridge? _____

d. Change C_u to a 0.005-μF capacitor, close S_1, and adjust R_1 for a null indication. Open S_1, and measure and record the value of R_1. Was your answer to step 2c correct? _____

3. a. Should changing the frequency of the generator change the resistance at which R_1 balances the bridge? _____

b. To check your answer, close S_1 and very carefully balance the bridge. Then change the frequency of the generator from 1000 to 800 Hz. Is the bridge still balanced? _____

15-5 LAB EXPERIMENT: MEASURING IMPEDANCE

PURPOSE

The purpose of this experiment is to measure the impedance of a speaker using the equivalent-resistance method. The impedance will be measured at several different frequencies.

MATERIALS

Qty.

1 signal generator, audio range of frequencies

1 DMM or VOM

Qty.

1 rheostat (or potentiometer), 10 Ω, ½ W, ±10%

1 speaker, 8-Ω rating

PROCEDURE

1. Construct the circuit shown in Fig. 15-6 and set the rheostat for about 50 percent of its maximum resistance. Adjust the generator output voltage until you can just hear the signal.

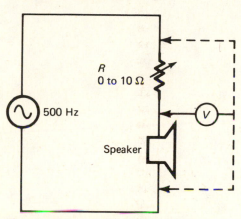

Fig. 15-6 Circuit for experiment 15-5.

The dotted lines in Fig. 15-6 indicate one lead of the voltmeter. These lines mean the lead will be alternately connected to measure speaker voltage and then resistor voltage. Now alternately measure these two voltages, while varying R, until the two voltages are equal. (If the speaker output gets too loud, reduce the voltage out of the generator.) After R is adjusted to achieve equal speaker and resistor voltages, disconnect the generator leads.

a. Without disturbing the setting of R, measure and record its value.
_____

b. What is the impedance of the speaker at 500 Hz? _____

2. a. Reconnect the generator and then change its frequency to 2000 Hz. Following the procedure outlined in step 1, determine and record the impedance of the speaker at 2000 Hz. _____

   b. Does the speaker have more or less impedance at 2000 Hz than it had at 500 Hz? _____

   c. Does your data show that a speaker is an inductive or a capacitive load? _____

   d. Change the generator frequency to 5000 Hz and again determine and record the speaker's impedance. _____

   e. Finally, determine and record the impedance of the speaker at 10,000 Hz (10 kHz). _____ Does the speaker still appear to be inductive? _____

15-6 LAB EXPERIMENT: MEASURING THREE-PHASE POWER

PURPOSE

This experiment will provide experience in measuring three-phase power. Both the single-wattmeter method and the two-wattmeter method will be employed.

MATERIALS

Qty.

2 wattmeters, 1000-W range, 300 V, 7 A (Note: This experiment can be done with one wattmeter, but two meters simplify the experiment.)

Qty.

3 lamps, 150 W, 120 V, incandescent, with lamp holders

PROCEDURE

CAUTION Dangerously high voltages are used in this experiment. All exposed terminals and connections must be insulated. Make all circuit connections (including meter connections) before the circuit is connected to the three-phase source. Once power is applied, do not touch any part of the circuit.

1. **a.** Construct the circuit in Fig. 15-7(a) but do not apply power. Double-check the wattmeter connections for correct polarity. How much power do you expect the meter in Fig. 15-7(a) to indicate? _____

   b. Apply power to the circuit and record the wattmeter reading. _____

   c. Do all three lamps appear to be lit to full brightness? _____

   d. Does the brightness of the lamps indicate that 450 W is being used by the three-phase load? _____

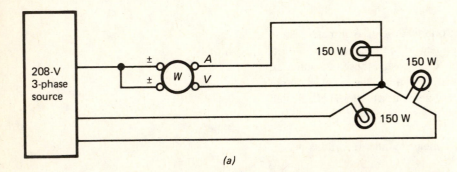

(a)

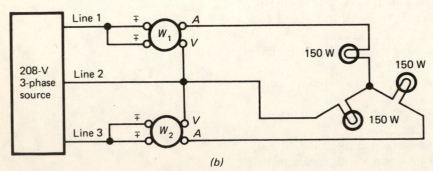

(b)

Fig. 15-7 Circuit for experiment 15-6.

e. Does three times the wattmeter reading equal the total power of the load? _____

f. Record the total power. _____

g. Disconnect the circuit from the three-phase source.

2. a. Now construct the circuit shown in Fig. 15-7(*b*) and double-check the wattmeter connections. Don't apply power at this time.

b. How much power should W_1 indicate? _____

c. How much power should W_2 indicate? _____

d. Apply power to the circuit and record the indication on each meter.
_____   _____

e. Does the two-wattmeter method indicate the same total power as the one-wattmeter method when the load is balanced? _____

Note: If only one meter is available, measure the power in line 1 first and then reconnect the wattmeter into line 2. *Remember to turn off the power* before making changes in the meter connections.

15-7 LAB EXPERIMENT: METER INTERNAL RESISTANCE

PURPOSE

The purpose of this simulation is to provide experience in determining the internal resistance of a voltmeter and an ammeter.

MATERIALS

Qty.

1   electronic-circuit simulation program
1   Fig. 15-8.ewb file (available from your instructor)
1   Fig. 15-9.ewb file (available from your instructor)

PROCEDURE

1. Use your simulation software to open the file labeled Fig. 15-8.ewb. Voltmeter V_2 has an input resistance of 20 MΩ. Using any, or all, of the components provided, determine the input resistance of voltmeter V_1. Submit a report detailing how you accomplished this task.

2. Next, open the file labeled Fig. 15-9.ewb. The maximum current rating of A_1 is 1 A. Using any, or all, of the components provided, determine the internal resistance of the ammeter. Submit a report showing how you determined the meter's internal resistance.

Appendix A

Construction Tools, Devices, and Techniques

This appendix will acquaint you with some of the common tools and techniques used to construct and maintain electric/electronic circuits.

ELECTRICAL TOOLS

Pliers and Cutters

The pliers and cutters shown in Fig. A-1 represent the major types used in

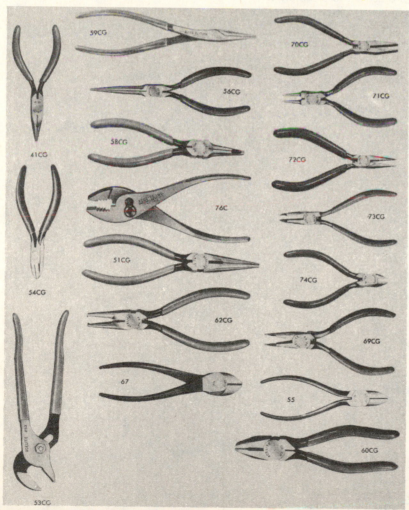

Fig. A-1 Pliers and cutters. (Courtesy of Xcelite, Cooper Industries.)

electricity and electronics. Each type of plier or cutter is made in a number of sizes and styles. For example, the cutters labeled 54CG, 55, 67, and 74CG are all *diagonal cutters*. The 74CG is a flush-cutting diagonal cutter and the 67 is a heavy-duty diagonal cutter.

The 60CG is a *side-cutting pliers*. It is often called *electrician's* or *lineman's pliers*.

The 62CG is an end cutter. It is useful for trimming excess lead length after a component has been soldered onto a printed circuit board.

The pliers labeled 59CG, 72CG, 41CG, and 51CG are all *long-nose* or *chain-nose pliers*. Some long-nose pliers, like the 51CG, also have side cutters in the jaws.

The 56CG pliers is a *needle-nose pliers*. It is used for bending light wire when working space is restricted.

The *round-nose pliers*, 71CG, is used to form a loop in the end of a conductor. The looped end of the conductor is then fastened under a screw head to make an electric connection.

Other pliers shown in Fig. A-1 are the *slip-joint* (76C), the *lock-joint* (53CG), and the *flat-nose* (70CG). These are general-purpose pliers used for twisting, turning, and squeezing mechanical fasteners.

Screwdrivers

Top views of common screw heads are shown and identified in Fig. A-2. Screwdrivers to fit three common head types (regular slot, Phillips, and clutch) are shown in Fig. A-3. The blades shown here fit into a common handle. A variety of bit sizes and lengths of screwdrivers are needed to assemble and maintain electric and electronic equipment.

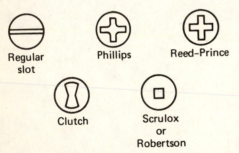

Fig. A-2 Screw heads (top view).

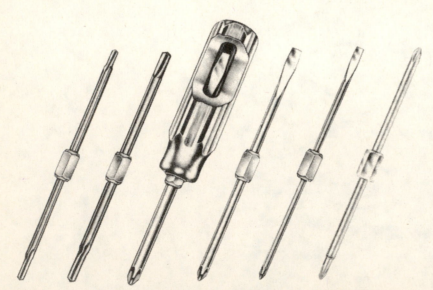

Fig. A-3 Common types of screwdrivers. (Courtesy of Xcelite, Cooper Industries.)

212

Hex and Spline Drivers

Knobs for electrical controls are often held in place with set screws. These screws may have hex or spline heads on them (see Fig. A-4). Drivers for these types of screws are shown in Fig. A-5(a) and (b).

Nut Drivers

Nut drivers are essential when removing or installing nuts in crowded enclosures.

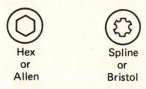

Hex
or
Allen

Spline
or
Bristol

Fig. A-4 Set screw heads.

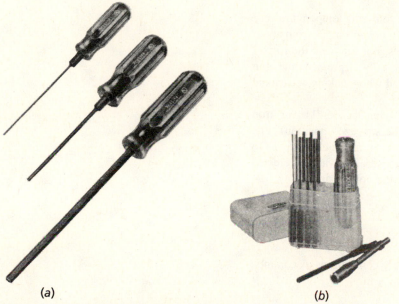

(a)

(b)

Fig. A-5 (a) Hex and (b) spline drivers.

Soldering Devices

Soldering delicate, heat-sensitive components requires a small soldering iron (pencil) such as the one shown in Fig. A-6. Pencil-style soldering irons range in power from about 10 to 60 W. A number of different styles of interchangeable tips (Fig. A-7) are available for small soldering irons.

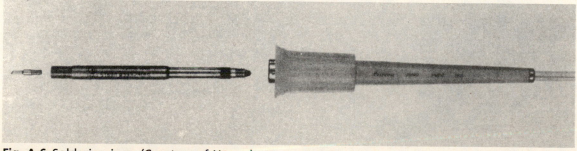

Fig. A-6 Soldering iron. (Courtesy of Ungar.)

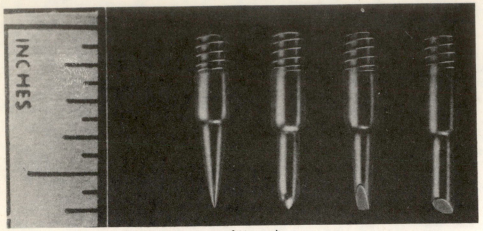

Fig. A-7 Soldering iron tips. (Courtesy of Ungar.)

Figure A-8 shows a temperature-controlled soldering station. The soldering iron in this type of station is electrically isolated from the power line. It operates at a reduced voltage, and it is grounded to reduce static buildup, which can harm some electronic components.

The soldering gun shown in Fig. A-9 heats up to soldering temperature very rapidly. Soldering guns like this one are available in power ranges from about 40 to 250 W. Some models have dual-heat controls. For low heat the trigger is only partially depressed. When the trigger is fully depressed, the gun switches to high heat. Soldering guns are very useful when making occasional soldered connections.

Desoldering tools are shown in Fig. A-10. In using the desoldering iron (top), the rubber bulb is squeezed (and held in the squeezed position). The hollow tip of the iron is then held to the connection from which solder is to be removed. When the solder melts, the bulb is released. The vacuum created by the released bulb draws the molten solder into the hollow tip.

SOLDERING

Materials and Procedures

An alloy of tin and lead is used for soldering electric connections. A common solder alloy contains 60 percent tin and 40 percent lead.

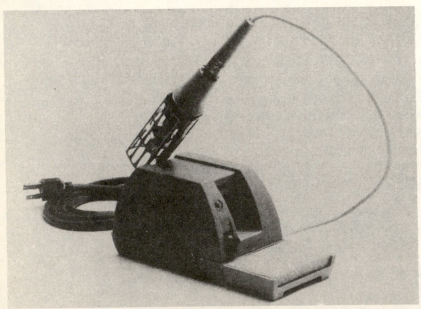

Fig. A-8 Temperature-controlled soldering station. (Courtesy of Ungar.)

Fig. A-9 Soldering gun. (Courtesy of Weller, Cooper Industries.)

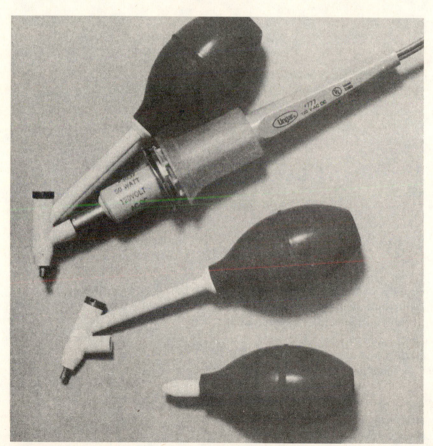

Fig. A-10 Desoldering tools. (Courtesy of Ungar.)

Soldering flux is a chemical solution which prevents metals from oxidizing as they are heated to soldering temperature. For electric and electronic connections, a rosin-base flux is used. Most solder used for electrical work contains the flux as a core within the solder wire. The flux melts before the solder and wets the connection to be soldered. Then the solder melts and flows over the joint (connection).

The parent metals (materials to be soldered) must be clean before a sound solder joint can be produced. Any contamination (grease, oxide, etc.) on the joint prevents a bond from forming between the solder and the parent metals.

The materials to be joined by solder must be held mechanically stable while being soldered. Wiggling or vibrating the electric connection while the solder is solidifying ruins the joint. The joint will be mechanically weak and it will have excessive electric resistance. Such a joint will have a dull grayish color. A solid soldered joint will have a bright, shiny silver color.

Finally, a sound soldered joint can be produced only if both parent materials receive adequate heat. Both materials must be hot enough to melt the solder. This is accomplished by having the tip of the soldering tool (Fig. A-11) make contact with both parent materials. The tip of the soldering tool must be clean and covered with a freshly applied film of solder. The soldering-tool tip is kept clean by wiping it on a sponge or rag moistened with water. After it is wiped, the tip is recoated with a thin film of solder. The solder film on the tip of a hot soldering tool soon oxidizes. Therefore, the tip should be cleaned and tinned (recoated) just before a connection is soldered.

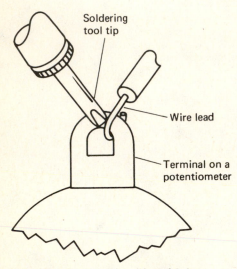

Soldering tool tip

Wire lead

Terminal on a potentiometer

Fig. A-11 Making a soldered joint.

Once the tip makes contact with both parent metals, touch the solder simultaneously to the tip and the metals. Then move the solder to the other side of the joint. When the solder has flowed smoothly onto both parent metals, the soldering tool is withdrawn. Figure A-12(*a*) shows a soldered connection (in cross section) in which both materials received adequate heat. Figure A-12(*b*) illustrates how the joint looks when one material was not hot enough. When both materials receive insufficient heat, the joint appears as shown in Fig. A-12(*c*).

The joint in Fig. A-12(*c*) is called a *cold solder joint*. An electric circuit may operate for a while with a cold solder joint. Eventually, however, oxides will form between the solder and metal and create a high-resistance (or open) joint.

Tinning

The process of applying a thin coat of solder on a conductor (or any object) is known as tinning. Stranded conductors are sometimes tinned to keep the individual wires together. This is often done when the stranded wire is to be fastened under a screw head. When tinning the stripped end of a conductor, start at the point where the insulation stops. When the solder starts to flow, the soldering-iron tip is moved along the conductor. The molten solder tends

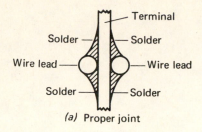

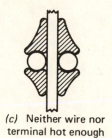

(b) Wire not
hot enough

(c) Neither wire nor
terminal hot enough

Fig. A-12 To make a good connection, all parts being joined must be properly heated.

to follow the hot tip. At the end of the conductor, the excess melted solder remains on the soldering-iron tip. This leaves a thin, uniform coat of solder on the conductor.

Care of Soldering Irons and Guns

Two types of tips are available for soldering guns and irons: ironclad and copper. Ironclad tips require very little maintenance. They need only be kept clean and tinned as they are being used. These tips are pretinned at the factory where they are made. Ironclad tips should not be filed or reshaped by the user.

Copper tips require some maintenance. A new tip needs to be cleaned with a file, sandpaper, or steel wool to remove the oxide. Then it is immediately tinned to prevent reoxidation of the copper. After considerable use, a copper tip becomes pitted and uneven. At this time it should be reshaped (with a file) and retinned. Like the ironclad tip, the copper tip should be periodically cleaned and retinned as it is being used.

When oxides form in the area where the tip joins the soldering iron, the tip may heat very slowly. If this oxidation problem is not corrected, it can become so serious that the tip never even reaches operating temperature. With a soldering iron, the oxidation can usually be removed by removing and reinstalling the tip. Occasionally the heating element also must be removed and reinserted. Removing and reinstalling these parts tends to remove the oxide from the threads (see Fig. A-6). With a soldering gun (Fig. A-9) the oxidation problem is cured by manipulating the two nuts that hold the tip. The nuts are loosened about a half turn and then retightened.

Safety

Protect your eyes with safety glasses whenever soldering or desoldering. Also be sure that those in the immediate vicinity of the soldering operation are wearing glasses. Wipe excess solder from the soldering iron on a damp sponge or cloth. Do not flick it off the tip.

Soldering irons can inflict severe burns. Do not leave a hot soldering tool where someone can accidentally come in contact with it.

SOLDERED CONNECTIONS

Chassis Wiring

Whenever possible, electric connections of conductors and components are made at a mechanically stable tie point. This not only makes soldering easier, but such a connection requires no insulation (see Fig. A-11).

Several conductors (or component leads) can be soldered together on the lug of a lug-type terminal strip. Terminal strips (see Fig. A-13) can have both grounded and insulated lugs. The grounded lugs make an electric connection to the chassis (box) on which the terminal strip is mounted. The insulated lugs are attached to the strip of insulation which is supported by the grounded lugs. When no electric connection to the chassis is required, a terminal strip without grounded lugs can be used [see Fig. A-13(b)].

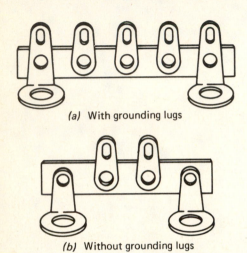

(a) With grounding lugs

(b) Without grounding lugs

Fig. A-13 Terminal strip with solder lugs.

Before conductors are soldered together without the aid of a tie point, they must be mechnically joined. Several mechanical joints (splices) are shown in Fig. A-14. These wire splices can be made with either solid or stranded wire. When using stranded wire, the strands should be tightly twisted together before the splices are made. The pigtail splice can be used to join together three or four conductors.

After a wire splice is soldered, it must be insulated. The joint can be insulated with multiple layers of electrical tape, or with a heat-shrinkable tubing.

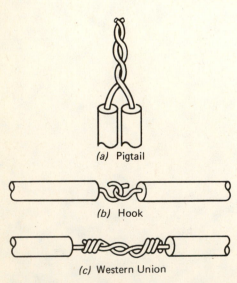

(a) Pigtail

(b) Hook

(c) Western Union

Fig. A-14 Wire splices.

Multiple layers of tape are put on a joint by overlapping each turn (or wrap) of the tape. As shown in Fig. A-15, each wrap should overlap the previous wrap about two-thirds the width of the tape. This amount of overlap provides three layers of tape over the splice. Several layers of tape should be folded over the end of a pigtail splice before it is wrapped with tape.

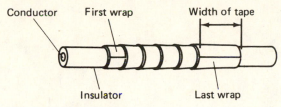

Fig. A-15 Taped joint.

When using heat-shrinkable tubing, select a diameter of tubing that just slips over the splice. The tubing should be 1½ to 2 times longer than the length of the splice. Center the tubing over the splice. Then heat the tubing until it shrinks tightly on the splice. The heat can be provided by the flame of a match. Keep the flame tip about 1 cm below the tubing and play the flame along the length of the tubing. Do not overheat or burn the tubing. A heat gun like the one in Fig. A-16 can also be used to shrink tubing. These guns blow a stream of hot air from the nozzle. The temperature at the nozzle exceeds 420°C. The temperature required to shrink the tubing depends on the type of plastic from which the tubing is made. The lower-temperature tubings require only 100 to 180°C. Most shrinkable tubings shrink about 50 percent in diameter and about 5 percent in length.

Printed Circuit Wiring

Wiring and soldering a printed circuit board present some additional problems not encountered in chassis wiring. Briefly, these problems are:

- Joints to be soldered usually are not mechanically sound.
- Circuit traces can be overheated and lifted from the board.
- Solder bridges (shorts) between adjacent traces can be accidentally created.
- Surface-mount components must be held in place until soldered.

A standard component like a resistor is prepared for insertion into the circuit board by bending its leads 90° from the axis of its body. The resistor's leads are then pushed through the appropriate holes in the circuit board so that the resistor body is on the nonfoil side of the board. Then, the leads are bent outward enough to keep the resistor from falling out (see Fig. A-17). The holes in the board should be as small as the leads will allow. If the holes are too large, it is difficult to establish a solder bridge between the lead and the foil.

After the component is inserted, the board is turned over and the component leads are soldered to the foil. Placing the component side of the board on a foam rubber pad will help hold the components securely in place—especially when components of varying heights are involved. Using the soldering techniques previously described, solder the lead to the foil. Use a low-power soldering pencil or station and remove the soldering pencil as soon as the solder flows around the lead and onto the foil. Use as little heat as possible. A good joint is illustrated in Fig. A-18(*a*). If a joint looks like Fig. A-18(*b*) or Fig. A-18(*c*), resolder it.

After the solder joint is completed, carefully inspect the area around the joint to be sure that no solder bridges were accidentally formed between two adjacent traces.

Fig. A-16 Heat gun used for shrinking tubing. (Courtesy of Ungar.)

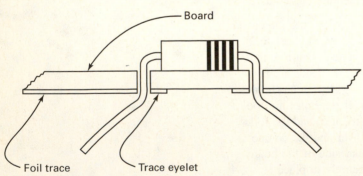

Board

Foil trace   Trace eyelet

Fig. A-17 Resistor of PC board.

CAUTION Always hold the end of a lead when cutting off the excess lead length. Otherwise, the cutoff piece of the lead may shoot out of the cutter and injure you or someone else.

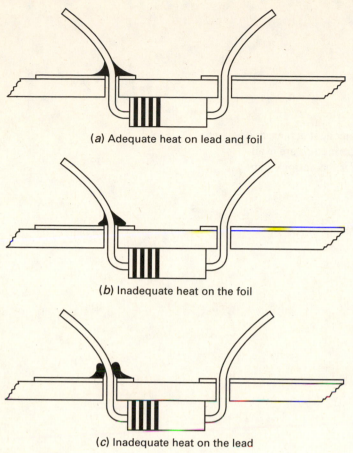

(*a*) Adequate heat on lead and foil

(*b*) Inadequate heat on the foil

(*c*) Inadequate heat on the lead

Fig. A-18 Solder joints on a PC board.

PRINTED CIRCUIT DESOLDERING

It is sometimes necessary to remove a defective part from a printed circuit board. This can be difficult to do when the part has several leads. Several tools and aids have been developed to make the job easier. There are two popular vacuum tools for this job. The vacuum desoldering pencil melts the joint, and then the bulb is released to draw the solder off the board (Fig. A-19). After all the leads have been desoldered, the part can be removed. A separate vacuum desoldering bulb (Fig. A-20) can be used with a separate soldering pencil to accomplish the same job.

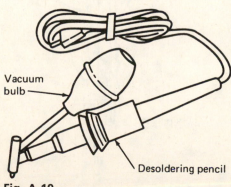

Vacuum bulb

Desoldering pencil

Fig. A-19

221

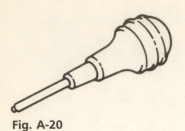

Fig. A-20

Some technicians prefer to heat all connections of a component at the same time, which also allows removal of the part. Special desoldering tips are available to accomplish this. Different tip styles are needed for the various transistor and IC parts (Fig. A-21).

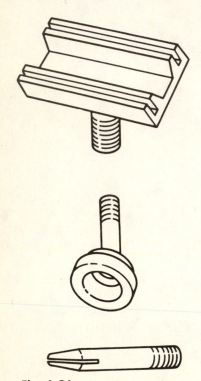

Fig. A-21

Yet another technique is to use finely braided wire. The wire and the tip are both applied to the connection. Capillary action causes the solder to flow off of the board and into the braided wire. Special wire made just for this purpose is available.

As circuits become more complicated, so do circuit boards. Many circuit boards are double-sided, with traces on both sides of the board. There are also multilayer boards with traces inside the board. Double-sided and multilayer boards are difficult to desolder. Since the holes for the component leads are plated through the board, the solder adheres to the sides of the hole.

Vacuum desoldering stations are recommended for removing components from circuit boards with plated-through holes. They contain a vacuum pump and circuits to control the temperature of the tip. A hand-held unit is connected to the station with a vacuum hose and a cable. The vacuum can be released with a finger control or a foot switch.

Figure A-22 shows the hand-held portion of a vacuum desoldering station. The tip is applied to the circuit board as shown in Fig. A-23. A back-and-forth motion is used. When the solder melts, the component lead moves freely. At this moment, the vacuum is released. The solder is drawn up into the tip and air enters the hole to cool the board and the component lead.

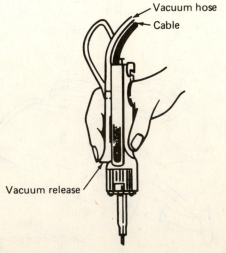

Fig. A-22

Vacuum hose
Cable
Vacuum release

222

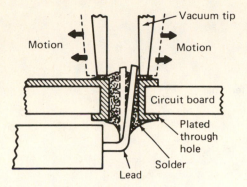

Apply heat and motion

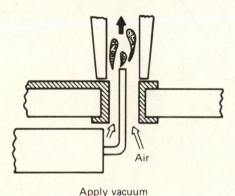

Apply vacuum

Fig. A-23

SURFACE-MOUNT TECHNOLOGY REPAIRS

Circuit boards that use surface-mount technology (SMT) can be difficult to repair. In fact, SMT has been developed with little consideration for component-level repair. It usually costs less to replace SM circuit boards than to repair them. However, there are instances when the repair of a SM board is appropriate: (1) a spare board is not on hand and equipment down time is unacceptable, (2) a replacement board cannot be obtained, or (3) a replacement board is too expensive.

SM repair requires the correct materials and tools. These include liquid flux, solder cream, special soldering tools, and good lighting including an optical magnifier.

The first step in the repair procedure is to apply liquid flux to each terminal of the device being replaced, as shown in Fig. A-24(a). Do not use ordinary paste flux. Desoldering is accomplished by using a soldering pencil with a collet tip or a dual-element tool as shown in Fig. A-24(b). Both tool types are designed to heat all of the device connections at the same time. Various collet sizes and shapes are available to handle the range of SM device packages. The same is true of dual-element tools. Desoldering can also be accomplished with a hot-gas tool. These tools heat an inert gas to a high temperature, and the hot gas is directed onto the connections for soldering or desoldering. When the solder melts, the SM device is twisted to break any adhesive bond between the device and the board. This can be done by twisting the soldering tool or by using a separate pair of tweezers depending upon which type of soldering equipment is being used. Tweezers, or a vaccum tool, are used to lift the device from the circuit board while the solder is still molten.

After the SM device has been removed, the circuit board must be prepared for the new device, as shown in Fig. A-24(c). Any excess solder must be

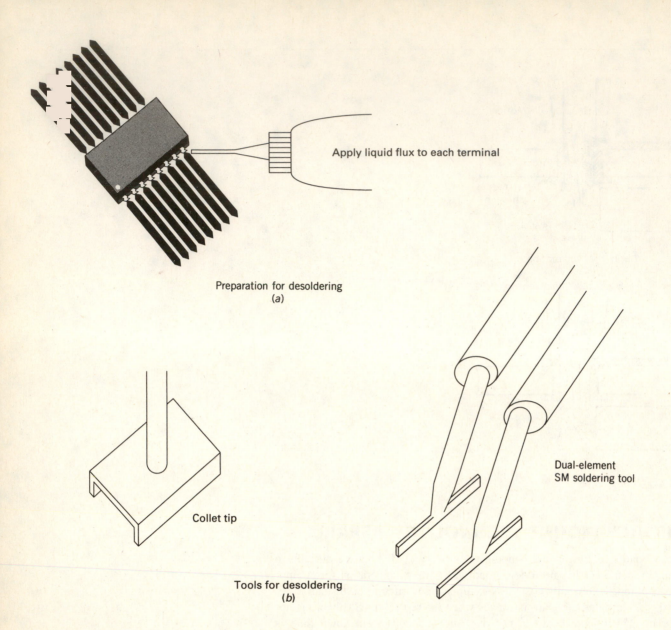

Apply liquid flux to each terminal

Preparation for desoldering
(*a*)

Collet tip

Dual-element
SM soldering tool

Tools for desoldering
(*b*)

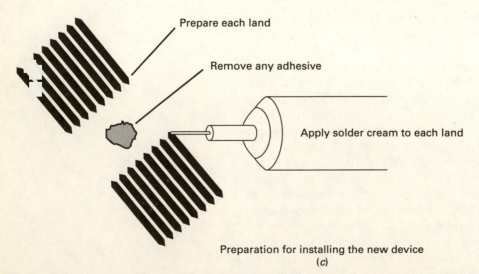

Prepare each land

Remove any adhesive

Apply solder cream to each land

Preparation for installing the new device
(*c*)

Fig. A-24 SM board repair.

removed from the lands. This can be accomplished with a fine-tipped soldering pencil and solder wick. Solder wick consists of finely braided copper wire
that is coated with flux. Additional liquid flux may be applied if needed to as-
sist in this process. If the original device was glued to the board, the residual
adhesive must be removed to allow proper seating of the new device. Then, a
small amount of solder cream is applied to each land. The new device is carefully positioned and then resoldered using the same tool that was used for desoldering. After the solder cools, the board should be inspected using magni-
fication. Each connection should be viewed to ensure a good solder joint and
to verify that there are no solder bridges.

SM board repair is easy to describe, but it can be difficult to do. On some
SM boards, the traces are only 0.020 in. wide and 0.010 in. apart. The repair
of circuits with such fine detail is meticulous and requires good vision, the
correct tools and materials, a steady hand, and practice.

SOLDERLESS CONNECTIONS

For many applications, solderless connections are quicker to make, more eco-
nomical, and as effective as a soldered connection.

The wire connector (wire nut) shown in Fig. A-25 is used extensively in
bonding together and in insulating pigtail splices. Wire connectors are available in several sizes to accommodate a variety of wire sizes. A wire nut is put
on a pigtail by twisting the nut in a clockwise direction. The pigtail splice
must be short enough so that the insulation on the conductors extends well
into the insulated cap.

Wire-wrapped connections are shown in Fig. A-26. The tool shown in Fig.
A-26 cuts, strips, and wraps the connection all in one operation. It is an air

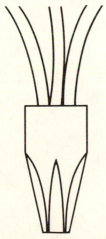

(a) Wire connector on a three–
conductor pigtail splice

Tapered, spiral spring or threaded cup

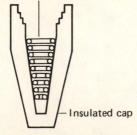

└─ Insulated cap

(b) Section of a wire connector

Fig. A-25 Wire connector.

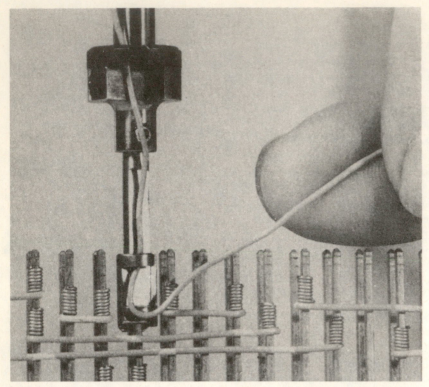

Fig. A-26 Wire-wrapped terminal connection. (Courtesy of OK Machine and Tool Corp.)

or electrically operated tool. A simpler, hand-operated wire-wrapping tool is shown in Fig. A-27. It is a type that can be used when only a few connections are to be made. Wrapped connections can be easily removed, for repair or circuit modification, with one of the tools shown in Fig. A-28.

Fig. A-27 Hand wrapping tool. (Courtesy of OK Machine and Tool Corp.)

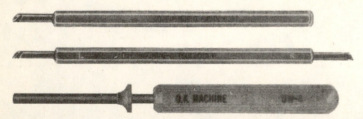

Fig. A-28 Unwrapping tools. (Courtesy of OK Machine and Tool Corp.)

Crimp-type terminals (Fig. A-29) are useful for terminating conductors on a screw-type terminal block (Fig. A-30). These terminals are available with either bare or insulated bodies. Some crimping tools (Fig. A-29) have separate grooves for crimping the insulated terminals. The top tool in Fig. A-29 is a combination tool. In addition to crimping, it has provisions for cutting and stripping the conductors.

Sometimes conductors are connected under a screw head without using any crimp-type terminal. In such cases, the end of the conductor should be formed into a loop under the screw head (see Fig. A-31). Notice in Fig. A-31 that the

226

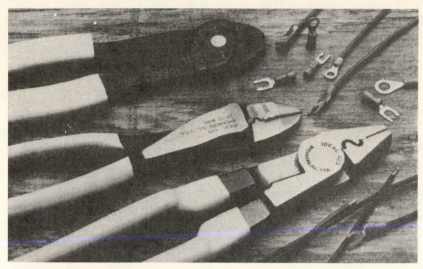

Fig. A-29 Crimp-type terminals and crimping tools. (Courtesy of Ideal Industries, Inc.)

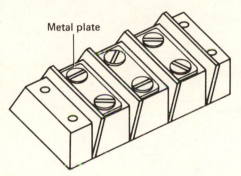

Metal plate

Fig. A-30 Screw-type terminal block.

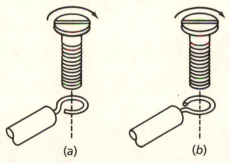

(a)   (b)

Fig. A-31 The right (*a*) and wrong (*b*) ways to connect a wire to a screw terminal.

loop is formed in the same direction as the screw turns. If the conductor is stranded, the strands must be twisted together and tinned before the loop is formed.

PLUGS AND JACKS

Some of the more common single-conductor plugs and jacks are shown in Fig. A-32. The jacks in Fig. A-32 can be obtained in either an insulated or an uninsulated style. The insulated style may have a plastic body, or it may be a metal

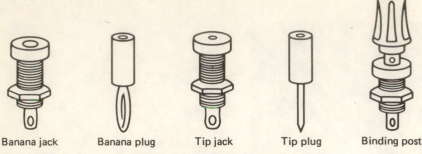

Banana jack   Banana plug   Tip jack   Tip plug   Binding post

Fig. A-32 Plugs and jacks (single conductor).

body with an insulating washer. The binding post in Fig. A-32 is designed to connect to either a bare wire or a banana plug.

Figure A-33 shows a variety of phone plugs and jacks. These devices can accommodate two or three conductors. They are used extensively for connecting audio circuits and devices. The jack in the center of Fig. A-33 is a closed-circuit (switching) jack. When the plug is inserted in the jack, the switch contacts open. Closed-circuit jacks are the type used for the headphone connection in radio receivers. When the plug is removed, the switch contacts close and reconnect the internal speaker to the receiver.

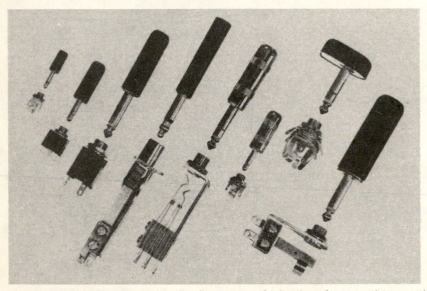

Fig. A-33 Phone plugs and jacks. (Courtesy of Switchcraft, Inc., Chicago, Ill.)

A four-conductor plug and receptacle is shown in Fig. A-34. The top half of the figure is an exploded view of the plug. The bottom half shows the receptacle, mounted in a panel, with the plug inserted. Notice the cable clamp in the body of the plug in Fig. A-34. This clamp prevents cable movement from putting excess stress on the soldered connections in the plug assembly.

MOUNTING COMPONENTS

All components in a circuit need to be secured. They should be attached to the chassis or to a tie point which is secured to the chassis. For example, resistors can be connected between the insulated lugs of a terminal strip. Fuses can be mounted in fuse holders like those shown in Fig. A-35. Of course, the fuse holder is mounted through a hole in the chassis.

A component can be mounted on, but insulated from, a metal chassis by using insulated washers. For example, the pin jack of Fig. A-36 is insulated from the chassis by two insulated washers.

228

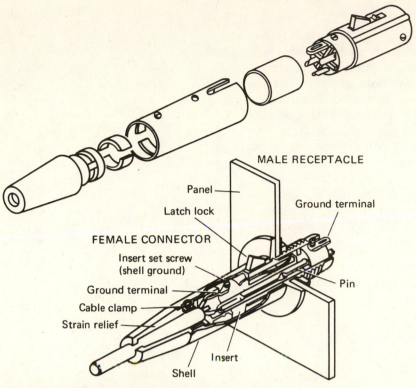

MALE RECEPTACLE

Panel

Latch lock

Ground terminal

FEMALE CONNECTOR

Insert set screw
(shell ground)

Ground terminal

Cable clamp

Strain relief

Pin

Insert

Shell

Fig. A-34 Cable connector showing plug and receptacle. (Courtesy of Switchcraft, Inc., Chicago, Ill.)

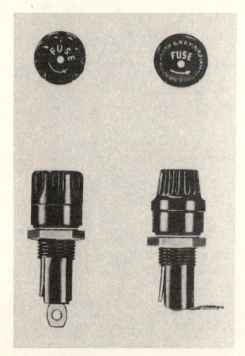

Fig. A-35 Fuse holders for panel mounting. (Courtesy of Littlefuse, Inc.)

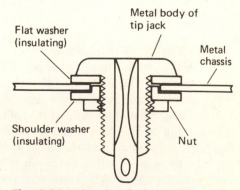

Flat washer
(insulating)

Metal body of
tip jack

Metal
chassis

Shoulder washer
(insulating)

Nut

Fig. A-36 Using insulating washers in a metal chassis.

SHORTENING SHAFTS

Often the control shafts on switches and potentiometers need to be shortened. This is done by clamping the excess shaft length in a vise and sawing the shaft off. Support the switch or potentiometer with one hand as the saw cut is being finished.

PRODUCING HOLES

Holes up to about ½ in. (1.3 cm) in diameter are easily produced with a twist drill. However, drilling thin metal, such as an electric chassis, can create problems. Unless the chassis is securely clamped, twist drills tend to drill a triangle-shaped hole. Also, the larger-sized drills tend to take too deep a cut and "grab" the thin metal of the chassis. Therefore, any small metal chassis or brackets must be clamped in a vise or a clamp before they are drilled. *Do not attempt to hold the metal by hand while it is being drilled.* If the drill catches the metal, it will jerk it out of your hand. The metal will then rotate with the drill and, very likely, cut and bruise your hand.

One way to avoid triangle-shaped holes is to drill the hole too small and then ream it to size. The hand reamer shown in Fig. A-37 is convenient for this purpose. This reamer will ream holes from ⅛ in. (3.2 mm) to ½ in. (1.3 cm).

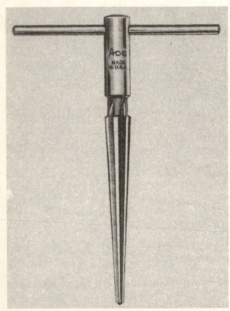

Fig. A-37 T-handle reamer. (Courtesy of Henry L. Hanson, Inc.)

Holes from ¹⁄₁₆ to ¼ in. in diameter can be quickly produced using the punch shown in Fig. A-38. Changing the punch and die size only requires removal of one screw. Producing holes with a punch practically eliminates the burrs found around a hole that has been drilled.

Holes larger than ½ in. in diameter can be made with a punch like the one shown in Fig. A-39. Chassis punches are available in sizes ranging from ½ to 3 in. They are also available in square and rectangular shapes. In using these punches, the smaller half of the punch is held stationary with a wrench or a vise. Then the bolt head is turned with a wrench.

INSULATION REMOVAL

When removing insulation from a conductor, caution must be used to avoid nicking the conductor. If a conductor is nicked, its cross-sectional area at the point of the nick is reduced. This, of course, reduces its current-carrying ability. It is especially easy to nick a conductor when removing insulation with a

230

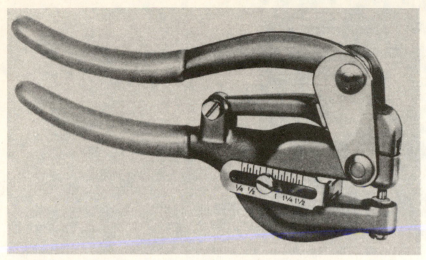

Fig. A-38 Light-duty punch. (Courtesy of Roper Whitney, Inc.)

Fig. A-39 Chassis punch. (Courtesy of Greenlee Tool Co.)

knife. To minimize the risk of nicking, make all knife cuts at a slight angle (rather than perpendicular) to the conductor.

The quickest and easiest way of removing insulation is with a wire stripper. For small conductors (up to about 10 gage) the strippers shown in Fig. A-40 are very convenient. Insulation on larger cables (stranded conductor) can be removed with the stripper shown in Fig. A-41.

Insulation is removed from magnet wire by a scraping process because the insulation is very thin. The wire skinner shown in Fig. A-42 is well suited for the job. Using a wire skinner properly requires practice. If too much pressure is applied to the blades, the wire will be nicked. If not enough pressure is applied, the blades slide over the insulation.

The outer insulating jacket can be easily removed from a multiconductor cable with the cable slitter shown in Fig. A-43. A cable slitter is especially useful if a considerable length of jacket must be removed.

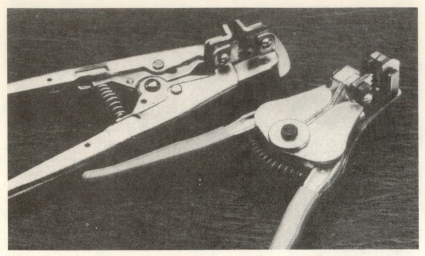
Fig. A-40 Wire strippers for small conductors. (Courtesy of Ideal Industries, Inc.)

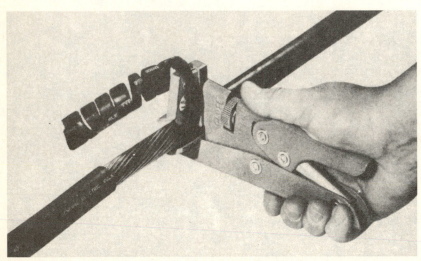
Fig. A-41 Cable stripper. (Courtesy of Greenlee Tool Co.)

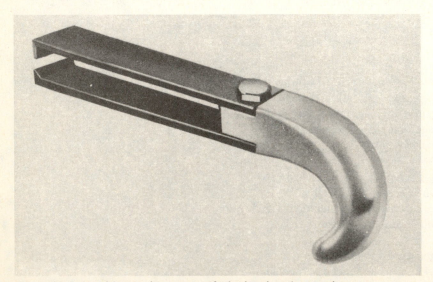
Fig. A-42 Wire skinner. (Courtesy of Ideal Industries, Inc.)

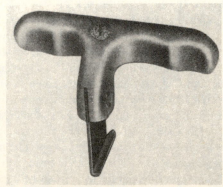
Fig. A-43 Cable slitter. (Courtesy of Mathias Klein and Sons, Inc.)

Appendix B

Breadboarding

CAUTION Breadboarding is generally limited to low-power circuits. High currents would cause high temperatures, and the breadboard would be damaged. High voltage could cause arcing and would be very dangerous. *If there is any doubt, consult your instructor before breadboarding a circuit.*

The name *breadboarding* has its origin in the early years of electronics, when circuits were sometimes fashioned on a flat piece of wood that looked like a breadboard (or actually was a breadboard). In case you didn't know, breadboards are used in some kitchens for working with dough or cutting bread. Today, wood breadboards are seldom used, and circuits are prototyped and tested using electronic breadboards, which are molded plastic with holes and internal metal contact strips. A circuit can be easily and quickly built by shoving component leads and jumper wires into the holes. Electronic breadboards are also called *prototyping boards*.

Figure B-1(*a*) shows how a series circuit appears on a typical electronic breadboard. Each group of five holes is electrically connected. Or, put another way, there is electrical continuity from any one contact to the other four contacts in that group. So, the top horizontal resistor is connected to the vertical resistor because each has a lead that is inserted into one group of five in Fig. B-1(*a*). Note that the vertical resistor and the bottom horizontal resistor are connected using another group of five.

There are also buses on breadboards. They are most often used for power, ground, or any signal requiring more than five common contact points. Figure B-1(*a*) shows two buses at the top and two at the bottom. Every contact along a bus is electrically connected to every other contact on that bus. Thus, the top source wire in Fig. B-1(*a*) is electrically connected to the top horizontal resistor via the top bus and jumper wire. Likewise, the bottom source wire is connected to the bottom horizontal resistor via the bottom bus and jumper wire. Note that the four buses in Fig. B-1(*a*) are electrically isolated from each other. So, one could use them as follows:

- +12-V bus
- −12-V bus
- +5-V bus
- Ground bus

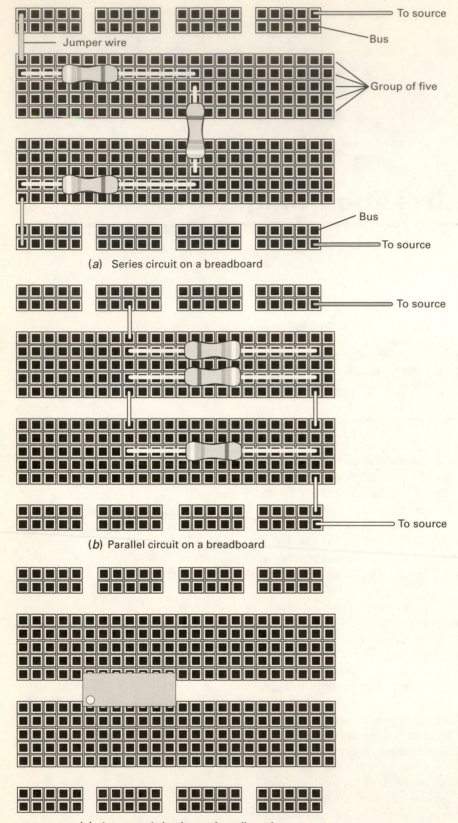

To source

Bus

Jumper wire

Group of five

Bus

To source

(*a*) Series circuit on a breadboard

To source

To source

(*b*) Parallel circuit on a breadboard

(*c*) Integrated circuit on a breadboard

Fig. B-1 Electronic breadboard.

Figure B-1(*b*) shows a parallel circuit. Notice how jumper wires are used to connect the top two resistors to the bottom resistor. There is a problem in Fig. B-1(*b*) in that both source leads are not connected to the resistors. Can you see why? How can the problem be corrected? Two possible answers are:

- Move the bottom source lead to the third bus down in Fig. B-1(*b*)

- Add a jumper wire from the third bus down to the bottom bus in Fig. B-1(*b*)

Figure B-1(*c*) shows that integrated circuits in a dual-inline package conform to the contact arrangement of the breadboard. The IC pins and the board contacts have the same center-to-center spacing of 0.1 in. Each IC pin in Fig. B-1(*c*) has four contact points available for interconnections. In cases when this is not enough, a jumper wire can connect an IC pin to an unused group of five, or two jumper wires to two groups, and so on.

Jumper wires are usually made from no. 22 or no. 24 solid, tinned, insulated wire. About ¼ in. of insulation is removed from each end. After a wire is used many times, the end might become bent and fragile. When this happens, cut off the damaged end. It is a good idea to use different wire colors, for example, red for positive, black for ground, green for negative, and white for signal paths. This becomes more of an issue when large, complicated circuits are breadboarded.

In classroom or lab settings, the component leads are usually left full-length, unless the ends are damaged as mentioned before. This is because the components are used over and over. This means that components might stand above the breadboard by an inch or more. This is usually acceptable, but be sure that they don't flop around and touch each other and cause short circuits.

Some component wires might be too big to fit comfortably into the contact openings. Do not force them. One solution is to solder a short length of no. 22 wire to the end of any wire too big in diameter for the breadboard. Some components cannot be soldered without ruining them. Fuses and lamps are examples. In these cases, fuse holders or lamp sockets will be required for soldering to the no. 22 wires. Consult your instructor in these cases.

RULES AND TIPS FOR BREADBOARDING

- High-power circuits should *not* be breadboarded.

- High-frequency circuits are usually not breadboarded. The higher the frequency, the more this is true.

- High-gain circuits might not perform well. There are often problems with noise and oscillation.

- Surface-mount components cannot be used without soldering leads to them or using special adapters (these are available for some surface-mount ICs).

- Arrange the placement of physical parts similar to the placement in the schematic drawing. This reduces errors and allows for easier checking. However, in the case of high-gain circuits, the output should be located away from the input regardless of how the schematic is drawn.

- Inventory all the parts before breadboarding. This reduces errors of omission and makes it less likely that an incorrect part will be used.

- Have your partner or a third party check your work for errors. He or she will often notice things that you will not.

- Work methodically. Wire all the power connections, then the grounds, and then the signal paths. Another method is to do resistors first, then capacitors, then ICs, and so on. Some people place a pencil check on the schematic for each interconnection and part as they are wired.

- Bypass the power bus or buses to ground with a 15- or 25-μF electrolytic or tantalum capacitor. Be sure to observe polarity and to use capacitors with an adequate voltage rating. Power-supply bypass capacitors will often correct strange behavior arising from noise or unwanted oscillation. The bypass capacitors should be located near any high-gain devices that could cause a problem.

Appendix C

Lab Notebook Policies

The world is shrinking. More and more companies and organizations are becoming players in the global marketplace. These developments are changing the way companies do business. Questions of quality, reliability, and liability have made it necessary that all critical procedures be accurately documented and closely followed by all employees. Any procedure that can adversely affect the quality and/or the reliability of goods or services is a critical procedure.

Perhaps the most organized current worldwide effort to develop standards in this area is the set of guidelines known as ISO 9000, or ANSI Q9000. The abbreviation *ISO* stands for the International Organization for Standards, which is based in Geneva, Switzerland, and *ANSI* stands for the American National Standards Institute. The ISO and ANSI guidelines are one and the same. These guidelines are elaborate and will not be covered here. However, they are mentioned because they are one of the major driving forces behind many of today's work requirements. Many employers use policies and procedures that are a subset of national and international guidelines.

Technicians and engineers work together in many companies to experiment with new ideas, to test new designs, to simulate product performance, to verify safe performance under adverse conditions, to find and eliminate possible interference to other products, and so on. What is learned in the laboratory must be clearly documented. Most often, the findings are recorded in a lab notebook.

The lab notebook policies and procedures given here are generic. They do not match those of any given company. Probably, no single organization would require all of them. Your instructor might assign several lab experiments and ask that they be reported using some of the following procedures. Such an experience could be very helpful to you since more employers are adopting and using such procedures.

The lab notebook is provided by the company and shall be:

1. Permanently bound. Three-ring bindings and the like are not acceptable.
2. Paginated. Every page must be prenumbered, in ink, and pages must never be removed.
3. Titled. The cover or the first page must contain the company name, the location, the room number or lab number where it serves, the beginning and ending dates of use, and any special purpose that it might serve within a given lab (for example, an entire notebook could be devoted to safety testing only in a multipurpose lab).
4. Located in the lab. It is not permissible to take a lab notebook home. Photocopying of any type is also not allowed in most companies.

Lab notebook entries shall be:

1. In ink. Pencils are not to be used. Nothing may be erased, and no whiteout or correction fluid may be used. Mistakes should be crossed out with a single stroke in such a way that they are still legible. All cross-outs must be initialed.

2. Clearly identified. Each job or procedure must have a title, a date, a job number, and the names of those engineers and technicians participating. Also, a customer name and/or a contract number might be required.

3. Complete. The information that is recorded should be brief but complete. The guideline often used is that the entire procedure could be duplicated by following only the information found in the notebook.

4. Traceable. Test equipment must be listed, including serial numbers and latest calibration dates. Material listings are sometimes extended to include complex parts such as ICs. The part history and all identification markings might be required. Since computers and computer software often play a major role in the lab, they are also listed and version numbers of the software are required.

In electronics labs, items often entered in the lab notebook include:

1. Statement of the purpose of the procedure.
2. Brief narrative describing the procedure.
3. Schematics and other relevant sketches.
4. Calculations and results. This includes documentation of the use of calculators and/or computers. Design calculations normally must be verified by independent means, and this too must be documented.
5. Results and/or data. This includes instrument readings, waveforms, and graphs. Use data tables where appropriate.
6. Notation of errors and possible explanations. Significant differences between calculated (theoretical) and measured values must be addressed.
7. References and related materials. This includes computer printouts, computer files, and equipment manuals. Small printouts might be taped or pasted into the lab manual. Or, the location and identification methods of the materials must be clearly stated. This policy varies from company to company. For example, in many organizations, some material will be found on a network file server.
8. Description of any equipment or component failures and possible explanations.
9. Any out-of-the-ordinary event that could possibly affect the results such as a lightning storm or power failure.
10. Conclusions and recommendations. If any part of the procedure was not entirely satisfactory, it needs to be stated here.

Don't forget to expect variations. Some companies require a table of contents in the lab notebook. This might be completed after the notebook is full. The table of contents can be added to pages 2 and 3, which have been reserved for this use.